IT TAKES A CHILD TO RAISE A PARENT

Vanessa

IT TAKES A CHILD TO RAISE A PARENT

Stories of Evolving Child and Parent Development

Janis Clark Johnston

For Vanessa,
stop. look, listen g love ♡.
Jan Johnston

ROWMAN & LITTLEFIELD PUBLISHERS, INC.
Lanham • Boulder • New York • Toronto • Plymouth, UK

Published by Rowman & Littlefield Publishers, Inc.
A wholly owned subsidary of The Rowman & Littlefield
Publishing Group, Inc.
4501 Forbes Boulevard, Suite 200, Lanham, Maryland 20706
www.rowman.com

10 Thornbury Road, Plymouth PL6 7PP, United Kingdom

British Library Cataloguing in Publication Information Available

Library of Congress Cataloging-in-Publication Data Available

ISBN 978-1-4422-2161-1 (cloth : alk. paper)—ISBN 978-1-4422-2162-8 (electronic)

∞™ The paper used in this publication meets the minimum requirements of
American National Standard for Information Sciences Permanence of Paper
for Printed Library Materials, ANSI/NISO Z39.48-1992.

Printed in the United States of America

In memory of Mark Emmett Johnston,
with gratitude for our exciting partnership;

and to our children,
Ryan and Megan, who raised us as parents,
with awe and joy.

CONTENTS

ACKNOWLEDGMENTS

The home is the centre and circumference, the start and the finish, of most of our lives.

—Charlotte Perkins Gilman, sociologist

Many people inspired the ideas on these pages. First and foremost, I am deeply indebted to my passionate parents, Lois Treasure Whitacre Clark and Robert Dale Clark, for being my first teachers and powerful role models for the basic values in my life. The public library is one of my poetic mother's many homes, as she visits there so frequently. My father turned into a voracious reader in his retirement years. Their love of learning started me on a lifelong search for knowledge and meaning. My maternal grandfather, Joseph E. Whitacre, was a writer of sermons. Both grandmothers qualify as writers. Bertha Fike Whitacre kept a daily diary for years. Vera Naragon Clark wrote long letters to family members who moved away from home. I always felt "rooted" as I read her newsy narratives when I left home for college and adult life.

My incredible parenting partner, Mark Emmett Johnston, taught me about being in the *present* moment. Mark's present moment enthusiasm for life touched everything he did, but it especially embraced his parenting style. My husband and I owe a huge debt of gratitude to our two creative children, Ryan and Megan, who "raised" us as parents. As adults, they also helped to raise this book, providing considerable help in their own unique ways. Ryan saved my fledgling chapter on creativity when my computer crashed. His wise and patient counsel on computer snafus throughout the years has been a safety net for this project. Megan gave significant editorial suggestions through reading many early versions of chapters. Her perceptive comments and brainstorming led me into new writing terrain on many occasions.

I owe my grounding in psychology to a Manchester University psychology professor, Donald Colburn, and my initial excitement in family psychology to two Boston University graduate school professors, Fran Grossman and John Gilmore. I gained much of my early expertise in child psychology during my first professional job as a school psychologist in Lexington, Massachusetts, under the caring supervision of Celia Schulhoff. My tutorial in problem-solving theory and practice began during the time I was a consultant to the Philadelphia public schools, where I taught Interpersonal Cognitive Problem Solving (now called "I Can Problem Solve") to teachers under Myrna Shure's guidance. Dick Schwartz, creator of Internal Family Systems, provided valuable mentoring in working with personality *parts*. Julia Cameron's book, *The Artist's Way*, inspired me to write my own ideas. Mary Pipher modeled how to write; her books, along with her writing class, provided soul food for me.

Many people supported me through the writing process. My book group supplied start-to-finish guidance: Cathy Pidek showed support for this work at its beginning; Liene Sorenson provided reference-librarian expertise; Nancy Leonard offered ongoing, enthusiastic support; and Carol Backe's graphic-design skills enhanced the line art. Writing teachers Julie Benesh, Brook Bergan, and Lisa Rosenthal suggested changes for clarity. Elizabeth Zack and Kelly Wilson contributed thoughtful editing. Many gracious readers read early versions of my work and gave valuable feedback: Tina Birnbaum, Frieda Brown, Lois Clark, Robert Clark (who said, "This is deep"), Jean D'Amico, Alice Epstein, James Garbarino, Marnie Gielo, Mary Rose Lambke, Jordan Rifis, Gretchen Schafft, Annie Tolle, Carol Wade, Melanie Weller, Lindee Petersen Wilson, and writing-group buddies at Chicago's Newberry Library, the Oak Park Public Library, the Palos Park Public Library, and the University of Nebraska summer writing conference.

Thanks to Deborah Preiser for her promotion advice and Hannah Jennings for her creative webmaster skills and to Virginia Bridges, Kathryn Knigge, and Julia Loy, for their behind-the-scenes hours in handling publication details. Grace Freedson's agent advice and Amy King's referral of the manuscript to her editor colleague are deeply appreciated. Finally, my heartfelt thanks goes to Suzanne I. Staszak-Silva, senior acquisitions editor at Rowman and Littlefield, for her understanding of the importance of this book.

While a book carries some original thoughts from an author, most of a book's ideas represent a compilation of learning from everyone who has touched an author's life. Just as many of our current roads are built on top of ancestral byways, theories and books build upon the footpaths forged by others. However, this book could not have been written without the ongoing tutoring in life struggles that I received from my children and the children in many client families. My understanding of human nature draws upon so many of their life stories. I have been privileged with a precious opportunity to journey with these children along some of their *raising roads*.

AUTHOR'S NOTE

Nothing is so delicate and fugitive by its very nature as a beginning.
—Pierre Teilhard de Chardin, French philosopher

Who am *I* as a parent? How am I supposed to *begin* parenting? Lamaze classes do not cover parenting technique. In fact, my Lamaze classes did not even mention the possibilities that my husband and I encountered in the labor and delivery of our first child. *It Takes a Child to Raise a Parent* compiles the developmental knowledge I wish I had in 1977, when I first gave birth. I never experienced parenting coursework in twenty-one years of schooling. Parent training was a do-it-yourself project. Apparently psychologists undergoing training in the 1970s were supposed to develop their own thinking about childrearing. I began my fledgling thoughts on parenting while I was a graduate student in psychology; I "practiced" on other people's children.

My parenting laboratory was housed in a dozen homes; each family had different rules, and each child had different challenges. My husband and I took on numerous live-in babysitting roles when the children's parents took vacations without their children. As a nanny couple, my husband and I puzzled over family snafus not covered in my child development textbooks; most of the dilemmas we faced were not covered.

Fortunately, my husband and I were schmoozers. We swapped stories about how our friends were raised. We dissected our own childhood memories. When our children were born, we shared many heart-to-heart chats about our parenting partnership over our thirty years of marriage. We might start out with different points of view, but eventually our runaway thoughts walked together as we debated our doubts in numerous dialogues with family, friends, and colleagues. We began to tell our *own* story about how to raise children who would be capable of reaching their potential. My husband and I did not agree on technique for every situation, but we agreed on these key notions of raising children:

- Communicate unconditional love for your children, knowing that some days this act seems easy and some days it seems impossible. Expressions of unconditional love, which call for being fully *in the moment* with your child, can happen in unexpected, everyday moments.
- Model the moral values that lead to hardy personality roles, knowing that your children constantly face cultural value systems that differ from your values. Stand up for *your* values.
- Collaborate with relatives, friends, and teachers in affirming your children's unique identities. Every child has special qualities.
- Treasure individual interactions with your children. Realize that your children share their learning with you, just as you share your learning with them.

One older parent told me, "I stood at the window in the hospital and just looked at my tiny baby girl. I thought to myself, 'I don't want to take you home, because I have no idea what to do with you.'" Where are classes to help her interact with her child for the next eighteen years? Another mother looks at her teenage pregnant daughter and sighs, "I'm too young to become a grandmother." In a second sigh, she shares her real worry: "My daughter is clueless about how to interact with a child." At the age of fifteen, her daughter has difficulty interacting with peers. Parents of every age ponder childrearing. Where are the road maps to guide parents along the raising road?

This book offers a guide for parent-child interactions for those who are thinking about becoming parents, for pregnant parents, and for current parents. I have looked far and wide to connect the dots in raising families well. An avid reader, I have turned to books for the big picture, to help me cope with life's challenges. Now it is my privilege to share one perspective on one of our most critical topics of the new millennium. My ideas stem not only from my years as a much-loved child but also from years of loving and learning as my two children helped raise my parenting potential. They also come from years of learning from children in both my private practice as a family psychologist and in public schools as a school psychologist. This book *maps* the healthy development of children within a context of developing parents. We are all parents in training, with not only a mandate to meet our children's basic needs but also an equal requirement to address our own basic needs along the raising road.

Sincerely,
Jan Johnston

INTRODUCTION: CHILDREN RAISE PARENTS, AND PARENTS RAISE CHILDREN

> Know yourself before you attempt to get to know children. Become aware of what you yourself are capable of before you attempt to outline the rights and responsibilities of children. First and foremost you must realize that you, too, are a child, whom you must first get to know, bring up, and educate.
>
> —Janusz Korczak, Polish pediatrician

Simplicity and complexity coexist within childhood. Many of us lack appreciation for our childhoods and the complex lessons we gather from them until we have a child of our own. We may show love for our child. We may teach our child moral values. We may celebrate our child's creative uniqueness. However, when our child experiences a crisis, we can lose our bearings. Our own internal crises jiggle loose. Just when our child most needs us, we are needy ourselves.

Our own needs echo so loudly in our head that we barely hear our child. Suddenly we find ourselves trapped in our personality's storehouse of replaying past problems and/or fixing the future. Meanwhile, our child ends up guiding us by *connecting* us to an earlier time in our life when we encountered distress. We dredge up a lesson. We adapt by changing the story that we tell ourselves about who we are. We find a way to steer our child in some turning point along the raising road of learning how to meet basic needs.

Unfortunately, one of the insights many parents lack concerns an overwhelming preoccupation with possessing *all* the complex answers that their children need. Actually, children help us grow up while we help them grow up. As caretakers, we discover that we are parents in training, having to learn how to meet both a child's changing needs and our own changing needs. But most of us lack parent-training coursework to guide us over the rough terrain. Instead, we receive our training from our parents or peers who have *their* own needs. Many of us parent through trial and error, finding that each child we have presents us with different challenges. Happily, each child also presents us with opportunities to learn new skills.

Parents raise children, and children raise parents. As parents, we renegotiate basic needs that surface from our own childhood memories as our youngsters pass through each of their developmental phases. Consequently, all parents come to find that as adults, they still have many raising issues that they need to address. "Yes, but how can I get my child to listen to me?" you may ask.

LEARNING TO LISTEN

My thirty-five years of experience as a psychologist confirms many therapists' observations. Psychotherapy models, with their varying techniques, are not as important to the process of change as a therapist's responsible or devoted *listening* is.[1] The same holds true for parenting: a caretaker's techniques seldom are as powerful in raising a child well as the underlying *interactions* or *connections* in relating with that child are. Devoted, responsible listening requires a caretaker to embrace a child's perspective in the present moment and address a child's predicaments one interaction at a time. We always want our child to listen to us, but frequently we lack the effort to listen well to our child. Often we do not find space in our crowded schedules for responsible listening when our child misbehaves. How can we train ourselves to listen to our child in a devoted way when we have so much of our own stuff happening? How can we learn to stop, look, and listen to our child one interaction at a time when we do not even come to a complete stop at every stop sign?

After experiencing many rolling stops and jerky starts throughout childhood, many offspring become parents in training, either choosing this role or happening into parenthood. Do-it-yourself parent training begins in middle school for some teen parents. Having a baby raises issues most people cannot comprehend ahead of the event. Also, not being able to have a baby delivers complicated issues. Some parents adopt children. Others face challenges in pregnancy, labor, and delivery. However, the reality of these developmental issues can surprise even those who prepare for them. Teens and adults discover that conception and pregnancy issues are more challenging than they ever imagined. And so, parents in training may not address some of their own unmet needs until a baby forces them to *listen* to their own multiple needs.

Pregnancy issues bring our daily needs into sharper focus. Potential parents reminisce about youthful escapades with a fondness they could not express earlier. When they were young children, they were concrete or literal thinkers; they could not grasp the special significance of their childhood years. As parents in training, they now recall some early times when their caretakers did not meet their needs and they faced dead ends along the raising road. However, they usually fixate on the future . . . until one day the baby arrives. Parenting a child exacts daily responsibilities. Romantic commitments shift and marital bonds crash in half of all American marriages today. Sometimes, jobs for parents in training disappear. An increasing number of dads today stay at home. Parents swerve along the raising road of learning to meet their basic needs, realizing that they not only "raise" their child but now have to "raise" themselves as adults and parents.

Unfortunately, we make many of the same mistakes our own parents made. Many of our parents did not listen well. We all travel a raising road of learning how to meet basic needs, and we all have the same basic needs. We fulfill many needs as time passes—but these needs keep recycling, and we constantly find that we have more and more needs. Some of our needs go unmet. The parent-training road consists of a Route 66–like highway that goes on and on, crossing generations and lifetime stories about meeting basic needs. *It Takes a Child to Raise a Parent* offers a raising road map for meeting basic needs.

PARENTING CROSSES GENERATIONAL LINES

Family intergenerational stories in parenting range from the simple (teaching teeth brushing) to the complex (teaching sex education). We forge through transitions or phases of developmental change. **Traveling story to story, the parenting trip provides parallel opportunities for adult and child growth**. We may not recognize this initially. Our culture primarily promotes the notion that adults grow up through their career responsibilities. However, at the end of life, many parents and grandparents say that they wish they spent more time with their children and realize that our best lessons in growing *up* happened with children.

Many kinds of families exist. Some parents do not raise their children, or they rely heavily upon grandparent help. Now the needs of three generations intertwine. An often unappreciated portion of the parenting population, many grandparents participate in parenting the second time around. Some grandparents pay the bills and house three generations. The fastest-growing type of U.S. households is one with three or more generations, growing by 38 percent from 1990 to 2000.[2] Grandparents who act as parents for their grandchildren entail a long history. President George Washington and his wife, Martha, became parents to Martha's grandchildren from her earlier marriage.[3] More commonly, parent-grandparent extended families raise the next generation together, with parents in the lead role. These families share precious childhood interactions across generations, savoring funny and wise child stories over many years. Even though many parents and grandparents mostly enjoy the raising road of each new child in the family, caretakers find certain parenting dilemmas totally frustrating.

CHAMELEON CHILDREN AND CHAMELEON CARETAKERS

This book introduces a travel guide for self-reflection and self-growth *through* parenting. Parents come to understand their own chameleon personality roles, or how their personality fluctuates in different situations. Each personality role acts as a leader when it comes to meeting certain needs. Caretakers can learn to embrace their own personality quirks while they learn how to dialogue with a quirky child *one interaction at a time*. They even learn to detect eccentric nonverbal signals from a needy child. Most caretakers recall seeing a child react nonverbally one way, and in the very next moment they see the child do or say something that seems *opposite*. Neither parent nor child understands that different needs and different personality roles of the caretaker-child pair are on a crash course.

To understand parent-child conflict, adults need to revisit their own childhood memories. As an adult, you have the capacity to think abstractly about your needs in your personality *story-house* of stored-up life memories. You put your childhood memories of meeting certain needs into context. You fast-forward into ramifications of your child's current difficulties in meeting needs, while at the same time you backtrack into the childhood dilemmas you encountered. You begin to grasp your family's "big picture." **You see, when you figure out something about your own childhood, it serves a double purpose: when you can acknowledge your unmet needs, you also can appreciate that your child may have similar unmet needs**.

And when you develop a philosophy of parenting that mostly meets *both* your child's basic needs as well as your own, you do not have to buy a how-to-parent book for every new issue that comes up in your child's life. Instead, you notice how life's journey highlights more similarities than differences between the generations. You begin practicing unconditional love for yourself and your child. You rediscover your values. You grasp the art of problem solving, looking for a number of alternatives for every conflict. You train yourself to appreciate the present moment.

PART I. WHAT'S THE STORY?

It Takes a Child to Raise a Parent brings psychology lessons into everyday language with personality-mapping exercises at the end of each chapter. In part I, we discover the importance of our shared, daily needs, an adaptation of psychologist Abraham Maslow's hierarchy of needs.[4] We find that our caretaker-child interactions lead us through many switchbacks in meeting needs along the raising road. Our parenting interactions help us to recall some unmet needs from our own childhood dilemmas. Perhaps we recognize, for the first time, our various personality roles. Marriage and family therapist Richard Schwartz's model of psychotherapy, Internal Family Systems, laid the groundwork for my understanding of personality *parts*,[5] or roles.

Each of our interaction stories depicts how family members' personality roles attempt to meet their basic needs. In addition to instructive stories regarding who we are and our cycles of meeting needs, a few overall parenting-trip tips highlight each chapter. For the reader who studies maps before ever putting the key into the ignition, a quick read of eight sets of parenting-trip tips provides an overview of where we are heading along the raising road of learning how to meet basic needs. For those who hopscotch their way through books, chapters cover these basic tips in the order in which they are listed. Each basic tip provides practical parenting steps.

And now, consider a family interaction story from my private practice. (All the names of the family members in this book have been changed.)

Jonathan (14)

> Jonathan explodes easily. When he cannot work algebra problems, he breaks his pencil, wads up his paper, and swears. In therapy, we map, or track, this one interaction. Just before Jonathan's angry outburst, he expresses a frustration role: he detects chest tightness and teeth clenching. Then he divulges a scared role: in the pit of his stomach, he wonders if he is smart. He detours to send a text message to a friend to "get some weed."

Jonathan has a parent who turns to substance abuse to soothe frayed nerves after difficult work assignments. Instead of looking for separate personality roles of parents and children, this developmental approach considers the similarities of family personality roles. After sixteen years working as a school psychologist and another nineteen years working as a family psychologist in private practice, I have met hundreds of wonderful youth from kindergarten through college, along with their caretakers. Each family member carries a burdensome backpack filled with the distresses of life.

From my work in schools, I learned how our educational systems expect children to be ready to learn when they come to school every morning. School staff members want students to leave any "outside" problems at the schoolhouse door when they enter. Somehow, children are expected to use only school *maps* from 8:00 a.m. to 3:00 p.m. Certain personality *maps*, or a person's network of emotional roles in their personality, are not welcome at school. Similarly, the workplace rejects certain adult personality roles. Parents are challenged in making sense of their personality roles, often begun in their childhoods, that refuse to part company at the office doorway. Both child and caretaker traumatic stories affect the parent-child relationship.

PART II. MEETING NEEDS, OUR CHILD'S AND OUR OWN

Part II explores how our personality roles attempt to fulfill five basic needs. Poignant child and parent interactive stories illustrate the common snafus many families face along the raising road. After we help our child navigate one treacherous stretch of their raising road, the transition stoplight changes, and we are challenged by a different topic. We are on a lifelong raising road of learning how to meet our basic needs as well as our child's basic needs.

Carly (11), Molly (44), and Dave (45)

> Morning brings another rat race. Dave wakes Carly. Then he walks the dog and comes back to find Carly still curled up in bed. Molly sleeps in. She works nights. Dave cajoles Carly out of bed, but she dawdles, complaining that she has "nothing to wear." Late again for work, just like yesterday morning, Dave smashes his "Mr. Nice Guy" role on the kitchen counter. A cereal box falls over and sprays Raisin Bran onto dishes that needed washing last night.

Carly, Molly, and Dave struggle with basic needs every morning. We all negotiate the same set of shared needs on our daily trek. **Caretakers share five basic needs with their children: energy, discipline, creativity, belonging, and ability. Needs recycle daily**. While we all have the *same* needs, we travel *different* paths to meet our needs. Our challenge as caretakers of children requires that we model how to meet these needs effectively so that everyone in the family thrives. Children, as well as parents, mostly fulfill birthright needs on good days. On other, not-so-good days, people collapse into ennui, fall into disorder, clone others in conformity, tumble into the "blues," and end up feeling apathetic. And yet our needs continue recycling. Parenting exists as a circular process, and this book reflects circularity. Adults do not recall their childhoods in chronological sequence, so composite stories of needs are told in varying ages.

PART III. MODELING HOW TO RELATE ONE INTERACTION AT A TIME

In part III, we learn to embrace *self-territory,* or the unifying foundation of personality that knows how to be *present*, in the moment, with both ourselves and others. We draw maps of our personality roles and their relationships. We now understand how our various personality roles and awareness of self-territory form the basis for all of our interactions with a given child. Hopefully, we gather travel tips for the raising road from each caretaker-child interaction.

Harriet (67)

> A grandparent revels in the birth of each newcomer in the family. She thinks of a special song for each new grandchild. She sings this song to the baby the first time she holds him or her. Each time she calls her daughter on the phone, she asks her to press the phone to a grandbaby's ear so she can sing to him or her. At eighteen months old, a grandson grins broadly, recognizing a *connection* as Grandma croons *their* song.

Harriet models how to relate to a child *one interaction at a time*. She prizes her grandparent role, because she discovers meaning within the present moment. In turn, she sets a powerful example for her daughter and grandchildren. Her daughter shares the here-and-now delight of her son and enjoys how her mother travels the grandparent road. Each family member's awareness of an inner space for relating in the present moment has implications for others in the family. If grandparents are not models of unconditional love in the family, then parents have to make a conscious effort to surround themselves with positive peers, planting their own roots for unconditional love.

Each day brings new opportunities for finding our roots. We learn to differentiate self-territory from our many personality roles. Descriptions of personality maps depict some journeys taken through both parent and child familiar personality roles, enhancing readers' understanding. **We create personal maps daily to meet our basic needs without realizing it. This book makes personality mapping a conscious act.** Drawing personality maps aids in the understanding of current growth pains for all ages. Maps offer concrete directions to help both children and adults in all of their interactions. Personality maps provide a simple mirror of who a person is at one transition point. Every child and every parent can discover new thinking about growing up when they train themselves to be aware of present moments in their lives.

WHAT YOU CAN TAKE AWAY FROM THIS BOOK

Some days are more challenging than others are. Some transitions are gargantuan. Growing up involves a lifetime cycle of delicate beginnings. However, you can learn to understand your child's basic needs and how they cycle, alongside your own basic needs, on the raising road. By taking this journey, you train yourself to recognize your basic needs and personality roles, as well as those of the children in your life. You learn to make *space* for relating one interaction at a time. You can find answers to many of your questions. What unmet potential exists for you? What roles of your personality hold you back from meeting your own potential? What unmet potential exists in some child you know?

Understanding the time crunch that adults experience, this book offers chunks—or brief, readable sections—to help you learn the answers to common parenting questions. Quotations throughout the book offer parental self-reflection. Learning chunks also appear in highlighted words and concepts throughout this parent-in-training road trip. Exercises at the end of each chapter offer another piece of chunking. You gather new chunks of learning when you approach your personality story-house of life memories from a new perspective. You evolve *your* self-authored story and connect the dots in understanding how to interact with your child *one interaction at a time*.

Part I

What's the Story?

I

LET'S UNDERSTAND THE FIVE BASIC NEEDS

"How can I get there?" asked Dorothy.

"You must walk. It is a long journey, through a country that is sometimes pleasant and sometimes dark and terrible . . ."

—L. Frank Baum, *The Wonderful Wizard of Oz*

We want to raise our child as wonderfully and effectively as possible. But as we face daily dilemmas, impatient thoughts wander around in circles in our mind: What does our child need? What do we need? Where is meaning found for the daily struggles we endure? Our questions outweigh our answers. We are somewhere in the evolving story of our life, but we have lost the story line. We are not sure which direction to take next. Our day can spin out of control; we head ourselves in one direction in the morning, but somehow we slip up and zigzag, ending up going in an opposite direction by evening. We feel lost. Where are basic parenting road signs? Does anyone have a *map*?

Maps are guides that pinpoint various locations; we use them when we plan trips or when we are lost in our travels. However, there is no map for parenting, and many parents weave a circuitous route in raising their children. Parents can feel as lost as Dorothy in *The Wonderful Wizard of Oz*. Without any maps, Dorothy and her hapless pals wander around in circles. Each character in the story has unmet needs, and each one perceives a lack of an internal compass that would help in meeting those needs. Dorothy defines her needs in terms of directions *home* after a cyclone disorients her. Her buddies also yearn for a self-definition, described as a "heart of kindness" for the Tin Man, a "brain with intelligence" for the Scarecrow, and "courage" for the outwardly timid Lion. In the story, they follow the yellow brick road to the wise wizard so that he can bestow guidance. The comrades appear unaware that they all have the potential to use their inner resources as maps, which can point them in significant and meaningful directions for their quest. The four friends discover an ancient truth: they expect external gifts to bring them meaning, when they already possess what they seek.

Our desire to gain external comfort often results in a circular yellow-brick-road experience for each one of us, too. However, solace and meaning in life are not external; we need to look within our own selves. If we plumb our personality story-house, or storehouse of life memories, we can come to use our own stories to uncover a philosophy or gain loving wisdom to meet our daily needs. We all have to look for our *own* meanings that we tuck into our assumptions or lay theories[1] about our needs. We cannot expect some expert—or wizard—to provide directions every time we are lost and cannot find our way. Similarly, we are responsible for driving our own parenting car. No agency exists to teach us and test our parental driving skills around the developmental hairpin curves that each one of us encounters with children. We issue our own parenting permit. So buckle up. Get ready for what I call the *raising road* of learning how to meet your child's basic needs . . . as well as your own.

RAISING *INTERACTIONS*

Our children often feel lost, not only at school or in an unfamiliar place but very often within the confines of our own homes. When they are at school, they wish for home; when they are home, they wish to travel to some other place. Their personality story-houses of their life's memories, like Dorothy's, are filled with fears and longing. Many times children wish for the wizard-like sources of strength they see on TV and in movies and video games. As caretakers, we are in the role of wizard or wise one, but often we feel a bit lost ourselves. Our thoughts jumble. We find we cannot focus on a child's plight as we bundle our brains around predicaments of our own. Many of us fail to recognize this very basic reality.

Often, parents imagine that others have smoother raising roads. One father describes his nine-month-old son as a "need machine." He is correct. He does not admit, however, that he also qualifies as a need machine. **As both adults and parents in training, we possess a high-rise personality story-house, the unique accumulation of life memories of trying to meet our basic needs.** Juggling constant needs weighs upon parents. Unfortunately, when we drive our minds through our early stories, we find some deep ruts—the places where we experienced unmet needs as children.

We seem to forget our "pothole" childhood memories until an incident jogs our attention. A child's behavior jiggles some of our early memories loose. In addition, we suddenly recall an earlier time when our own need machine broke down. Alternatively, joining in our child's turn to meet these same needs, we confront memories of our childhood in similar time frames. We sense certain sights, smells, or other sensory triggers of a particular event in our life. Sometimes we have very few words to describe our memories, but our needs in the remembered situation loom large. Encountering such childhood memories of needs, some met and some unmet, raises questions for us.

Embedded within each story-house personality of life memories are underlying age-old questions: Who am I? What do my memories mean for my life? Where am I on the yellow brick road of my life? Where is home base? Sometimes we have so much sorting through of our own needs to do that we do not travel patiently, or slow down often enough, to consider our child's needs seriously. We struggle in looking at a child's needs *one interaction at a time* because we have not examined enough of our own needs *one interaction at a time*.

Many caretakers feel lost. As one young mother confides to her mother, "I never knew parenting an infant would be so difficult. . . . I'm having to raise myself at the same time I'm raising my baby!" What do we mean when we say parents are *raising* children? What kind of raising road prepares a person for meeting the basic needs of a child?

- The word "raise" comes from *re* and *alier*. The Latin prefix *re* means "again" or "backward." *Alier* comes from Old French and means "to join."

- "Raise" literally means "to join again" or "to join backward."
- Thirty-two examples of the verb "raise" are in my dictionary. Several useful definitions include "to lift up," "to set upright," "to set in motion," "to care for and promote the growth of," and "to serve in the capacity of parent."[2]

Notice how the word "up" appears in several of the definitions. Elizabeth Barrett Browning, in her poem "Aurora Leigh," writes of rearing *up*: "Women know / The way to rear up children (to be just)."[3] The up or upright connotation lends a positive, moral tone. Parents join their stories of growing up with morals with those of other generations. The "raising up" definitions capture the idea of parents recognizing their own stories of growing up and knowing right from wrong. **Additionally, the "joining again" and "joining backward" definitions convey a central theme of this book: in most families, children join in raising their parents just as much as parents raise children.**

"GROWING UP"

A young father juggles parenting with his career as a family-practice doctor. He admits, "I never would have learned certain things about myself if I had never had children. I don't admit this to single people. . . . I don't want them to feel bad . . . but it's true. I didn't grow up until I had children." Families' raising stories illustrate challenging personality-role transitions in both child and adult development. Certain developmental transitions in growing up are universal. For example, the wonder of birth and the mystery of death touch everyone. **We come to share some similar stories because we all have the same basic needs. However, we all meet these basic needs in a variety of ways, which is what makes developmental phases seem so different among family members.**

In this chapter, we consider our basic needs, our underlying self-awareness, our personality struggles, and our often ignored or misinterpreted nonverbal communication signals.

Parenting-Trip Tips

- Identify the basic, or birthright, needs—energy, discipline, creativity, belonging, and ability—that both you and your child encounter every day.
- Recognize the underlying *self-territory* in each person.
- Acknowledge and accept your *own* struggles in meeting needs through discovery of your personality *story-house* of life memories.
- Detect nonverbal communication in your relationships. The majority of interactions between people do not contain language. Parenting missteps often occur because we fail to recognize nonverbal behavioral cues.

BIRTHRIGHT NEEDS

All people face basic, or birthright, needs for survival everyday—energy, discipline, creativity, belonging, and ability needs. Our energy and discipline needs clamor for our attention as soon as we awaken. As parents, we may not have the luxury of meeting some of our own energy needs if our crying baby's energy needs reach our ears before a clock arouses us. For the parent in training who wants to exercise first thing in the morning, a baby's exercising lungs demand a detour from the "First I run on my treadmill" routine. "Feed me" is the alarm clock in many families and calls for a caretaker's discipline to know what to feed a child at a particular age and to have the wherewithal to provide it. Meeting energy and discipline needs helps caretakers organize plans for the morning's first tasks: helping family members eat a nutritious breakfast and move on to school, work, home, and community commitments. Backing up, basic energy and discipline needs call for a good night's sleep the night before, giving the next morning's needs a reasonable chance of being met.

Do family need machines ever stop? Actually, we barely covered the beginning and ending basic needs of the day. Families juggle needs all day long. Parents in training can learn to employ creative problem solving to find ever-new ways to travel the raising road of meeting family basic needs. Belonging needs weave their way into family members' need machines at every turn. Acknowledging ability needs takes thoughtful and creative planning to enable each family member to fulfill their birthright potential. While adults and children have the same basic needs, they have different ways of coping with them.[4] Young children frequently require adult help in meeting these needs. Our ongoing task as parents in training requires us to model how children can learn to meet their own needs successfully as they grow up. However, this modeling role challenges even the best caretakers. In order to model how to meet needs well, we have to address our own basic needs and come close to answering them as well.

Some people ignore their own needs. As anthropologist Daniel Miller points out, many parents tend to focus most of their efforts on the development of their children.[5] When do parents pay attention to their own development? Realistically, most adults desire some amount of modeling and companionship in meeting their own basic needs. In healthy families, the members keep learning positive ways to meet basic needs every day of their lives.[6] Children help parents and grandparents meet basic needs by reminding them that everyone requires exercise. Youngsters often pitch in to help their parents meet basic needs when illness or disability issues exist. Complex interactions among family members happen along the trail of needs.

While birthright needs are listed in a linear fashion to help you remember them easily, energy, discipline, creativity, belonging, and ability needs intertwine in varying ways. All needs relate to our most basic of needs: our instinctual need for survival. In this model, each survival need interconnects with other needs, both within a person and among family members. For example, obtaining enough sleep affects how well parents and children use their energy abilities each day. A child's energy needs intertwine with a caretaker's energy needs. To facilitate remembering the birthright needs in our development, I have created the following "need machine" image. It presents an ascending and descending escalator of needs to illustrate how closely needs feed into one another.

THE NEED MACHINE

Picture a moving stairway, an escalator that transports a person from one basic need to the next. Just as real escalators transport people from one story of a building to another, our needs escalator takes us from one story in our day to our next event or story.

ABILITY
BELONGING
CREATIVITY
DISCIPLINE
ENERGY

Yet, while standing still on escalators, we continue moving, for escalator steps run along looping tracks pulled by chains. In the same way, the needs escalator runs along, one need dissolving into the next, followed by successive needs moving in step-wise motion. However, our basic needs can change directions, just like escalator steps. An up escalator turns into a down escalator when directionality shifts—for example, during rush hours, to accommodate a flood of workers leaving a building. At the top and bottom of the escalator, tracks level off, allowing steps to flatten. The flat spaces allow people to step on and off safely.[7] When it comes to meeting our needs, we step off our needs escalator periodically, as we have to attend to our child's needs. Some basic needs among family members are met jointly, but others veer toward us at the "wrong" time or place.

There are other escalator parallels to human functioning. After taking care of one need, the next need moves into place just as the next step of an escalator rises up routinely. You see, we always seem to need

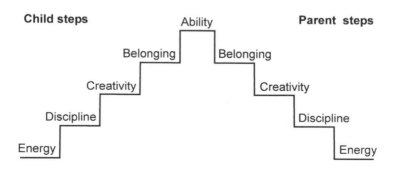

Figure 1.1.

something. We tell ourselves that our cycling habits are our "story." We meet energy needs with food, exercise, sex, rest, relaxation, or meditation. We require discipline or simple rules and values to run our day successfully and safely. Creativity improves our attempts to problem solve effectively and enhances meaning in life through various innovations we can envision. Belonging at home, on the job, and with significant others (as well as having a sense of belonging to ourselves) gives social meaning to our days. Last, but certainly no less important than any of the other birthright needs, ability needs help us fulfill our potential and progress as a planet. In this way, our cyclical need machine repeats telltale sequences many times in the same day.

WHOSE NEEDS COME FIRST?

Children's needs also follow cyclical patterns. Consider the cranky child before dinnertime; the child becomes soothed and energized after the nutritious meal. Not too long afterward, sleep needs emerge to restore energy. The most adept caretakers set a few discipline rules to smooth a child's path to bedtime. They also satisfy a child's belonging needs by setting up playdates and spending quality time with him or her. However, parents often find themselves in the position of having to meet more than one person's needs at a time. For example, the time after dinner often presents the first opportunity in the career parent's day for belonging, because he or she can return personal e-mails or phone calls. Whose needs come first? Parents also possess cranky roles in their personalities. However, with practice, parents in training learn how to shift the gears on the family-needs escalator so that everyone can meet their basic needs.

A smooth-running family escalator of needs represents an *ideal* relationship, a close-knit caretaker-child bond through which family members are free to develop skills, meet basic needs, and realize their potential. Instead of a "hierarchy" of needs, this developmental progression is an interactive model. Needs of parent and child appear as revolving steps on a more or less continuous cycle. **Child needs and caretaker needs *interact*, repeating sequences in habitual cycles like escalator levels that loop from step to step. Some of our days reflect *in-sync* family escalator movement through needs. On**

other days, we collide while attempting to meet needs, facing breakdown and heartache.

Each of us requires time to step off the conveyor belt of meeting continuous needs. We become weary. We require sleep. Escalators are built to receive "rest"—speed-control mechanisms cut down escalator energy costs by making them run at half speed when they're not in use. Guided by photoelectric sensors, an escalator returns to full speed when a person gets on the first step.[8] Similarly, our body sensors know when to run at half speed, although we pay little attention to these nonverbal cues. Sometimes escalators break down. Passengers trudge upward or downward on steps that seem glued in place. Sometimes people get sick or discouraged. Meeting a daily diet of needs with low energy results in a difficult climb. Similarly, our busy need cycles can obscure our capacity to tune into meeting our needs in any measured sense. We sometimes lose track of how best to meet our needs. The family need machines keep needing and moving anyway.

UNMET BASIC NEEDS

Some family members seldom experience the pattern of meeting one basic need after another. Instead of taking imaginary escalator steps *up*, they cascade downward, as if they are out of control on some icy ski slope. They breezily go through days, without seeming to take the time to breathe very much. Some parents use physical force on their children in attempts to *make* them meet certain needs. Sometimes a parent is the victim of domestic violence. Family violence erodes everyone's energy, leading to mental and physical exhaustion for both caretakers and children.

Other parents face energy crashes after a death in the family. After her husband's sudden death, one grief-stricken mother confides, "I have the kids to raise, the house remodeling is in the middle stages, and my job has changed. I am tired all the time." Family unmet needs collide. **On collision days, a downward slope cascades one misstep into the next. As shown in the diagram that follows, apathy can drop into "the blues," which can slip into conformity, slide into disorder, and eventually descend into ennui or listlessness.** Again, this is only one sequence following unmet basic needs. Each family member's bumpy pattern can take somewhat different turns.

When one family member experiences a state of regret or exhaustion, emotional fallout shadows those nearby. Like a child navigating a summer slip-and-slide water toy, we all experience some slippage along the way in meeting basic needs. One father sighs as he relates, "I feel guilty that my son is just like me." He clarifies that he wants to cool his hot temper whenever he senses his teenage son spinning out of verbal control, just like him. When we do not meet some of our own basic needs, we have difficulty in modeling how best to meet daily needs for our child.

In the words of one young struggling mother, "My mother told all of us kids we were losers. . . . When I got pregnant, she didn't believe me. She thought I wanted to get married at twenty just to get out of the house." This parent worries about her own reactions to her children. She does not want to repeat the negative cycle of blame-then-shame parenting. All caretaker actions have reactions. Caretakers affect children's needs and children affect caretakers' needs. Some days we slip more than glide through our day of negotiating needs. When we do not slow down our pace to have awareness in present moments and connect with self-territory, we can feel as if we have lost our footing in meeting basic needs.

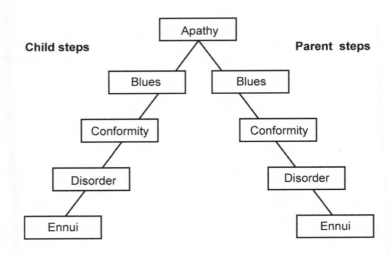

Figure 1.2.

In fact, along the raising road of learning how to meet basic needs, caretakers and children travel at many different energy, discipline, creativity, belonging, and ability speeds. Either party speeds up or slows down interactions. Most family interactions speed along in high gear, with rapid hairpin turns of needs, actions, and reactions. Youth do not know how to calibrate their reactions, and they feel lost on a regular basis. Similarly, many parents in training do not fine-tune their motors either. When we consider that each interaction in family life echoes as a reciprocal action-reaction whereby adults and children influence one another's life stories, we grasp the meaning of parents raising children and children raising parents. When we slow down the race-horse pace and encounter our child *one interaction at a time* from self-territory, we are in a better position to connect with our child's needs and our own needs.

SELF-TERRITORY

The ideal way to raise *up* a child considers the basic needs of both parent and child, as we make a conscious effort to relate one interaction at a time. Consider meanings for "one interaction at a time":

- "Interaction" comes from the Latin words *inter* (*inter* means "between," "among," "reciprocally," "together") and *actus* or *acta* (*actus* means "a doing," and *acta*, the plural form, means "things done").
- The word "interaction" means "reciprocal action" or "things done together."[9]

While reciprocity, or doing tasks together, best characterizes how to raise our children well while raising ourselves as caretakers, the dual effort required to juggle our needs with those of one or more family members takes considerable energy. Jobs and careers also take energy. Household management takes energy. Everything we do in our day takes energy. Sometimes, several needs pile up at the same time, as if the gears on the family needs escalator went into high speed. We have to learn how to slow down our pace so that we can respond to our child one interaction at a time. The action of relating to a child in one interaction sounds deceptively easy. However, there are many times during our busy day when we simply are not aware of a child's present needs, because we are thinking about our own unmet needs.

Often we are unaware of self-territory. We also find ourselves blind to our child's underlying self-territory. **The first step in addressing** *any* **parenting snafu requires a few deep breaths to feel centered within your inner home base, or self-territory.** While many have described the concept of self, probably each person has a slightly different idea of the meaning. Marriage and family therapist Richard Schwartz defines a "core self" as becoming aware of "a state of calm well-being and lightheartedness."[10]

"Self" (from an Old English word, *zelf*), as it applies to our parenting purposes, suggests a foundation for one's personality: "the uniting principle, as a soul, underlying all subjective experience" and "that which knows, remembers . . . as contrasted with that known, remembered."

Secondary words help us comprehend further self-reflection meanings:

- "know" from the Latin word *(g)novi*, "to understand as truth . . . to be aware of";
- "remember" from the Latin *re*, "backward or again," plus the Latin *memor*, "keep in mind; remain aware of"; and
- "soul," from the Old English word *sawl* (related to sea, fancied habitation of the soul): "the spiritual part of man regarded in its moral aspect."[11]

Perhaps our special linkage with the sea reflects our earliest lives in our mothers' wombs. While we have strong connections with water, we have equally powerful ties to water's opposite, land. All of us function within some kind of land or external territory. However, we also function within interior territory.

With the word "territory," we initially conjure up images of land, turf, and boundaries, as the Latin word *terra* means land. Psychiatrist Albert Scheflen describes how territories are necessary for the survival for each flock, pride, or troop of animals; each group has communication within its own territory.[12] A dictionary definition providing the underlying meaning for "territory" for our use suggests an interior *space*: "a field or sphere of action, thought . . . domain."[13]

A definition for *self-territory* therefore encompasses several meanings: a uniting principle underlying our personal experiences, a knowing as truth, a spiritual/moral sphere, and a field of awareness. The sphere of *self* includes both action and thought, or *territory*.

UNCHARTED TERRITORY

When you hear someone say, "I am not myself today," the person means that she feels preoccupied and has not made a *connection* to *self-territory* today. She feels as though she has uncharted *territory*. She has not taken time to breathe deeply, listen, or reflect. When we do not listen well to one another, different moods—or mind divisions—whether acknowledged or not, keep us from being able to focus on the present moment, even when that moment involves ourselves. "When we look into the mirror, we initially examine our features, but then the mind 'loses it.' Our thoughts wander; we think about what happened that day, our jobs, our relationships. We drift off into another world, plan our day, and think about how nice it would be to sleep for another hour."[14] Sometimes our minds are so wrapped up with different mind divisions in our personalities that we miss the *present* moment altogether. Can you think of a time when your child asked you a question and you totally spaced out, even though the two of you were standing right next to each other?

The self-sphere we inhabit is one of continuous meaning making that undergirds the daily steps we take. Yet we do not take the time to recognize our own self-territory often enough as we rush from need to need, action to reaction. Similarly, we do not slow down long enough to acknowledge the inner presence, or self-territory, in those around us.

Knowledge of your inner self-sphere helps provide a map to "making it" through life's difficult journey. Having the presence to relate to your child one interaction at a time requires intention and awareness. What do you have to do in the present moment in order to mobilize self-territory for one interaction at a time?

- Slow down your racing thoughts by taking three deep breaths. My tai chi teacher, Beatrice DeFranco, instructs, "Find the place

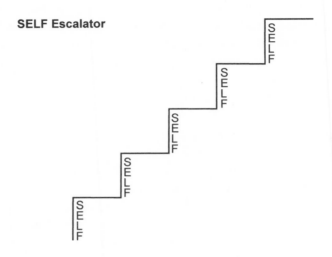

SELF Escalator

Figure 1.3.

where your breathing interacts with your navel." I like this image. All of us *first* breathe in interaction with our mothers; deep breaths that feel as though they touch one's navel are symbolic.

- Become aware of the intuitive, reflective nature underlying your personality. Just like vast, uncharted land and water territories, self-territory has a quality of *spaciousness* that awaits your discovery. Your recognition of self-territory continues to grow as you focus on becoming aware in present moments.
- Have patience. Devote yourself to becoming a responsible listener.
- Do not give up when you "mess up" and yell at your child. Collect your runaway thoughts and take some deep breaths. Say that you are sorry that you yelled and that you want to say something *different* now. There are multiple daily opportunities to practice relating to others one interaction at a time.

Like the territory of an underground stream always running in several different directions, our self-territory connects us to the self-territory of others. When we are in contact with our self-territory, we have the best chance of meeting our own daily survival needs along with our child's daily survival needs. We find space to relate to our needs and our child's needs one interaction at a time.

For example, can we notice that our child has an aching need for more energy if we have an acute need for belonging at the very same moment? Therefore, we see the *present* situation with clarity and acceptance. This perspective allows us to make wise choices in deciding how best to meet the various needs of family members. We come to appreciate the personality story-*house* in everyone's life—the remembered lessons other people keep in mind and their perceptions of truth—along with our own story-house. We come to perceive that we are the ones who create our own adult story and set our own internal compass for the directions we want to take in the present.

We perceive ourselves as *aware*—able to stop what we are doing in the moment, able to look for our child's nonverbal messages, and able to have a capacity for *responsible listening*. When we enter such self-territory, we have the capability to hold, or contain, opposite roles in our personality with equal respect for their messages. Self-territory allows acceptance for opposite roles and opposite needs in family members. We can bring order to chaos in our conflicts in the family by asking ourselves, "What do I have to do in the *present* moment?"

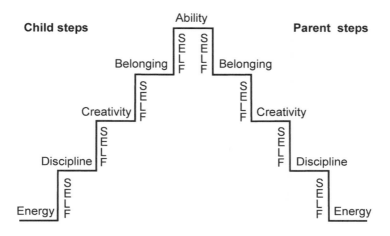

Figure I.4.

BE HERE NOW

The key for caretakers is being present, being here now, and able to engage in one interaction at a time, thereby experiencing self-territory with our child. In addition to tuning into self-territory, all of us have energy, discipline, creativity, belonging, and ability needs we simultaneously seek to fulfill. The juggling act of fitting our issues into some kind of meaningful pattern that enhances our own unique opportunities in life while meeting the basic needs of our child presents challenges. We often fail to perceive any common ground among family members' needs. Some parents view their own agenda as more important than a child's daily docket. Other caretakers overlook their own needs to elevate the issues of someone else, often their child's, in the family. **Frequently, problems in our family life stem from the ways in which we define both our own and others' needs.**

The major challenges of parenting are dismantling our own childhood need baggage, discovering ways to connect with every kind of child, and forming empowering relationships with each child. We often struggle to find any self-territory for one interaction at a time because we are too busy multitasking our way through life and making up for past unmet needs. When we have not been able to experience self-territory for myriad reasons, parenting may appear as an enormous hardship. Perhaps we did not learn enough positive empowering steps from the previous generation, but this lack of knowledge does not mean we are doomed to commit the errors of our ancestors. In fact, each generation has new opportunities for raising *up* its members. These opportunities are parent-in-training remodeling, or changing the story we tell ourselves about who we are. What if we do not view family needs as conflicting needs but learn to view them as complementary needs? What if families learn how to help *each* family member negotiate meeting *each* kind of need along the raising road?

I find parenting has similarities to gardening. Most gardeners do not amend the soil before planting. They are in a hurry to plant seeds or tiny transplants, so they stick them into the ground without first improving the garden soil with organic material. Often, any fertilizer is added later and may not be as helpful. In the same way, many parents attempt to rear children without first preparing *themselves* for the job. However, preparing for parenthood by making amendments in our own growing up yields a better crop of children.

PERSONALITY STORY-HOUSE IN THE MAKING

Each person gathers stories of their day-to-day interactions while traveling the raising road of learning to meet basic needs. Stories are learning tools for all of us, not just for youngsters who love to hear stories read by a caretaker. In fact, before books were printed, people shared their learning through fables and storytelling. In Europe during the Middle Ages, many stories flourished as painted legends upon the outside walls of buildings; each floor held a different tale, and these various floors were called "stories."[15] Certain themes ran through a collection of the stories on one building. Similarly, each person stores certain themes within particular life roles in the various levels of their personality story-house. We keep remodeling or evolving our life story as we age.

We begin to construct the foundation for our personality story-house even before we have language development, as bodily memories from early childhood carry their own story versions. One father recalls nightmares from his childhood. He dreamed he was being born and was positioned "upside down, like in a well," with sensations of "doing a headstand to right himself." This young father carries uncomfortable memories of his mother telling him that he had a "terrible birth." Whether we link pictures to tell a family story in our personality storehouse or piece together images and sensations from our memories of prior events, we use stories to make some meaning out of life. Our stories influence our lives and our relationships with others.[16] We store these stories in our personality story-house. Our stories create a cocoon in which we live.

STORY-HOUSE MEMORIES

We build our story-house of memories one story at a time, and throughout our lives, we keep plastering our story-house walls to evolve certain aspects of our "story." Our personality story-houses are not set in "hard plaster"; in fact, research supports a "soft plaster" personality that changes "gradually but systematically throughout the life span, sometimes more after age 30 than before."[17] Significantly, the personality traits of conscientiousness and agreeableness were found to increase for both women and men throughout early and middle adulthood, while the trait termed "neuroticism" declined for women but did not change among men.[18] In other words, women were found to become less emotionally dependent and more "competent" with age, while men started adulthood less dependent and feeling "competent," traits that remained with them over time.[19] Life can seem scary to many young women.

When we face scary terrain though, we often bury the details of the painful stories we stash in our personality storehouses. We do not think about problem solving; we shut down our need machine temporarily. While we may not be able to focus our present attention in a traumatic event, our brains store the ordeal in nonverbal form.[20] Whether we acknowledge frightening details from our past or not, story fragments exist in the basement of our story-house, making up our personality foundation. We then function as if we have shoved such details—sometimes whole memories—down the basement stairs of our story-house.

We forget about the basement of our personality story-house, consciously preferring to live on higher ground. However, some basements flood. One child's situation, or even one neighbor child's experience, can cause a deluge of forgotten memories to rise from the walls of our personality basement. Like ancient hieroglyphics, old stories beckon us to decipher their meaning. **Suddenly, we can feel five, or ten, or fifteen all over again when our child reaches five, ten, or fifteen years of age and their experience draws forth one of our stories and its meaning.** In this regard, our children raise us *up* into greater consciousness of our life's meaning through one story at a time.

I offer composite stories of families in the pages that follow. Actually, all of our stories are composites, as we frequently incorporate bits of other people's stories into our own personality story-house. Like the wooden Russian doll that houses many smaller dolls inside, we layer our life stories within stories when we recall our earlier experiences. Later, our story fragments combine in remodeled renditions as we tell our stories to others. As psychologist Dan McAdams suggests, we tell others who we are by the stories we share from our experiences. Storytelling appears across cultures and helps us organize our lives:[21] "We become the stories that we tell; our stories aren't single authored."[22]

The following composite stories reflect the themes that habitually come into play as families seek to survive everyday life. Many relay some universal sagas and lessons we all live out. Each story has an accompanying developmental milepost and age marker to provide "travel tips" for particular ages. However, developmental phases do not hold to rigid age norms. Every person has unique patterns of growing up. Developmental tips for certain ages reflect issues that are typical of many children at a particular age.

INCONSISTENT BEHAVIOR

"Eddie" begins our caretaker/raising road stories. Children are not consistent creatures, and we are not consistent caretakers. One minute we espouse one parenting philosophy; the next minute we express a conflicting notion. **We can understand the chameleon patterns of our own children when we embrace our own chameleon ways.** Eddie's story illustrates why it takes a child to raise a parent.

Eddie (9)

> Nine years old and not demonstrating even a hint of kid chatter, this belligerent boy bellows at his tall, stately mother. Like a rooster with puffed up feathers, Eddie swaggers in a pseudoadolescent gait. He boasts, blames, defends, and defies. He taunts, teases, and dares his mother to discipline him. Hands on his hips, he demands to go to the store for a video game. He brings a video magazine to therapy, showing me all the violent selections he wants. He alternates between glaring at his mother and curling up next to her, like a cat who desires mealtime. Scampering off in one direction but ending up in the opposite direction, Eddie has ever-changing moods. He cries when someone treats him badly at recess, yet he bullies other children who are smaller in stature.

There are some other angles to Eddie's personality though. Talking alone with me in a therapy session, Eddie speaks in a soft, high-pitched voice that sounds much younger than his bravado voice of earlier. He has tears in his eyes when he recalls one time when his friends deserted him at lunch and an older student bullied him. He sheepishly admits that he gets scared when he watches violent movies; he has bad dreams about movie characters who commit murder on-screen. But Eddie worries what his friends will think if he confides in them that he does not like horror movies. When asked what he would like his parents to do differently, what they could do to help him, Eddie takes his time in answering. He sucks in his breath and wheezes out muscled air. I take a long deep breath along with Eddie. Thoughtfully, Eddie finally speaks in a small, quiet voice to say he wishes his parents would not hit him.

DEVELOPMENT DIRECTIONS

> I believe that any people's story is every people's story, and that from stories, we can all learn something to enrich our lives.
> —Harriette Gillem Robinet, *If You Please, President Lincoln*

A child's needs signal a number of similar needs for caretakers. We often do not confront the unhelpful, nonilluminating dead ends of our early travels until we become parents and find ourselves face-to-face with some triggered memory in our own childhood story-house. Here, Eddie struggles with discipline and belonging needs. Eddie's mother squirms when she relates her own difficult childhood with an alcoholic mother. She turns sideways, unable to face me eye to eye, as she recalls some unhappy memories. She has her own discipline issues with drinking too much. She struggles with the guilty role this behavior engenders: "I always thought in raising my children, I would do things differently."

Sometimes parents do not share their painful excursions along their raising road with their children, thinking that they can protect them from the dangerous developmental highways that children don't know about. Sometimes parents grasp their child's plight quickly, and they steer their problem solving in creative directions. Many times, however, a child's needs drive the family car into reverse, jolting the parents into recalling their *own* developmental collisions at a similar age. Perhaps, for the first time as an adult with the capacity for abstract or cause-effect thinking, parents grasp the significance of their own childhood tortures that, until now, were buried in the basement of their personality story-house.

Tip for Raising Nine-Year-Olds

Boys need permission to express scared and sad feelings. "Emotional isolation wears many faces. Sometimes it comes in the guise of anger, sarcasm, or hostility. . . . Boys . . . see almost everyone and everything as unworthy of respect . . . [when] it's they [the boys themselves] who feel worthless."[23]

Burying certain memories serves a protective function. We dislike feeling fear or pain on our life journey. We feel ill equipped to navigate our way through such bumpy roads. Some parents lose or divorce some of the other passengers in their family car, thinking that their life's trip can progress better with fewer backseat drivers. Still others travel along some of their family's old pathways while trying to add some new routes along the way. When we have a new child join us for the family expedition, suddenly we face an *awareness* of the enormity of our choices. Our questions create more baggage than we would like. Are we ready for the parenting open road? Which gears are best for parenting a moody child? And why do *we* feel so moody so much of the time?

STOMACHACHE-HEARTACHE

Frank (10) and Susan (35)

> Frank misses a day of school due to a stomachache of undetermined causes. Susan calls her son's teacher to obtain his missed homework. Now, Frank does not want to go to school the next day, as he will have to take three tests. He studies for one test and feels overwhelmed; his energy slips away. Only at his mother's urging does Frank put in three and a half hours of studying. Yet during this time, he does not focus on what he knows and learns but on his notion that he knows "nothing." Susan detects Frank's increasingly jittery mood, yet she too feels an energy drain. "Why does Frank always procrastinate? Why doesn't he have discipline or willpower? Why didn't I make him go to school today?" In a tense argument, Susan yells her brand of discipline at Frank and sends him to his room for a time-out

"for the rest of the night." Meanwhile, another child takes cover in
his bedroom to stay clear of his mother's verbal missiles. He knows
the pose—"I'm angry and you better not cross my path"—just looking at his mother's contorted face.

Now Susan reflects upon her own plight. She knows she is edging
closer and closer to a cold war with her spouse. Her husband is working
late—again—and the entire burden of parent homework has fallen on
her shoulders after a stressful workday at the office. Lately, it seems to
Susan as if her husband belongs more to his office mates than to his
married mate. Susan smolders with anger as she considers all of the
household work before her this evening. She procrastinates, her own
discipline falters, and she does not begin any of the house homework.
Then she remembers an earlier phone call. Frank's teacher blithely
says, "I don't see any stress at school; is Frank stressed at home?" Susan
starts to cry as she flashes upon a scene from her own childhood. Her
father, "the original homework tyrant," rants and raves at her own with-
ering attempts at evening homework assignments. Susan suddenly
makes connections between her ineffective student status and the yelling from her father, her own yelling at her son, and her son's inept
homework efforts. The parenting road stretches at least a few decades.
Susan regrets that she hated school (and her father) on a frequent basis
when she was a child.

Susan wonders in a later therapy session what she might have done
career-wise if she had studied more. She grieves her lost ability potential. Susan fast-forwards to the present situation with Frank. She finds
Frank in his room, burrowed under the covers in his bedroom bunker;
he cries also. Spent, mother and child console each other with hugs and
kisses. They have finally made space in their hectic day for one peaceful
interaction. They do not have all their needs met, but they take a break,
a respite from their needs. Backtracking, Susan wishes for a peaceful
interaction with her father, but she doubts it will ever materialize. Then
she fast-forwards to the present moment again. In this moment, she can
make something happen. Susan apologizes for yelling; Frank says he
will go to school the next day.

DEVELOPMENT DIRECTIONS

> In the mirror, I could see both myself at ten and my mother at eighty. . . . I could still catch a glimpse of that same bewildered, lost kid I sometimes was. In the mirror, I could see the old woman I was becoming.
>
> —Barbara Hamilton-Holway, *Who Will Remember Me?*

Both Susan and Frank struggle with having enough energy, discipline, creativity, belonging, and ability. Developmental growth challenges the energy needs of both caretaker and child. Homework for children and housework for parents flows more smoothly with a few simple discipline rules in the home: When do children begin their homework each school night? Who washes dishes after dinner? How many family members participate in laundry loads? Next, our development progresses with more ease with a little creativity in household problem solving. One family puts their creative suggestions for house cleaning into an empty tissue box. Everyone draws a suggestion from the box and pitches in to clean up. Evening time in the home can ebb from one stream of activity to the next without major snafus. All members of the household will feel a sense of belonging to every other family member and solidify their familial bonds if each one tells the others how much he or she loves them. Each person, regardless of age, benefits from the encouragement to use their abilities to meet their potential. Susan plans to encourage Frank as much as she can, especially as she regrets her lost ability as a youngster and struggles to find satisfaction in a lackluster job that does not challenge her abilities. She does not want Frank to repeat her story as an adult.

Tip for Raising Ten-Year-Olds

Ten-year-olds are very aware of a parent's criticism. "But some—boys more than girls—feel that mother is always trying to improve them."[24]

Tip for Raising Thirty-Five-Year-Olds

Parents need support just as much as children need support. "There is no 'present' for us parents who do too much. There is only past and future. If we take time to stop, in the midst of our whirlwind schedule, we can tell you what we just 'did,' and what we now 'have to do.' We are going from 'here' to get to 'there.' We are not experiencing life; we are only living it."[25]

TEENAGE ANGST

The teenage years challenge most parents in training. Many times, our teenagers grow to be taller than we are as parents. Their everyday emotions also appear to grow tall.

Hanna (16), Helen (38), and Ethan (40)

> Mornings are terrible; nights are worse. Hanna tests every discipline limit that her parents set for her. Helen and Ethan say that a curfew on school nights protects study time, and they make 8:30 p.m. the weeknight curfew. Yet Hanna saunters home anywhere between 8:45 and 11:00 p.m. Helen takes away Hanna's phone privileges as a punishment for the curfew violation. Hanna then sneaks Helen's cell phone into her bedroom after her mom goes to bed, and she keeps her social, or belonging, life percolating long into the night. Ethan has a rule that no guests are allowed if adults are not home, so he takes away Hanna's house key after teenage boys accompany her home after school. A friend of Hanna's picks the door lock, allowing several teens to come into the forbidden domain. When ongoing punishment results in ongoing retaliation, a stalemate exists between the warring family members.

At family therapy, tense nonverbal poses flash knowing signals among Hanna, Helen, and Ethan. Unspoken family patterns dictate the rules for engagement. Each one speeds into the room and then collapses into a sofa, winded and devoid of energy before anyone even speaks. Their tightly coiled anger saps their energy. Accustomed to yelling, the sparring trio rages at one another within minutes of walking into my therapy office. "I hate you!" sputters Hanna. "You never listen to me," spits back Helen. Ethan raises his voice at them: "Just shut up!" Critical glares and angry stares appear in each personality's repertoire of poses; all other possible emotional roles hide under a personality stage cramped with fury. As each person snarls, I roll my office chair a few inches forward into the referee zone. I validate each personality role. Then I begin to identify unmet needs.

DEVELOPMENT DIRECTIONS

> A good start is only a start, though. Focused on the beginning of life, Western societies see later needs far less clearly.
>
> —Penelope Leach, *Children First*

Hanna's anger erupts when she does not perceive acceptance for her social or belonging issues. Helen worries about Hanna's basic energy needs and her ability issues at school. Ethan wants discipline to reign at all costs. All three of them have legitimate points of view. Each believes that his or her perspective deserves attention. It does, but creativity has not entered their problem solving. Each operates out of his or her personality story-house of memories with little awareness of the roles he or she plays. Only when each family member acknowledges and accepts his or her particular communication style does a more promising dialogue ensue. We are capable of finding common ground in the present moment in self-territory by listening with present ears and working on the underlying value of trust in any relationship. Conscious, aware thinking has a quieting effect.

Tip for Raising Sixteen-Year-Olds

Brace yourself with deep breaths; teens test limits. "Knee-jerk reactions kick back! Ask, listen, discuss, and decide together especially when you feel a knee-jerk reaction coming on."[26]

Tip for Raising Thirty-Eight-Year-Olds

Seeing a child develop an adult body raises fears in adults. "This is not a phase that my child is just passing through, this is it: my child is becoming a grown-up, and I am becoming old."[27]

Tip for Raising Forty-Year-Olds

Model the behavior you want your teen to follow; then model the behavior repeatedly. "Children need models rather than critics."[28]

UNDERSTANDING THE IMPORTANCE OF NONVERBAL POSES

What parenting techniques will Eddie, Frank, and Hanna stash in their personality story-houses for future parenting? Through these composite stories, we can detect a number of nonverbal messages that tell something important about each one's needs. Eddie's swagger, Frank's stomachache, and Hanna's sneakiness speak loudly. **In our verbal society, we give little credence to nonverbal feeling states. We ignore others' nonverbal signals as well as our own. We assume that words are necessary for every message.**

I took my parents, both in their eighties, to see a 1920s "silent" movie. It had only a few subtitles; they introduced a new scene or gave a brief conversation clip. However, there was little doubt as to what the "silent" mouths might be saying. The exaggerated bodily poses told the story without needing verbalization. My parents and I laughed almost nonstop at the ironic and silly antics on screen. We are mammals who sense others' actions by "reading" body poses.

Our culture devalues those who do not speak well. For example, the word "dumb" formally means "without the power of speech or mute."[29] However, the words "dumb" and "stupid" plague our playgrounds daily and misconstrue the idea that nonverbal behavior equals less intelligence. We forget the wise adage of Benjamin Franklin: "Well done is better than well said." We tend to discount people in our world who do not have facile language skills—children, developmentally disabled people, mentally ill people, the hearing impaired. We instead look for bold words and people who can deliver them, in spite of the fact that words often mislead. If we operate predominantly from our left hemisphere's language base, we make mistakes in perceiving nonverbal communication in others. We do not consider any self-territory. We focus on fleeting speech; we do not notice that swaggers, stomachaches, and sneakiness have a way of speaking that lingers in story-house walls like hidden mold.

Thus parents "misread" pieces of behavior they see in their child, often taking messages from verbal cues rather than noticing the more prevalent nonverbal language offered. **Most of us experience a reading disability in the realm of "reading" nonverbal snippets of behavior in others. Then we construct a whole line of thinking based upon *our* assumptions and *our* needs.** Often we are wrong in our interpretations of children's behavior. We assume the worst about a particular child behavior, or we interpret devious behavior lurking in front of our nose as positive. Whatever the nature of our miscues, these behavioral roles and poses we envision in children's personalities often are not the real story. Not only do we misinterpret which roles of a child's personality are most prevalent, but also we overlook their basic needs and self-territory.

BODY TALK

The physician who helped pioneer biofeedback, Elmer Green, finds that changes in our personality roles link with corresponding nonverbal changes in our bodies whether we realize these changes or not.[30] Picture the pose of a person filled with incredible rage: the eyes narrow, the face flushes, and the teeth show a menacing grimace, which brings to mind the popular phrase "in your face." Remember the saying "If looks could kill"? Such "looks," or body poses, speak loudly to us, even though words are not used. The word "pose" is a derivative of the Latin word *pausa*, meaning "to halt or stop." Two definitions define these nonverbal reactions or poses: "bodily attitude or posture" and "a mental attitude or posture."[31] We pose, or pause, in habitual nonverbal postures in unique body talk throughout our daily interactions, often without considering what message(s) we convey.

All of us send certain body-talk poses to our children, and they contain powerful messages. Ray Birdwhistell, a researcher in anthropology, studied body language or nonverbal poses. His analyses of body poses suggested that no one movement ever stands alone; a person's moves always are part of a pattern.[32] Such patterns require two ingredients for nonverbal communication—giving a message and receiving a message. Unfortunately, delivering a message does not ensure that the communication sent matches the message received.[33] Remember the child's game of telephone? One child whispers some tidbit into another's ear. The second child relays the message to the next child. By the time the whispered message makes it around the circle of children, the final tale often has little or no resemblance to the initial story. Here lies the crux of human miscommunication: **we assume that our children *listen* to our words, yet, many times, they do not ingest our meaning because we offer messages that are more powerful through our nonverbal poses.** Think of the old saying, "Do as I say, not as I do."

We believe our verbal messages reach our children. However, almost everyone uses multiple nonverbal poses to send a message; vocal loudness, speed of talking, and the amount of talking mix with facial cues, activity cues, and bodily movements.[34] The body talk messages we send often carry more than one intention. Mixed messages are so commonplace in daily family communication that it is no wonder that people frequently mutter, "I can't understand anything he says." Psychologist Albert Mehrabian outlines our ordinary conversation in percentages:

- Seven percent of our communication comes from our words;
- thirty-eight percent comes from *how* we say something; and
- fifty-five percent comes from how we *look* when we say something.[35]

We miss the most valuable communicating in a conversation because it takes place nonverbally, without any boisterous fanfare. We erroneously read others' personality roles predominantly from their words, missing the communicating they deliver through nonverbal poses. It is as if we constantly send message missiles and they miss their intended targets. When we do read body poses, we rely on our translation of another's nonverbal posture, signaling, and voice quality. As in the folk-wisdom saying, we do not "see the forest for the trees."

YOU CRITICIZED ME (AGAIN)

We criticize others for not hearing our self-important messages. Likewise, we receive criticism from others almost continually. We live in an assessment-bound culture, so we assess ourselves and others from dawn until well beyond dusk. Others assess back. We continuously weigh our thoughts and behaviors along with others' words and actions; sometimes we measure every single word. Many of our measurements weigh in as heavy or negative: "Who does she think she is? She thinks she is somebody," mutters a tired mother to me after she has a conflict with her daughter's teacher. When we misinterpret another's comments and needs, we analyze them based upon our own personality roles. Misinterpretation of a child's nonverbal body poses occurs. We calculate our own thoughts as solid evidence, in spite of the fact that all measuring has a bias due to the measure maker's perceptions. We often miss the opportunity for relating to our child one interaction at a time. In order to relate in the present moment, we have to listen more with our eyes focused, our nose, mouth, and intuition ready to pick up cues, and our posture attuned to our child.

Hands on both hips, a father demands of his teen son, "Who in the —— do you think you are?" Undaunted, the son (who qualifies as *somebody*) puts his hands on his own hips and fires back, "Who in the —— do you think *you* are?" We can guess that this popular swear now files itself in the teen's repertoire for future use. Our physical poses to our children are nearly constant. **Having observed our caretakers handle difficult situations, not only did we learn certain fears and voice inflections from their example, but we also copied their body language poses.**

Another body-language example comes to mind. I turn a corner inside a store's aisle. A woman's sharp voice slashes the air: "Stop swinging my damn purse." The glare on her twentysomething face hardens more with each punctuated word. I pick up danger in thin air. I stop in my tracks. The two young children accompanying her (their mother? their babysitter?) stop, too. I quickly gather careful words, but I do not say anything as a child steps onto center stage. After a few seconds of silence, the younger one (a sibling of the child who received the reprimand?) looks contrite and begins a soulful rendition: "Twinkle, twinkle little star / how I wonder what you are . . ." The woman appears chagrined. Her youngest charge, in one interaction at a time, raises the bar for civility in a simple song. In the softest of chameleon-caretaker tones, the harried woman switches roles and offers, "Come on, let's go." Which personality poses will imprint themselves on the children's personality portfolios?

Parent poses have the possibility of modeling beneficial roles and/or harsh roles. Many different adaptations exist in the memory rooms of our story-houses; some children copy their parents' exact behaviors, while others pledge they will never copy their actions. One mother admits, "I never thought I'd say this . . . I tried so hard not to be my mother, but now I keep hearing my mother's voice every time I discipline Joana. I'm even starting to look like my mother!" While people's wording may change, body posture can repeat similar moves through the generations. Many moves receive so much practice that they become our poses, or our regular nonverbal posture, for given situations.

MOODY BODIES

While we are often unaware of how our bodies pose our personality roles, sometimes we recognize our moody moves, even trying to stand or move in a particularly exaggerated way to get a certain kind of reaction. Teenagers master the mechanics of flirtatious poses; a head toss, a hair twirl, and a sidelong glance become second nature to girls who want to attract a boy. Actors know moody body poses well; in fact, our culture rewards those adept at performing personality poses so clearly that we cannot tell if their actions are insincere. Some actors repeat certain poses so frequently that we say they are "typecast," or incapable of playing out a variety of personality postures. One businessperson casts his personality in these words: "I am just an actor—I just role play." Like the typecast actor, we repeat frozen-in-time poses in our personalities.

Body-mind psychotherapist Susan Aposhyan suggests how indelibly posture reflects our personalities; we practice certain body postures, movements, and breathing, which become anchors[36] of our personality roles. **Our personality story-house resides in our bodies as well as in our minds.** As body-mind psychotherapist Babette Rothschild points out, body, or "somatic," memory appears neither more nor less reliable than other kinds of memory. Over time, the accuracy of cognitive memory and body memory can shift. [37]

These altered memories of our story-house link up with our practiced personality poses. As adults, we carry with us early images from the poses demonstrated repeatedly by our caretakers. The power of parental nonverbal influence lingers well into old age. Ancestor voices echo in our ears. Ancestor poses creep into our limbs. One grandparent reminisces how his father looked at him when he did not meet his father's stern expectations: "I always knew what that look meant—I'd better get to my chores right away or I'd get a beating with the horse whip." I ask how he looked at his own son in the growing-up years; he seemed surprised when he answered that he had copied his father's stern gaze on a regular basis. We are not so conscious of our own nonverbal communication.

CONSCIOUS STORIES

In a family restaurant, I walk into the middle of parents dishing up an extra order of frustration. A mother: "I've asked you plenty. Now I'm going to put my hand over your mouth if you don't stop." A father: "You are going to sit and you are going to eat." A mother: "OK, I'm going to ask you nicely, and then you are going to do it." A father: "We are not arguing—sh-sh-sh." A mother: "Do you want a nap?" A father: "We are moving over to another table. Shut up!" I silently wonder what goes on at home if these admonishments are "public" family fare. If I am losing my appetite, what happens to energy in the stomachs of these children? How can anyone enjoy his or her meal? What discipline will work when these youngsters reach adolescence? I eat quickly, and when I wrap myself in the outdoor warmth of the final weekend of summer, I mull over possible transition stories such a family encounters: the end of a family vacation, the beginning a new school year, a parent's job promotion, the illness or death of a relative or friend, the early decay in a marital relationship. Are these parents conscious of their personality story-houses? Maybe these families are experiencing several transitions at once. Transitions happen with such roundabout regularity in families that most days we seem to drive the family car around in circles.

We forget to look into our own evolving personality story-houses, our own storehouse of memories we gather from earlier moments of our lives, for insight into our actions. Battling roles in our personality clamor for different directions, and we become confused along our developmental highways, unable to decide which way to turn next. Where are the "right" turns on the yellow brick road of family life? How different would our family story be if we turned "left"? As discussed earlier, we often look for external wizards to guide us to some imagined Oz. We want parental Munchkins who can help us find our way.

We mistakenly believe the old saying, "The grass is greener on the other side of the fence," thinking that somebody else knows exactly what parental direction to take next. As caretakers, we hold a responsible role. We want to make wise decisions, as we know we have some influence over our young charges. **However, as we are all creatures of habit, when we face a crossroads, we are likely to rely on decisions we have made on other occasions regardless of past negative outcomes.** I watch a rabbit chew on prized hosta plants in my garden; my rapid walking toward the gourmet diner always causes it to take cover under the same evergreen bushes in the side yard. All of us take cover in familiar poses of behavior, just like scared rabbits returning to safe turf. What do we teach our children about choices and postures for scary situations? How can we help them find safe territory on a daily basis? There are few pat answers for the multitude of child development questions.

SELF-TERRITORY THROUGH A CHILD'S EYES

Who rates as *somebody*? Everyone is somebody with basic needs and self-territory. A five-year-old boy tells me proudly, "I'm somebody at school!" His father grins and notices the joyful body cues of his expressive youngster. The dad explains that his son's teacher assigns rotating jobs to each child each week. This week, his son has the important job of helping his teacher when she says, "I need somebody to . . ." Listening to his father's explanation, the son beams and adds, "I like being somebody!"

All of us are important *somebodies* to ourselves and to those around us. All of the ways we describe who we are help us understand that we are not lost, that we are somebodies meeting basic needs. When we can calm ourselves and find inner self-territory, we face our struggles with new eyes for meeting our energy, discipline, creativity, belonging, and ability needs. Psychologist Kristin Neff calls this capacity "self-compassion," or being able to "hold painful thoughts and feelings in balanced awareness."[38]

Kenny (10)

Kenny faces academic-ability challenges at school but feels good about himself when he uses his athletic ability in baseball. He thinks about self-territory with this pitch: "Your self is kind of like the home base inside of you. It is where you are headed. . . . When you get there, you can breathe easier . . . you can relax . . . the pressure is off . . . you have arrived 'home.'" Kenny then tells about a recent baseball game in which his friends all came up to him, tapped him on the shoulder when he reached home base, and said to him, "Nice job." I use a child's language to continue our dialogue: "Yes, it is something like that when you reach your inside home base. Only this time, you can tap all the different parts of you from your inner self and say, 'Nice job for helping me out today.' What else could you say as your special inside coach?" After laughing and giving himself love taps all over his feet, legs, hips, rear end, chest, arms, neck, face, and hair, Kenny says repeatedly, "Nice job for just being a kid and trying your best." He then asks for paper. Kenny draws self-territory as the Land of Oz.

DEVELOPMENT DIRECTIONS

Generally, Oz is a gentle land where the good are rewarded and bad forgiven.

—Michael Patrick Hearn, *The Annotated Wizard of Oz*

Many children have a strong sense of self-territory by age ten. Our job as caretakers requires that we reinforce a child's inner resources just as much as we reinforce their external deeds.

Tip for Raising Ten-Year-Olds

Talk with your child about seeing his or her life as a "nice job for just being a kid and trying your best." "Boys need . . . a sense of self that includes the desire to grow into men who are kind, disciplined, and caring. Someone must spend the time making sure that they know we care more about the quality of their hearts and their spirits than we do about their clothes and their haircuts."[39]

STORY-HOUSE MAPPING

Owning your personality story-house takes a lifetime. Some people die without owning up to the "facts" and transitions they endured as children in training or parents in training. The reason to own our memories—to learn to search through the various roles in our personalities as well as the personalities of significant others for clues—rests upon our search for meaning in life. When no senior family members are available to help you sift through your family stories, consider the other ways in which you can gather stories of your early history:

- Look for family pictures of yourself at various ages. Sometimes, one picture triggers a memory about life circumstances at the developmental age captured in the snapshot.
- Consider family pictures as still life art. Take time to notice the background, the clothing or other props, and the overall posture of family members, including everyone's facial expression.
- Write a brief story about special family pictures. Your stories can take a fairytale approach or a more realistic tone. No one will grade your writing, so feel free to put down whatever comes to mind. Record your mapping entries in a journal, or jot down your ideas on loose-leaf paper that you keep in a folder. If writing seems cumbersome, you can either tell your stories to another person or record them for your children to listen to at another time.
- Include pertinent personality roles in your story. You may discover some roles that do not seem very much like you today. Just collect the roles as they occur to you, and jot them down for future reference.

- Consider the stories you write or tell others. Look for overall themes across stories. Owning more stories about your past impacts your present life. One seven-year-old boy came to a therapy session saying, "I had the worst dream I ever had last night, but I can't tell anybody about it." Do we tell our children, "It's just a dream," and dismiss too readily the role of fear that lingers in their thoughts? All life events have some meaning for us.

- **Recognize the worth of your daily stories. You are in a better position to help children own and translate their daily stories one interaction at a time when you have encountered your own stories in your childhood's developmental transitions.**

2

DISCOVER WHAT A PERSONALITY STORY-HOUSE SAYS ABOUT US

We do not discover ourselves through myth; we make ourselves through myth. . . . Main characters work to personify our basic de- sires . . . the warrior, the sage, the lover, the caregiver, the humanist, the healer, and the survivor.

—Dan McAdams, psychologist, *The Stories We Live By*

We begin building our personality story-house of life memories at birth. Our first stories have enormous importance, but many parenting books jump into the middle of childhood without covering opening chapters of either a child's or parent's life. I believe we can avoid some mistakes our parents made when we consider our family's whole story. As psychologist Dan McAdams suggests, the caregivers with whom we spend our first year of life influence the kind of story we tell about ourselves as adults.[1] Like an old-fashioned hand-me-down article of clothing, the optimism and pessimism they pass to us ultimately find places in our closet. We hang on to first pleasures as well as first trau- mas, whether we remember the specific details of each event or not.

As we live and grow, we hopefully gain awareness and come to acknowledge the influence of both our early glad rags and sad rem- nants. However, more happy or traumatic events follow, making it diffi- cult to sort through our first memories later. Some closet doors in the rooms of our story-house can remain closed off for years. However, becoming a parent can heighten our awareness of our past. **As parents**

in training, we need to revisit our personality story-house and even engage in some remodeling. We also need to recognize where fairy tale accounts—and those that are closer to the truth—exist in our story-houses.

THE MEMORY STORY-HOUSE

This is my version of the story-house that Jack and Jill built.

 This is the memory
  That lay in the story-house that Jack and Jill built.
   This is the trauma
   That ate the memory
   That lay in the story-house that Jack and Jill built.
    This is the awareness
    That soothed the trauma
    That ate the memory
    That lay in the story-house that Jack and Jill built.
     This is trauma two
     That fought the awareness
     That soothed the trauma
     That ate the memory
     That lay in the story-house that Jack and Jill built.
      This is trauma three with the crumpled past
      That tossed trauma two
      That fought the awareness
      That soothed the trauma
      That ate the memory
      That lay in the story-house that Jack and Jill built.
       This is the caretaker, her roles cast
       That ignored trauma three with the crumpled past
       That tossed trauma two
       That fought the awareness
       That soothed the trauma
       That ate the memory
       That lay in the story-house that Jack and Jill built.
        This is the partner, way too "fast"
        That kissed the caretaker, her roles cast
        That ignored trauma three with the crumpled past
        That tossed trauma two

That fought the awareness
That soothed the trauma
That ate the memory
That lay in the story-house that Jack and Jill built.
 This is the priest who stood at the mast
 That married the partner, way too "fast"
 That kissed the caretaker, her roles cast
 That ignored trauma three with the crumpled past
 That tossed trauma two
 That fought the awareness
 That soothed the trauma
 That ate the memory
 That lay in the story-house that Jack and Jill built.
  This is the baby with cries so vast
  That surprised the priest who stood at the mast
  That married the partner, way too "fast"
  That kissed the caretaker, her roles cast
  That ignored trauma three with the crumpled past
  That tossed trauma two
  That fought the awareness
  That soothed the trauma
  That ate the memory
  That lay in the story-house that Jack and Jill built.
   This is the grandparent, sowing her last,
   That kept the baby with cries so vast
   That surprised the priest who stood at the mast
   That married the partner, way too "fast"
   That kissed the caretaker, her roles cast
   That ignored trauma three with the crumpled past
   That tossed trauma two
   That fought the awareness
   That soothed the trauma
   That ate the memory
   That lay in the story-house that Jack and Jill built.[2]

Our lives are not the stuff of common fairy tales or nursery rhymes. They only seem like repetitive stories because we all must meet the same needs that tumble down through our lives, one need after another. Thus many people's life stories echo parts of others' stories. In terms of parenting, connecting the dots to realize unconditional love for our new baby includes the following steps: recognizing our expectations about the birth, acknowledging there are opposite roles within a parent's personality, discovering our ongoing need for personality growth, and nurturing our personal resilience.

Parenting-Trip Tips

- Share with your significant other how your expectations in having a baby might differ from the reality of conception and childbirth.
- Recognize that the birth of your child and his or her personality opens up your awareness, as a parent in training, to opposing roles within your own personality.
- Begin to notice a network of roles in your personality story-house and how these roles relate to meeting your basic needs.
- Cultivate survival and resilience skills by practicing unconditional love for your child one interaction at a time.

RECOGNIZING OUR EXPECTATIONS AND MISCUES ABOUT OUR CHILD'S BIRTH

There can be little surprise that we do not have accurate expectations of having a baby. The staggering complexity of this, our first parenting interaction, daunts scientists. Even our nonscientific thinking misses, or overlooks, some of the basic facts. Consider the science of the egg-meets-sperm tale: after a sperm reaches an egg, its genes stay separate from the genes of the egg for one or more days. Then, once merged, the genome needs another day to take control of the cell. The so-called moment of conception actually requires twenty-four to forty-eight hours![3] Of fertilized eggs, only one-fourth to one-third continue growing; many eject or abort spontaneously. The intricate juggling of bodies and genes, with most genetic pitches ending up as "foul balls," describes the first interaction of parenting. Baseball itself never approaches this much uncertainty!

Now, contrast a poetic version of giving birth with a "just-the-facts" scientific version. First, here are excerpts from Alma Luz Villanueva's poem, "The Planet Earth Speaks," written to a precious newborn: "I spin through time and darkness: I glue you to me with love. I house your body with earth, your soul with air. You swim toward me each night crying, 'Mother' . . . I am spinning through the fabric of your dreams. I am ever present. I am an ancient pattern within you, without you, and you've never escaped my scrutiny or my stare. You are glued to me, but, yes, I've also taught you flight . . . and I made you to love me whole, small echo of my womb: to love me as I love you. Unconditionally."[4]

Words that are just as true as this beautiful portrayal of a mother's belonging attachment to her newborn come from psychologist Steven Pinker: "Every time a woman has sex with a man she is taking a chance at sentencing herself to years of motherhood . . . committing a chunk of her finite reproductive output to the genes and intentions of that man, forgoing the opportunity to use it with some other man who may have better endowments of either or both. The man . . . may be either implicitly committing his sweat and toil to the incipient child or deceiving his partner about such intention."[5] Such issues rarely surface in the heat of romance. Whether either individual intends to have a child, each parent in training must come to decide upon degrees of commitment if gestation occurs. **Indeed, the whole concept of giving birth floods our brains with multiple perspectives before the little tyke's official arrival on planet Earth.** Even for those who are actively planning to have a baby and are involved and committed in intimate partnerships, conception stories are complicated.

WHEN IS A PARENT A PARENT?

The first interaction in raising a child breeds complexity. First, it takes two parents in training interacting to create a child. Science helps us comprehend a few details. Romantic attraction relates to elevated levels of at least one brain stimulant, dopamine—the same brain chemical that underlies mammal attraction in prairie voles, a type of rodent that looks like a mouse.

Anthropologist Helen Fisher discovered that 90 percent of prairie voles live in monogamous relationships their entire lives. However, during research trials in which female prairie voles receive injections that reduce their dopamine levels, they lose their preference for monogamy and play the field like some humans. Then, when the female vole has an injection with an increase in dopamine, she again begins to have a preference for a certain male, the one who is with her at the time of the injection.[6] "All of the basic drives are associated with elevated levels of central dopamine. . . . Romantic love is a need, a craving. We need food. We need water. We need warmth. And the lover feels he/she needs the beloved."[7] A baby can be conceived from what are the cravings of chemistry.

Our romantic love also is linked with two other mating behaviors: lust, or a craving for sex, and attachment, the belonging need for secure and long-lasting relationships. Each of these three mating behaviors has accomplice neurochemicals. We already know that romantic love has ties with dopamine (and possibly with norepinephrine and serotonin); lust predominantly links with testosterone in both men and women, while attachment relates to the hormones oxytocin and vasopressin.[8] Our attachment behavior predisposes us to keep up a *connection* with a partner. However, as the neurochemicals in romantic love, lust, and attachment link with various other networks in the brain,[9] each Jack and Jill travels up the hills of parenting differently wired. For example, one or both parents may fail to grasp their creation connection with another. They may have been drunk or otherwise drugged when a parenting "pitch" reaches home base. In this way, parenting spring training arrives as a surprise to many. One estimate has about half of the six million pregnancies reported annually in the United States as unplanned.[10] Some parents in training can identify with the simple poem of sexual romance too early: "When I met you, I liked you. When I liked you, I loved you. When I loved you, I let you. When I let you, I lost you."[11]

Babies can be created from an intimate partnership, a casual "hookup," or, unfortunately, a rape. They can also be created in petri dishes through the aid of technology. Each kind of interaction creates its own story in our personality story-house of life memories that we carry with us over the years.

Other missteps can occur before we actually begin parenting. For example, relationships between couples can change during the nine-month pregnancy. Complex decisions abound regarding sexual intimacy, and straightforward conversations about intimacy threaten many individuals.[12] Thus complications gather on the doorstep to parenting. For many, meeting their sexual energy needs does not include the idea of parenthood. Unwanted pregnancy thrusts people onto the parenting highway at a very high speed. In stark contrast are those who discover that the filling of their sexual energy needs does not produce a child that is wanted. Fifteen to twenty percent of parental hopefuls experience some type of infertility.[13] An infertile couple faces invasive medical testing, much waiting, and considerable disappointment along the path that eventually leads to conception, adoption, or the difficult decision not to experience parenting.

INFERTILITY AND LOST DREAMS

Let's have a closer look at how baby-creation stories impact parents.

Elise (32) and Marvin (35)

> Married for eight years, Elise and Marvin begin creating a homey nest for a newcomer. A handy guy, Marvin remodels the family bungalow to include special details for a child's room, and Elise makes her own window treatments for the bedroom. The young couple saves money, works on strengthening their relationship, makes strong friendships with other couples, and appears emotionally ready for the parenting developmental transition in their coupledom. As parents in training, they enjoy sexual intimacy, too. Then "it" happens—or, rather, "it" does not happen. Their wish for a child does not materialize. They do not use contraception for more than a year, and no baby forms. Elise and Marvin go for medical tests, but the results are inconclusive. Fertility treatments begin. Still no child emerges from all their careful efforts. The couple investigates the option of adoption but realizes that grief is blocking their way. The lost dream of having a biological child is haunting Elise. Wisely, Elise and Marvin take a two-year period to reassess and regroup upon their foiled transition to parenthood. Yet two years later, they still have more questions than answers.

DEVELOPMENTAL DIRECTIONS

I knew that my "boys" had problems—they don't swim well at the deep end of the pool and even if they get to the deep end, there aren't that many of them.

> —Al Roker, weatherman, *Don't Make Me Stop This Car!*
> *Adventures in Fatherhood*

The loss of the ability to give birth affects each couple in unique ways. Some couples become so tense with the underlying uncertainty shadowing them everyday that they have marital conflicts, each blaming the other for being infertile. Other couples pull together, partners in problem solving and getting through this painful transition. Typically couples do not know much about their fertility potential until they attempt to conceive. The miscues involved with infertility therefore appear mysterious. Infertile parents in training experience disruption in meeting their daily energy, discipline, creativity, belonging, and ability needs. The natural order of creating the next generation eludes them. Their dream of creating life together becomes a precious and unattainable holy grail, an elusive dream they desire even more.

Tip for Raising Thirty-Two-Year-Olds

We say the biological clock ticks for women when they reach their thirties and their desire to have a baby appears thwarted. However, infertility affects the feelings of both women and men. "Emphasis is placed on trying to see infertility as a problem shared by the partners, despite the reality that most investigations and procedures are directed towards women."[14]

Tip for Raising Thirty-five Year Olds

Men experience the sting of infertility just as much as women, but they may not express their feelings on the topic. "For some men, infertility can denote a lack of virility and masculinity, and it is this aspect that is often more troubling than the denial of an opportunity to parent."[15]

Dead-End Sign on the Parenting Road

Loss finds every family. **We all lose many dreams in life, but we are not taught how to grieve any of them.** Many of us adopt a stone-faced pose, taking on a stiff upper lip and denying our sadness in public. Time off from work after the death of a loved one traditionally equals only three days in corporate America. A tragic event like learning of one's infertility does not even rate in our culture's loss column. Similarly, the impact of losing the opportunity to produce a child gets overlooked in most parenting books. Yet I find that parents in training sometimes learn the harshest of life lessons even before becoming parents of a healthy baby. Signs pointing the way to a hoped-for child disappear, and infertility seems like a dead-end sign on the parenting road. Suddenly the terrain becomes hostile, the pavement ends, and parents in training wonder, "Why me?" A "What did I do wrong?" pose characterizes many grieving issues.

The transition from parent-in-waiting to parent-in-grieving temporarily blurs the way to finding meaning in life. When experiencing infertility, daily issues appear daunting, but parents in training can still take steps to meet energy, discipline, creativity, belonging, and ability needs. All parents in training have the challenge of learning how to remodel their personality story-houses.

MISCARRIAGE: BIRTH'S SHORTCUT TO DEATH

The two most powerful life transitions we face are those of birth and death. Ironically and sadly, "giving birth" to another human being sometimes includes "receiving death." There are many kinds of breakdowns along the conception trail. Some of them occur before a child's birth, and some develop right after. The loss of a baby ranks as one of life's tough transitions.[16] Stillborn babies happen less, statistically speaking, than miscarriages, but much grief and sadness accompanies both losses. Miscarriage, or the pregnancy loss that occurs before a fetus reaches twenty weeks, happens with such frequency that many parents in training do not even know "it" happened in the first place. And many couples who realize they are pregnant never receive signs that warn them of impending danger for their baby-to-be.

In spite of the frequency of miscarriage, little open discussion about the topic happens in our culture. Families may keep secrets about babies that did not thrive. Stillborn babies and miscarriages rate as some of the trauma that can arrest the memory in the story-house personality of parents in training. Miscarriage researchers Marie Allen and Shelly Marks met after both suffered miscarriages in the same year. They interviewed one hundred women who also experienced miscarriage. Over two-thirds of these parents in training referred to the event as "the death of their child."[17] Half of the grieving parents in training experienced a sensation of closeness with their babies even after the miscarriage, and three-fourths of the women admitted to vast feelings of confusion over what had happened to their child.[18]

Physicians sometimes may gloss over the death of a miscarried child with words they imagine as encouraging: "You are healthy. You can get pregnant again." But a grieving mother may sense that her mourning does not seem completely valid to her physician. One gynecologist who tried to show empathy said to a crying mother after her dilation and curettage procedure, "You already have one child. Lots of women have one or more miscarriages before having a pregnancy go to full term." These words do not provide the comfort a mother in mourning needs. It is a myth that fathers do not grieve a miscarriage; their grief is often dismissed.[19] The parent-in-training transition after miscarriage, as with infertility and stillbirth, deserves to be recognized as a significant event along our raising road of learning how to meet our basic needs.

Lucia (35) and Tomas (36)

> Both Lucia and Tomas are at work. Late one morning, Lucia starts to feel unease. She goes over a few possibilities in her mind, silently crossing each off the list. She does not consider the termination of her pregnancy as one of the possibilities. Elated at being pregnant, both Lucia and Tomas have been fantasizing about their child. They take pride in their lucky aim; their due date is Valentine's Day. Fast-forwarding to February 14 in their imaginations, they have spent hours happily imagining how the three of them will be valentines together. They joke about how their "homemade" sexuality has made the ultimate "valentine": their child.
>
> Lucia wisely decides to eat lunch, thinking that pregnancy surely has strange sensations. But the carefully chosen meal lurches precariously inside her, and she loses her lunch, along with her confidence. As cramping engulfs her back and abdomen, fear envelops her body. Then the bleeding begins. At first, there is only a trickle, but Lucia begins to sense the inevitable. She fights tears and makes excuses to

leave work early. Later, Lucia cannot recall how she ever made the trip home on the train. What she can remember focuses on the depth of the loss: an attachment to the child she never sees.

Lucia grieves over the fact that no rituals exist in our society for the proper send-off for her child made out of love. She shares her grief with her female friends and her mother. Tomas's experience is vastly different from Lucia's. He tells very few people about the miscarriage. The couple receives no conclusive medical findings about what went wrong, so telling others "something" went wrong seems inadequate to him. His internal trauma does not express itself verbally, like Lucia's. Tomas starts to spend more time at his job, and in spite of the nice weather, coolness fills the air at their home. Meanwhile, Lucia wants to talk about her complicated feelings. Who wants to hear her?

DEVELOPMENT DIRECTIONS

One of the reasons for tragedy is that you learn important lessons from it. Appreciation for your normal life for one thing. A new longing for things only ordinary.

—Elizabeth Berg, *Range of Motion*

How do these preparenting interactions affect personality roles? As hope dims and fears escalate immediately after a miscarriage, energy, discipline, creativity, belonging, and ability needs flounder for varying periods of time. Some women blame themselves for the miscarriage, although some of their partners are apt to feel some burden of guilt, too. In fact, most parents in training who lose a child feel totally unprepared to handle their grief. Perhaps the most important thing partners and grieving parents can do involves giving themselves permission to express their grief one interaction at a time. For example, upon seeing someone else's thriving baby in the supermarket, those who miscarried may cry. Some people will not be able to handle their expressions of grief, but there will be others who can. Talking about your grief and getting in touch with your pain is helpful down the raising road of meeting your basic needs.

Tip for Raising Thirty-Five-Year-Olds

Whether or not you are a "parent" before your miscarriage, you are now a parent in training, and all parents deal with raw emotions regarding babies. "Some of us are not accustomed to expressing our emotions, yet we can always start. The more we express them, the more accustomed we become to doing so and the more we learn we will survive and feel better afterward."[20]

Tip for Raising Thirty-Six-Year-Olds

Being a parent in training has many ups and downs; share your concerns with your partner, friends, and extended family. "Fathering does not come 'naturally' to men along with penises and stubble—it has to be learned."[21]

CHILDBIRTH AND EMOTIONAL STRETCH MARKS

Becoming a parent creates emotional stretch marks for mothers and fathers alike. However, mothers especially are challenged, as a "combination of psychological stressors and hormonal events . . . make women so vulnerable to depression during the childbearing years."[22] **The sheer responsibility of creating a child can dazzle or befuddle your brain; it likely does both.** Psychologist Dan McAdams researches the life stories of people; he finds that a child's birth rates as the single event most frequently given as a "life-story high point."[23] The high point dazzles, but sooner or later, fears surface for most parents.

We spend our lives vacillating between feeling hopeful and feeling fearful, two opposite roles in our personalities. On the one hand, we wish for a life in which a healthy child thrives, growing up with as few bumps in the road as possible. On the other hand, we have silent but nagging suspicions that, at one point or another, our child will face difficult times. We know we faced challenges, just as our parents and our grandparents before them did. Some of us prefer to ignore the road bumps we encountered as children, pretending they are insignificant now that we are in the fast lane of adulthood, the parent lane. However, raising *up* the next generation well takes acceptance of both our child's struggles and our own childhood difficulties. How can we help a child consciously problem solve their way through snafu after snafu if we do not acknowledge our own dilemmas? In this way, again, it takes a child to raise our parenting potential.

Tony (28) and Carrie (48)

There are no foolproof ways to prepare for childbirth. Parent in training Carrie strains to delay the birth of her son because the nurse tells her, "The doctor is not here yet." In fact, the nurse's hand forcefully holds back the baby's head to keep him from being delivered spontaneously. Many years later and with no one having recounted to him this unbelievable behavior, Carrie's son, Tony, tells of extremely uncomfortable sensations whenever he thinks of being born.

A generation later, Tony finds that his own son's birth challenges him, albeit in different ways. Tony feels unsure about his ability to be a good-enough parent, but he and his wife lovingly plan for a child and take Lamaze classes to make sure they understand their coach and player roles. They wait for game time, but soon three weeks pass from the estimated due date. The doctor suggests a hospital visit the following week to consider the possibility of inducing labor.

Sick with apprehension, Tony wonders what he has signed on for. In addition to worrying about the impending birth, now he feels stress whenever he looks at his wife. She is uncomfortable because of back pains. Her walk turns into a waddle. Will she drop the baby at a moment's notice? If not, why not? Tony takes his wife to the hospital, since she hasn't yet delivered naturally. On the way, another car hurtles into the passenger side of Tony's car. Tony is overwhelmed. Why didn't he see the car coming sideways at them? Has his baby been harmed? He speeds to the hospital.

The nursing staff does not rush when they arrive and takes no heed of the pain radiating from his wife's ankle. Soon, Pitocin-created contractions overpower her ankle pain anyway. A healthy heartbeat helps relieve everyone's stress. The nurse tapers off Pitocin drips, and Tony is instructed to take his wife home and wait for the onset of real contractions. As he watches his wife limp down the hallway, Tony feels drained and disappointed. The baby, after all, is still hiding in the dugout.

The following week, as Tony and his wife are about to see the doctor again, green water gushes down his wife's legs. Tony races them to the doctor's office. An out-of-breath Tony and his wife stumble into the office, and the doctor breathes hard as well. The words the doctor directs at the nurse resonate within Tony: "See if you can get a heartbeat." Thankful again when they find the baby's heartbeat, Tony is told to go to the hospital. On the way there, Tony runs one traffic light after another.

The hospital doctor detects trouble; the baby's head is not in the correct position for delivery. Meanwhile, the hospital has run out of labor rooms, and Tony finds out that he cannot stay with his wife in the "common" labor room because of hospital rules. With his wife's contractions in full throttle, Lamaze coach Tony gets thrown off the birthing field. Tony puts up a terrific fuss and demands that decisions about his wife and baby's immediate care take place before he leaves. Another doctor arrives with an epidural and pronounces that if Tony's wife pushes hard, the baby will turn around for a proper delivery. Tony is escorted out of the room.

Now stripped of his coaching role, Tony anxiously awaits far away from the action. Not constituted for the sidelines, Tony sends regular messages of encouragement through a nurse. He even manages to sneak back into the cramped pit to squeeze his wife's hand. Yet Tony feels like he dropped the ball as a coach. Finally, he is called off the bench. Allowed to reenter the game for the final play, Tony arrives just in time to see his son leave the dugout.

DEVELOPMENT DIRECTIONS

> If you seriously want to learn about life, having and raising children is probably the single best thing.
>
> —M. Scott Peck, psychiatrist, *In Search of Stones*

Newborn children and their families are partners in transition. For all, the transition of birth differs person to person. Some births are traumatic; others are peaceful. Some are guided by a wise doula, or labor support person;[24] others by the more traditional doctor-and-nurse team. Some babies arrive with music in the background and relatives gathered to welcome them to the family. Others experience the shock of a baby coming weeks, even months, early, or they hear the unsteadying news that their little newcomer is not well. Whatever the details of a baby's entry, each parent in training has fleeting questions about their own birth. Also, feelings opposite in nature to one another—happiness and sadness, fear and joy—flood their consciousness.

While some deliveries happen without a hitch, complications may exist in the relationship between the parents in training. Perhaps one parent desires this new long-term family partnership, while the other prefers single status. Each person's perceptions stem from their personality story-house of life memories, and having a baby occupies a much larger space in the life of a parent in training than any previous transition. Energy, discipline, creativity, belonging, and ability transitions are about to make emotional stretch marks in ways most new parents cannot even imagine.

Tip for Raising Twenty-Eight-Year-Olds

Becoming a father changes the priorities in your life. You view the transition as one of the most meaningful experiences of your life, or you fear the responsibility of parenting; on many days, both of these thoughts crisscross through your mind. "It takes more than love and good intentions to do a good job [of parenting]. There are certain very concrete skills that are necessary in order to work with children."[25]

Tip for Raising Forty-Eight-Year-Olds

When a parent becomes a grandparent, she is no longer "in charge." The new role requires careful actions, as her advice giving often falls upon deaf ears. Consider this Chinese proverb: "Govern a family as you would cook a small fish—very gently."

THE BIRTH OF PERSONALITY

Just as each of us experiences some unique entry into this world, each of us begins to express our fledgling, unique personality shortly after being born. "Even the youngest babies, while lacking the full capacity of spoken language, exhibit complicated and well-organized patterns of communication. Shortly after birth, not only do they have a full range of emotions, but, using gaze, facial expressions, vocalizations, and gestures, young infants can effectively relay information regarding their emotional state to their caregivers."[26] This infant communication about their nonstop needs steadily goes on both day and night. As any new parent knows, personality roles in a newborn flux as often as patterns and colors change in kaleidoscopes. As parents, we too surge through moody moves. Overtired and new at the task, many new parents face opposing emotional roles in their personalities. Who wants an emotional tug-of-war in the middle of the night?

Many conflicts reside within each of us when we are deciding which of several caretaking moves might best take care of the current child crisis. One father commiserates, "I didn't know whether to pick up B.J. when he cries or to let him cry it out." There is not just one answer. For example, a parent can adjust day and night rhythms. But, with infants' early crying, a factor should be considered: seemingly nonstop crying generally peaks at about six weeks of age.[27] Like a fencer, the questioning father can internally parry his own rage when nothing seems to quiet or soothe little B.J. All parents in training feel en garde as they uncertainly prepare for the next childhood "lunge."

Even so-called experts experience uncertainty in raising their own children during particular developmental transitions. As psychiatrist Erik Erikson points out, all of us make some assumptions about being "positive"; we assume that we can secure a positive stance for ourselves, such as having a sense of trust, "once and for all." However, we cannot "omit all the 'negative' senses (basic mistrust, etc.) which are and remain the dynamic counterpart of the 'positive' ones throughout life."[28] **Therefore, all of us experience times of trust and times of mistrust in our key relationships, both with significant others and with our own children.** Much of this mistrust translates into personality-role conflicts over some sense of wanting to feel safe or not lost. Frequently, our personality struggles with our own opposite roles occur during transition times in family life. And, as I have mentioned, the act of giving birth rates as one of life's major transitions.

POSTPARTUM DEPRESSION CHALLENGES

The childbirth transition exacts an energy toll on most parents in training. In some instances, postpartum depression follows, making parenting interactions actually feel impossible. What begins as elation during pregnancy can turn into the opposite feeling afterward, plunging a new mother into the depths of depression. Postpartum depression occurs when "there is an imbalance of certain neurotransmitter systems in your brain. . . . Serotonin and norepinephrine appear to be abnormally low."[29] Without any training on the topic of depression, many new parents suffer initially in silence.

Actress Brooke Shields describes her postpartum depression in terms of not having any preparation: "[My daughter] came without a call sheet or stage directions. . . . I wanted to smash violently through the window. . . . This urge was so strong. . . . How ironic that she was saving me from hurting myself."[30] **Even babies help "raise" their parents in training.** Another mother describes her postpartum experience as being in a maze where she cannot "find herself" and cannot relate to her newborn. New mothers attempt to talk themselves out of feeling "the blues," or their depression.[31] Fathers can be very confused by their postpartum partner's distance and moodiness. They struggle to connect with their spouse's intensity levels; they continually ask themselves, "What has happened?"

For the child who lives through her mother's postpartum depression, the trauma of rejection and alienation can invade story-house memories like a bad dream.

Lee (57)

> Lee remembers her early childhood with an acute sense of how her energy spiraled into depression or ennui. Her older sister was in the hospital at the same time that her mother was battling postpartum depression over the birth of her stillborn baby. After Lee lived with relatives awhile, she went home at age three to face a mother with an energy gauge pointing to "Empty." Lee recalls having to fend for herself; her mother put breakfast and dinner on the table but spent the bulk of her day in bed. Lee stayed outside all day on the family farm, entertaining herself as well as a three-year-old could. When hungry midday, she went back into the house and asked her mother for something to eat; she was told, "Find cereal."
>
> Lee remembers the ordeal of making her own lunch. She had to find a chair to open the refrigerator. A gallon of fresh milk from her father's cows felt heavy, but she managed to pour the milk without spilling. A few times, she went without milk on her cereal, because

heavy cream had settled on the top of the 1950s milk jug, and she could not lift the milk container high enough to jiggle milk through the cream. Lee ate dry cereal so as not to upset her mother with another request for assistance.

At birth, Lee was an Rh baby. This designation signals a condition whereby a mother and infant have different antigens in their red blood cells. Lee therefore has blood transfusion scars on her ankles and arms, a sign of her survivor status. Lee often overheard her mother saying to others, "Lee was not supposed to live." When Lee's older sister eventually came home from the hospital, Lee's mother trudged into a caretaking role but had the expectation too that Lee could share in the care of her six-year-old sister, a child three years older than Lee. During this time, Lee noticed that her sister "[got] everything," including everyone's attention, after her extended illness. Lee pondered internally, "Why do other people get taken care of and I do not get taken care of?" Her mother expected Lee to stay indoors and play with her sister, but Lee refused. Instead she went outside to take care of herself, as she learned to do before her sister came back home. Her anger turned inward over her mother's treatment of her and her sister. Lee admits as an adult that she has learned to sidestep confrontations: "I go out of my way to avoid conflict."

DEVELOPMENT DIRECTIONS

> Probably everyone has a more or less concealed chamber that she hides even from herself and in which the props of her childhood drama are to be found. Those who will be most affected by the contents of this hidden chamber are her children.
>
> —Alice Miller, psychiatrist, *The Drama of the Gifted Child*

Lee literally raised herself during much of the time of her mother's acute depression. She had few choices; her energy, discipline, creativity, belonging, and ability needs were not satisfied by her parents. Her father busied himself as the breadwinner, leaving the childrearing to his wife. However, Lee's mother had many things on her mind: grief over a stillborn baby, postpartum depression, and a hospitalized older child. Yet she lived in a culture that expected her to "pull herself together." Undoubtedly, this stretched-to-the-limits parent juggled opposite roles in dealing with her youngest child; she loved her, but she could not muster the energy to take responsibility and nurture her. As an adult, Lee now has a better understanding of her mother and her unmet needs. Postpartum issues of mothers are frequently misunderstood. The cultural values in the 1950s supported a stiff-upper-lip pose, not grief counseling. As a result, Lee practiced that pose for decades.

Tip for Raising Fifty-Seven-Year-Olds

It is high time to remodel our 1950s story-house, consciously accepting our past and choosing to meet our current needs in the best way possible. "Fiftysomethings usually have a capacity to integrate and become at one with their experience."[32]

THE PERSONALITY-TRANSITION ROLLER COASTER

Transitions, or changes from a time of familiarity to a time of incredible uncertainty, define parenting. Therefore, opposite reactions, or changes that occur from taking on different roles within our personalities, are normal occurrences for all caretakers. While we aspire to have present-moment awareness guide our daily actions, each of us falls short of this goal. Just when we think we have one stage of family life figured out, our child slips into some chameleon pose that we cannot even recognize as being that of *our* child. We experience growth pains. Who *raised* this kid? Where did our happy baby go? What Frankenstein clone has climbed out of his crib? Your happy baby experiences growth pains . . . and so do you. Sometimes your baby's growth spurts bring up satisfying memories from your own past.

Other times, your child's normal childhood transitions dredge up some old trauma from your personality story-house. These previously forgotten memories remind you of the mistakes your parents made with you when you were a child. You seldom recalled such painful early stories on a frequent basis because they are frightening, reminding you of times when you felt off-track or lost. Now your child's stress triggers your own, often-unresolved, earlier distress, and you are thrust, often kicking and screaming, into a new phase of your own development. Whether such transitions in our lives appear to us initially as happy or sad, they produce growth spurts and the taking on of lots of opposite roles within our personalities.

As caretakers, we are thrust into meeting transitions rapidly, ready or not. **You see, as children undergo certain developmental phases, their parents renegotiate, or work through once again, many of their *own* transitions in these same developmental time frames.** In adults' story-houses of memories, previously closed doors are opened when a child undergoes their developmental issues. As one parent said, "I never thought much about my childhood until I became a parent." Another caretaker winces after criticizing her mother; she takes a long breath and lowers her voice, saying, "I see myself in my mother." Most of us have considerable growing up ahead of us after becoming parents. And it's okay to grow up with children. It takes a child to raise a parent, after all.

Still, such change unnerves us. Therefore we struggle in meeting basic needs, either our own, our child's, or both. For example, consider a typical preschooler who shivers with fear of separation whenever a parent leaves him. In reality, the stress of separation affects parents more poignantly than the child. As soon as a child gets inside a classroom with a caring teacher or into the living room with an attentive babysitter, fearful roles in the child melt away. However, this transition takes much longer in a parent. One mother's blaming role in her personality makes her think, "I must have done something wrong because Carmella cried so hard. . . . I should have sneaked out the back door before she knew I would leave. . . . Maybe I should have given her a bottle when I left. . . . Maybe I shouldn't leave her at this age. . . . Maybe the sitter won't be able to calm Carmella. . . ." Then, these thoughts might waft their way to the top of a parent's consciousness about their own separations: "I remember when my mother left me the first day of kindergarten," or "When I was left with a sitter, _____ happened." Another parent recalls this separation misstep: "I remember how I got a spanking when I cried as my mother was leaving the house; she said, 'Now you'll really have something to cry about.'"

Remembering these fragments from your personality story-house of memories helps you parent. You gain an appreciation of the complexities you endured in growing up. What part of your personality hates to feel left behind? What pose does your body take when you experience fear? How do you model anxiety in your face, body, and tone of voice?

When an anxious role of your personality "takes over" your functioning, how does your role modeling affect your child?

All of us clutch insecure, vulnerable, and scared roles somewhere within our personality story-houses. We practice, over time, habitual ways of expressing our personalities, both in repeated verbal scripts and bodily poses. However, some caretakers are so accustomed to ignoring their fears that they do not acknowledge ever being scared. What happens when we can recognize that fears in separating from someone are not only universal but also one of the ways in which we protect both ourselves and our children from harm? To drive our family safely through the inevitable transitions in our child's life and in our own life with a sense of well-being, we need to back up the family car on a fairly frequent basis. Our parenting trip does not travel a smooth or straight highway. We encounter many detours and obstacles along the raising road of meeting basic needs.

MOODY PARENT ROLES

Anonymous Father (Age Unknown)

> One weekend morning at a restaurant, I overhear a conversation between two couples at the next table. The main speakers are the two mothers. One dad engages only through his "yeah, yeah" agreements: "Kids bring out emotions you never knew you had." "Yeah . . ." "The rage . . ." "Yeah . . ." "Then you just spiral." "Yeah . . ." "They know to stop when you are ready to blow." "Yeah . . ." "I was exhausted." "Yeah . . ." "Sometimes I just don't know what to do next." "Yeah . . ." "Should I try to calm her or should I just let her cry it out?" "Yeah . . ." "I second guess myself a lot."
>
> The second father remains mute, holding his head in his hands. What does his resigned pose say—frustration, helplessness? Does he want to run from the table, or does he just want to have a quiet breakfast with his wife and friends without the intrusion of the kids for a change? Does he have thoughts about the kind of fathering he received as a child, or does he simply feel exhausted from hearing about all the emotions of parenting?

DEVELOPMENT DIRECTIONS

> When my first baby was born . . . I looked at this tiny, mysterious thing and felt so stupid. I felt small, weak, and feeble.
>
> —Abraham Maslow, psychologist

Fathers frequently are left out of discussions about childrearing. Does this omission occur because fathers are not expected to engage in care-taking as many hours as mothers or because they exclude themselves? The truth is, every child longs for a close tie with both parents, and many fathers tell me that they now regret not having spent much time with their children when they were young. Some make up for these lost nurturing years by becoming close to their grandchildren. Others seem stymied, not knowing how to playfully engage with a youngster. At some point in their lives, they give up any aspirations of having a healthy attachment to children. No adult has to give up such goals. Wonderful volunteer organizations focus on pairing retired men, who can offer relationships that involve belonging, with youth who may not have a father figure in their lives. Single men can mentor in volunteer groups throughout their lives. And dads of all ages can make today the first day in relating with children of any age.

Tip for Raising Dads of Every Age

Grab every opportunity you can to be with your child one interaction at a time. "Younger fathers . . . spoke openly about affection and tender-ness. . . . It's healthy."[33]

BALANCING OUR OPPOSITE ROLES AND FINDING SELF-TERRITORY

How can we turn our painful transitions into meaningful directions? **One way for turning around a difficult life story consists of ac-knowledging our opposing thoughts and emotions in any situa-tion.** Becoming a parent in training enlarges our awareness to the op-posing roles within both our personalities and our children's. Swiss psychologist Carl Jung refers to the adult challenge of balancing or reconciling our opposites.[34] Opposite roles are termed "polarized parts" by marriage and family therapist Richard Schwartz.[35] One moment in parenthood we feel hopeful and resilient, believing in our capacity to raise up the next generation. Another moment, and possibly not too many minutes after our earlier hopeful pose, we focus on the fearful and stressful roles of our personality. For example, one diligent mother feels proud of modeling good work habits for her preteen son. However, in the next breath, she unleashes her worry: "I see Rafael picking up on all my stress mannerisms." We are more likely to tip in the direction of our fears when we cannot center ourselves in self-territory. To understand this, picture a seesaw as the continuum of our opposite roles.[36] When fear frames our parenting roles, hope seems to bottom out. We cannot imagine our hopefulness ever rising again.

All we notice when our fearful role dominates is a precarious hanging sensation, as if our feet and arms are dangling helplessly. We even may hyperventilate, breathing in such a shallow fashion that we almost reach a breathless state. While control over our current predicament is our wish, we realize how little in parenthood we actually control. In one poignant moment of crisis, such as when our baby refuses to sleep, we focus initially on only our fears. After a while though, we usually are able to flip-flop our position. Everyone flip-flops.

We first meet one pressing need, perhaps something as simple as preparing food; through eating a nutritious meal, we gain some energy. As we soothe the clamors of one need, hope revs our parenting motors; fear subsides. Perhaps a restless baby finally begins to sleep through the night. Or perhaps our independent teenager follows curfew rules and comes home on time. We let out a huge sigh of relief; we believe that we can raise this child after all. We go to sleep. And even our fears begin to sleep through the night.

Figure 2.1.

HOPE ETERNAL

Fortunately, we do not have to careen from one extreme end of the personality seesaw to the other. There is another path to helping ourselves. We can learn to balance our fears. A fulcrum, or support, exists at the center of our personality seesaw of opposites. This pivotal mechanism holds both our emotional ends in balance. **In the human personality, self-territory exists in this inner holding place.** We have an underlying point of calmness in our interior; here, we balance our chatty hopes and boisterous fears. We are all comprised of more than our opposite roles, more than our fears and hopes.

When we are babies, we rely on our caretakers to provide this *holder*, or balancing fulcrum, for us. But as we grow up, we learn to be our own holding fulcrum for the opposite roles in our personality. This life learning takes place at different ages for people. Sometimes children grasp this inner strength on their own. Most often, caretakers model for children how to balance the ups and downs of each day. They teach children how to live with changes, and children teach their caretakers how to live with changes, too. In many families, a child raises our consciousness so that we learn to embrace certain opposite roles in our personality. When we learn to take drawn-out, deep breaths during an interaction, we can bring our personality seesaw into the centered position of self-territory. We make space for relating, both to ourselves and to our children, one interaction at a time.

OUR PERSONALITY NETWORK OF ROLES

What starts out as a few nonverbal poses from a baby's personality later develop into a person's story-house of roles and practiced personality poses. However, we are kept so busy meeting our basic needs and those

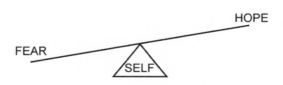

Figure 2.2.

of our children that, some days, we scarcely notice our collection of personality roles and poses. Seemingly blind to much of our own personality functioning and expressions, we may criticize others' conduct while engaging in the same roles and poses ourselves. Psychologists Hal and Sidra Stone predict that we grapple with people during our lifetime who frequently act out roles of our personality that we do not like; they also assert that often we marry people with such "disowned" qualities.[37] Certain family postures become predictable over time, and yet we are unaware of our part in repeating these seasonal patterns. One husband's summary of his wife's opposite personality roles takes this path: "I am comfortable being uncomfortable [with her personality roles]."

While we watch, criticize, and endure the changing roles in others' personalities, we relate by recognizing in our chameleon personalities many of our *own* changing roles. Psychiatrist Daniel Stern's research with mother-infant pairs reveals how very young children (before the age of eighteen months and before spoken language) begin to accumulate a story-house of memories; in fact, by the age of three or four, children are verbalizing their autobiographical stories.[38] Preschool and kindergarten children gather up powerful images that can underlie their sense of "who am I."[39] A five-year-old girl, who grapples with her fear of the dark, tells me this story about a puppy puppet that learns how to fall asleep and not be afraid: "Pretend like I'm making light coming out of her, 'cause she's going to disappear magically. . . . She's going to form a different way. . . . I have a really good feeling . . . she's already changing. . . . We change all the time!"

As we grow up and construct our personality story-house, we remodel certain memories along the way as we make plans for the future: Every person incorporates "the reconstructed past and the imagined future into a more or less coherent" narrative or story.[40] Our stories have an impact upon us as we function to meet our basic needs. However, it is when we become conscious of our various childhood stories that we are better positioned to discover their meaning and purpose for our current life.

The common phrase "So-and-so has no personality" has no truth at all; everyone has a *map*, or a network of emotional roles in their personality story-house, to meet daily needs. Every person's map is as unique as a zebra's stripes. All zebras have distinctive stripes, and all people have distinctive personal maps. The reason our stripes may resemble another's is because all of us have the same basic needs. We share similar personality roles to meet these needs, but our network of roles plays out its nonverbal poses and verbalized expressions in unique patterns. All of us have networks of personality roles, some known to us and some hidden for periods of time. The more we learn who we really are and how we can meet our basic needs, the better the chance that we can teach our children who they really are and how they can meet their needs.

Unfortunately, with so many of our different personality poses speaking a language we may or may not recognize, sometimes we can confuse ourselves and our children: "It is a big problem when a thousand parts of your mind are all speaking at the same time."[41] For example, we dislike some thoughts we hear in our daily thinking, and we judge many of our own personality roles harshly. We can feel that certain of our personality roles are "bad." Likewise, we can judge these same roles in our children with disgust. When we communicate from this critical role, we are not responding one interaction at a time, and we are not connecting with self-territory to focus on the present moment. Instead, we offer echoes of past fault finding or are consumed by worries about the future.

INTERNAL FAMILY ROLES

Marriage and family therapist Richard Schwartz suggests our multidimensional personality parts, or roles, can act internally in sequences that are similar or opposite of relationship patterns in our family.[42] I tend to use the word "part" when I talk with children and the word "role" when I talk with adults. We experience roles of our personality as thoughts, emotions, or sensations. All of these personality roles desire something positive for each person—there are no bad roles. However, some of our roles, like an angry role, may hijack our personality at times and seem to "take over" our functioning.

Schwartz conceptualizes one model of understanding the various parts of our personality. He identifies three categories of personality parts or roles: managers, exiles, and firefighters.[43] Manager roles run the day-to-day functions of organizing the day, making plans for future events, controlling many situations, and protecting a person from feeling any hurt or rejection. For example, one teacher-mother has a manager role she refers to as "Sarge"; she relies on this role of her personality to control her classroom and organize her home every day. Her "Sarge" role meets her needs for discipline, as she turns the authority thermostat up or down to suit classroom and home situations. Another mother terms the organizer role of her personality as the "Energizer," and she initially thinks of herself as predominantly comprised of this energetic role. **All of our personality roles reflect our attempts to meet our basic needs, but both children and adults may require a *map* to understand how these roles network.**

The exile parts of our personality in Schwartz's model are roles that sometimes derive from trauma in childhood. Isolated from the rest of the personality, exile roles represent painful memories that are shoved to the basement of our personality story-house. The story-house basement offers a source of protection that keeps people from further pain or fear, and stories relegated here are not always included in our conscious map of our personality. One parent, for example, buried her memories of incest in the basement of her mind until she became a mother and faced her child's belonging needs. Suddenly, unwelcome images of a much earlier, scary time with her father forced their awareness upon her consciousness through a troubling dream. Her drunken father's incestuous behavior shows a distortion of how he met *his* belonging needs. This man's childhood story includes beatings from a stern father, who likely struggled with his own belonging and discipline needs.

Schwartz describes a third group of personality roles as firefighter parts, which appear on the scene when our exile parts or roles are activated. Our internal firefighter roles protect us by moving quickly to extinguish any feelings of pain. Firefighter roles attempt to manage inner conflicts like manager roles do, but they take more drastic poses. For example, a father uses marijuana daily to neutralize the anxiety resulting from his demanding career, which he senses thwarts his ability needs. A mother becomes addicted to pain medications prescribed for a back problem. She numbs her unmet belonging needs through continued pill popping long after her backache improves. And, perhaps, a grandparent nurses one beer after another to blur his awareness of his persistent energy/health problems. All of the roles in our personalities have ties to meeting our basic needs.

SPLINTER PERSONALITY FUNCTIONING

Often caretakers operate from splinter personalities[44] or use only certain roles in their personalities to meet needs. Whether we label groups of our personality roles or not, many of us have the A team (the roles we use most) and the B team (the roles we prefer to bench, or do not use consciously in our personalities). Such groupings develop and change over a lifetime. We all have certain personality roles that we practice over and over. But expressing splinter personalities can hinder us from meeting our basic needs and those of our children. We want to understand how we can best use our personality roles to meet both our own and our children's *present* basic needs *one interaction at a time*.

Research on monkeys reveals how easily our parental poses groom the early behavior of our offspring. For example, if an infant monkey *senses* its mother acting afraid in the presence of a snake, the wee monkey learns to fear snakes.[45] Apparently, these juvenile monkeys hold on to powerful memories (their mother's acting fearful) just like young human children hold on to stirring memories. A mother who tells of her extreme fear of spiders also sheepishly admits that her young son now shares her fear, because he has seen her scream at the sight of a spider. Such fears foster early personality roles that our children can carry for years.

DAILY REBIRTHS OF UNCONDITIONAL LOVE

Babies and toddlers make nearly constant bids to meet their belonging needs. Children coo, smile, gurgle, and flirt outrageously with their caretakers during their first year. In the second year, they banter, sometimes continuously, with chirpy chatter. Often our young children connect with us most closely when they amuse us with their early logic: "Don't talk so loud. You'll wake up the dark!" advises a youngster at bedtime. However, toddlers' tantrum-like behavior just as easily makes them disconnect with their caretakers. **Your child's expression of opposite roles can throw the family's functioning into reverse gear within seconds.**

Biologist and educator Carla Hannaford reminds parents that the so-called terrible twos behavior does not qualify as manipulative: a child's cognitive structures are not in place to hold such a complex motive. Rather, toddlers imitate others' behaviors in exaggerated forms (for example, kicking and screaming) instead of verbally complaining.[46] Parents in training can learn to model appropriate behavior calmly to a toddler, although this approach is hard to remember when child needs call with such loud drama.

Mary (2) and Marilyn (24)

Mary is a bundle of joy, as she lives her days making endless discoveries. Her mother is seduced by many of her youngster's happy antics and lovingly joins her in precious moments of shared delight. One day, Mary finds a fascinating bathtub for many of her toys: the toilet bowl. Marilyn carefully takes each toy out of the toilet and washes it before making another bathtub arrangement in the sink. However, later in the day, she recoils when Mary's toddler behavior steamrolls into protests, sleep disturbances, and increasing agitation. When Mary screams in a seemingly uncontrollable screech, Marilyn also raises her voice and yells menacingly, "Stop it right now!" Marilyn ends up scaring herself more than she scares Mary, who recoils from the "monster" voice. Marilyn hears her mother's words and intonation in her own and wonders how this has happened. Her intentions are noble, after all, when they come to her child. She believes that she qualifies as a good mother, yet who *owns* the voice she hears raging at the top ranges of her own vocal cords? Is she a duplicate of her mother? Will her child also turn into a screaming clone someday?

DEVELOPMENT DIRECTIONS

Parents constantly reencounter the childhood of their own children and the child that they carry within themselves, their own childhood selves. Thus in struggling to deal with their children, they are also struggling to deal with the children they once were.

—E. James Anthony and Therese Benedek, psychiatrists, *Parenthood*

Every parent in training experiences moments that contain throwback scripts from our youth. Our best intentions falter, our voice changes octaves, and we find ourselves in a "twilight zone" of past relating. Old messages surface with alarming speed: "If I told you once, I've told you one hundred times not to . . ." When you recognize you are losing your temper, the best approach is a simple apology: "I'm sorry. I got so mad I couldn't think about what I really wanted to say to you." Then take in a few deep breaths and encourage your child to breathe with you. Start over with your preferred message from another role in your personality. Not only can you teach your child to learn from mistakes, but you can repair the broken belonging connections that occur when you rage in your out-of-control angry role. Your young child watches your personality poses and mimics many of them throughout the day. So make a conscious effort to model poses you want your child to copy.

Tip for Raising Two-Year-Olds

All of us go through a phase of exploratory messiness. When asked if her grandchild reminded her of her daughter at age two, the grandmother replied, "Oh yes. A great deal. She was very independent. . . . It was hard to keep track of her, and a lot of work."[47]

Tip for Raising Twenty-Four-Year-Olds

Stay open to the creativity of your toddler; each day brings new learning for both you and your child. "As a new mother [or father], your responses to the world at large change and you develop completely new sensibilities with regard to what you notice, hear and smell."[48]

BALANCING ACTS

Our personality teeters off in one role or another all day. Being balanced in *self-territory* is difficult. Remember though, we are becoming *aware* of our personality roles that we have practiced over the years and not trying to rid our personality of its particular stripes. Our personality roles are not bad. They serve a protective function, and each role along the personality continuum has an equally important moral or message. For example, our grief over some loss has as much merit as our productivity on some project. As we grow, we detour back many times along the raising road of learning how to meet our basic needs to our upbringing and early parenting memories. In the words of one mother, "I did not grow up until I became a parent. I had to become responsible, to think of someone other than just myself."

A grandfather's caring role invests in a newfound interest in environmental issues: "As a new grandfather, I'm concerned about the environment for my grandson." Addressing even one child's needs leads caretakers to make changes in our world so that all children can thrive. In this way, having a child raises a caretaker's awareness levels. Caretaker-child unconditional love happens in such *present* moments, through *one interaction at a time.*

Children hold many tools to help us remodel our ways of thinking about ourselves and the world: "We are continually stimulated to re-think our childhood by the birth and development of our own children."[49] If you do not have any children at this time, spend some time with a relative's child. Youth can raise your consciousness about your own life in ways that may surprise you. Playing with a young child can bring both of you into the present moment, into self-territory. Additionally, certain life experiences lay the groundwork for our later parental reactions. Through watching a child totally engage in some activity, we learn to embrace memories of our own childhoods and come to carry our personality story-house backpack with a lighter step. We find self-awareness in a variety of starts and stops along the raising road.

SELF-RECOGNITION BY TODDLERS

A young child prompts a caretaker's self-awareness, but scientific data also indicates that a baby develops self-awareness at an early age. German researcher Wilhelm Preyer and American psychologist Gordon Gallup Jr. have found that children gain their first self-recognition at approximately the age of sixteen months.[50] Psychologist Jerome Kagan finds that youngsters substitute a toy for their self in their imaginative play in the months just before they turn two years.[51] As children master more language skills, they share more of their thinking process as they relate events to themselves.

Children sometimes raise their parents' consciousness of here-and-now issues through their candid ability to notice present moments. For example, my daughter at age six noticed a young man with a punk hairstyle. Wide-eyed, she whispered discretely to me, "That guy has hair standing straight up!" When I asked if she liked it, she shook her head no. I told her that the teenage boy just wants to be different from other teenagers, and I then asked my daughter if she would like to be different. She said, "No. I like the way I look already." I responded, "Me too." We squeezed hands and continued walking. Such self-territory exchanges between parent and child take only a few moments, but they create strong relationship connections.

REMODELING PERSONALITY ROLES

Story-houses have powerful precedents for each of our personality roles, whether or not we acknowledge family memories from earlier years. For example, input from peer groups and our societal culture also influence our personalities. This book acknowledges such *outside* influences, but it focuses most of its attention upon the *inside* remodeling. These changes constantly occur through the daily transitions that take place in our families while we meet our basic needs. Every day we remodel our personality story-house of life memories in large or small ways. We do not recall every small transition. There are simply too many of them, but each does help define our current personality.

In remembering key transitions from our past, however, we gain a new appreciation of our internal personal strength, or self-territory. Everyone, after all, experiences rough raising roads of one kind or another. Fortunately, we learn that inside each of us there exists a *holder* of self territory, or an inner navigator that does not get lost when the going seems so tough. The holder of our stories, much like the fulcrum in a seesaw, holds up the possibility of experiencing both sides of our emotional roles. Through balancing opposites, such as fear and hope, we find personal balance as we go through one interaction at a time.

Contrast these two parent-in-training scenes. A mother tensely admonishes her two young sons during a shopping trip: "I have to spend my time looking for you. The entire reason we are still shopping is you!" She then takes off, disgust distorting her pretty face. The boys run to try to catch up with their mother-turned-angry-whirlwind. Another parent carefully plans her shopping outing by giving her sons a few instructions before opening the car doors at the mall: "Remember our shopping rule: stick beside me. We are buying socks and jeans. Each of you can choose the color of socks you want. We may not find everything in one store. When we are finished, we can stop by the park playground for a few minutes on the jungle gym." The sons share grins. They know their mother's shopping story, and they are looking forward to the three of them hanging together like monkeys.

Some days, we wonder how many details we can juggle and hold in our minds at the very same time. The number of thoughts, perceptions, emotions, and sensations that torpedo our awareness seem endless. Becoming a parent in training seems to speed up further our busybody existence. However, we can make *space* for self-territory moments. We can focus on unconditional love for ourselves and our child. Having a resilient and loving attitude helps solve even the toughest of life transitions. As we learn to acknowledge our personality story-house of memories, we gain a perspective about life. We recognize and accept that we have opposite roles in our personality. We also trust ourselves to keep growing *up*. We notice when our child learns from us, and we learn from our child. We raise *up* each other. We express unconditional love for our child *one interaction at a time* whenever we are able to do so.

RAISING *UP* FAMILIES TO MEET BASIC NEEDS

Raising our children by teaching them how to meet basic needs, *one interaction at a time*, covers the rest of these pages. However, as caretakers, we need to pay equal attention to "giving birth" to our own daily needs. **Every day we keep on raising ourselves. All of this raising requires that we take stock of what we *value* in our many worlds—worlds such as home, work, friends, spirituality, education, and leisure pursuits.** Probably everyone has differing explanations and experiences of the worlds that are important to them. Whatever labels we give to our spheres of influence, though, all of us have daily births, or beginnings. Then, for some of us, day-to-day transitions appear fairly easy; for others, these transitions through energy, discipline, creativity, belonging, and ability needs catapult both caretaker and child into daily struggles and grief. The reasons for such difficulty vary for each person, but find comfort in the fact that every age of human history has struggled with raising roads of learning how to meet basic needs.

Remember always that there is a home-base position for parenting well-being. We can act in the present moment to raise our children well. There we cultivate unconditional love for ourselves as well as for our child. We affirm and respect ourselves. We affirm and respect our child. **While we may not agree with a child's choice of actions in a particular moment, we can hold our many personality roles at bay and listen to the opposite role that is being expressed by our child's behavior.** By engaging in one interaction at a time, parents in training find resilience as they continually meet transitions. In each transition, we embrace hope for our child and embrace our child's immediate need. Similarly, we need to hold on to our own potential rather than limit ourselves by gripping only on to our fears.

BIRTHRIGHT MAPPING

Scan your memories for your most important life events or transitions in your life. There are no right or wrong ways to represent these life changes. A few suggestions follow, but you may have another idea for mapping the transitions in your life and discovering how they still have meaning for you today. You may record your various mapping entries in a journal or jot down your ideas on loose-leaf paper that you keep in a folder.

- **One way to acknowledge transitions utilizes a timeline.** Draw a line vertically or horizontally, or make a huge circle that fills the entire page.
- Choose a beginning point. It may be at the top or bottom or on one side of the page. Make a small cross line on your timeline and jot down the date of your birth.
- On a separate page, make four categories: "Facts," "Questions," "Roles," and "Translations." Jot down any "facts" that you know about your own birth process. If your parents are accessible, ask them questions about your first transition. If you have older siblings or other relatives, ask them for the family stories about your birth.

- After you gather any possible details of your birth, such as a thirty-six-hour labor, think of any questions that linger for you. Are there some unknowns? Do not worry that your questions may not receive ready answers. Many of our questions in life fall into a similar category.
- Make a third entry. Write down whatever personality roles pop up regarding your birth. For example, one mother realizes rejection over her placement in an orphanage.
- Now consider a fourth entry. When you size up what you have put together so far, how does this information translate to your life now? For example, another mother recalls her preemie status; everyone thought, because she was so small at birth, that she might die. She gets in touch with fear. As a youngster and adult, she overeats. Later, she expresses rage toward her parents for "allowing pigging out at every meal." As an adult, she also carries self-directed anger. Scanning these understandable roles, she begins new eating patterns.
- Continue adding transition points to your timeline as you recall them. Give facts of family moves, other births, deaths, school transitions, and friend transitions. Indicate on your timeline whatever changes you consider important from your life. This exercise helps you continue mapping your particular story-house.

Part II

Meeting Needs, Our Child's and Our Own

3

ENERGY NEEDS: ARE YOU AN ENGINEER, OR ARE YOU ENSLAVED TO ENNUI?

Everyone knows on any given day that there are energies slumbering in him. . . . Most of us feel as if a sort of cloud weighed upon us. . . . Compared with what we ought to be, we are only half awake. We are making use of only a small part of our possible mental and physical resources. In some persons this sense of being cut off from their rightful resources is extreme.

—William James, 1906 presidential address to the
American Psychological Association

We live in a world of cycles. The corona, or array of concentric circles of light surrounding our sun, sizzles at 2.7 million degrees. Scientists explain our sun's exterior as an energy carpet with more than 50,000 magnetic patches, each containing positive and negative charges. Energy heaves from these magnetic loops thousands of miles across the sun's surface, like giant train tracks connecting the patches. When the loops cross or touch each other, heat waves emit energy. As reported by Paul Hoversten in a *USA Today* article on March 11, 1999, these powerful magnetic tracks then break up and disappear, only to be replaced every forty hours. Twice monthly our sun's "search engine" finds Earth and our moon in a relationship that creates stronger-than-usual tides on Earth. Other sun alignments recycle over time as well; for example, a total eclipse repeats itself every eighteen years, ten and one-third days.[1]

While discoveries about the sun dazzle our imaginations, back on Earth, we ourselves tend to engage in more mundane rotations. We eat (more or less) three meals a day, sleep (more or less) seven hours a night, and work (more or less) forty hours a week. We do not think often about the sweeping energy changes of the sun. Many of us overlook our individual need for exercise cycles, whereby we can replenish our energy with walking, jogging, dancing, biking, yoga, martial arts, sports, or weightlifting regularly. Frequently, we trap our body's energy with our cramped personal agendas. Replenishing energy takes time, and we often perceive ourselves as "time strapped." **We therefore take our body's energy for granted, not realizing that our steam for the day exists as an engine both hitched to a star and to a train of personality cargo.** As you now know, some of this "cargo" is buried deep within our *story-house* of memories.

We have the ability to direct or turn our energy cycles in different directions. We can put our energies into unconditional love for our child through the following: examining our energy needs, examining our child's patterns of energy, exploring how these patterns affect both our minds and our bodies, and planning family rituals to replenish energy that we can practice on a daily basis.

Parenting-Trip Tips

- Recognize the early energy messages you gathered in childhood.
- Consider your energy cycles throughout the days and weeks; contrast your cycles with those of your children, parents, and grandparents.
- Understand your feelings as *energy perceptions* trying to keep track of what happens to you in your body and mind.
- Establish simple family rituals for developing healthy habits in eating, sleeping, and exercise for you and your child.

FAMILIAL RECYCLE BINS

Our brains are storage bins that recycle their contents constantly. **We have every story that happened to us stashed somewhere in our brain's filing system.** Our personality roles form out of our story-house of lifetime memories, and they keep recycling themselves in our lives as we attend to our daily needs. Psychologist Shad Helmstetter considers that our personality roles relate to messages we heard repeatedly early in life: "Parent-talk" sets up a child's internal "self-talk." Indeed, even if you as a parent tell your children things that are not true, if they hear the same refrains over and over, these words can echo into their future.[2]

The recycling of one generation's energy thoughts and actions to the next generation may or may not receive our conscious attention. Many of our energizing and energy-challenged roles emerge from the first eighteen years of our life and represent stories that are influenced by caretaker stories.[3] Families often have a common identity comprised of certain personality poses for relating to one another and certain habitual postures for handling our daily existence. A frazzled woman sounds stressed when she describes a conversation she had with her husband the previous day: "I could tell he had a bad day. I warned him, 'Don't take it out on me!' But that's exactly what he did. He acts just like my father!" You may not plan to replicate your caretakers' patterns, but you are likely to do just that if you are not aware of them. Too often, our awareness for relating one interaction at a time seems blocked from view.

RECYCLING A PARENT'S FEAR ENERGY

Noreen (47)

> Noreen has a nagging sense that there must be some reason for her nervous overprotectiveness of her three children. When I ask her about any childhood memories of being hurt, she initially replies that she does not remember her early years. Then, a few seconds later, Noreen thoughtfully responds from a different role of her personality, saying that she can recall *one* incident. Her voice softens. Noreen revisits her role as a four-year-old helper; in her memory, she visualizes herself carrying some glass jars down a set of stairs.
>
> Noreen does not recall how the accident that follows happened, but she has a vivid ending image in her mind: she is lying at the bottom of the stairway, and her mother is frantically screaming, praying over Noreen and picking shards of glass from out of her daughter's limp and bloody hands. Initially, Noreen has no words to describe her own reactions to the incident from her story-house of life

memories. All of her attention focuses upon the fear she reads in her mother's eyes. "I was worried about *her*," is Noreen's only stated recollection of the trauma. Noreen continues her big-girl helper role by remaining as quiet as possible about this recollection. In an incident that occurred years later, Noreen remembers how her infant son tumbled down a set of steps in his stroller, and she considers how she now takes on the role of worrier every time one of her children screams. Each time Noreen finds herself in the role of worrier, she finds her other roles in her personality do not have a chance for expression. In this way, traumatic memories have a way of eating into one's energy-supply pipeline.

DEVELOPMENT DIRECTIONS

> By becoming aware of family messages, you can decide for yourself whether or not you want to maintain these roles and beliefs.
>   —Monica McGoldrick, psychologist, *You Can Go Home Again*

We all have memories in our personality story-house that we do not appreciate because they seem far removed from our daily lives. But *are* these memories "far removed"? There are many linkages that exist between our childhood story-houses and our energetic functioning today. We probably will never consciously recall all of the vast number of personal stories from our youth, but some of them do shed light upon current dilemmas. Reminiscing about each age period in our lives turns up fascinating directions for our current developmental travels.

Tip for Raising Forty-Seven-Year-Olds

Jot down early memories as they return to your consciousness. "At midlife, we are challenged to look at our lives from new perspectives, and if we remain open to this new energy flowing through us, no part of our life will remain unchanged."[4]

The Only Constant Is Change

Sometimes we forget that as parents in training, we need to grow up our own personality roles along the developmental track. After all, our children watch us intently. Their circumstances can jolt us out of any sense of complacency along the raising road of learning how to meet our basic needs. "As when they tell us to 'chill out,' our children remain our best teachers in pushing us to make . . . changes. Not only do they send us important messages, they are almost as active in shaping us as we are in shaping them. They are superb in getting us back on track when we have strayed too far from the parenting they need."[5] When our child has trouble with a particular issue, we are forced to face the issue on our own terms, whatever they may be.

We might prefer to keep some painful issues from our past in the basement of our personality story-house, desiring emotional amnesia as protection from further suffering. However, when our child experiences pain along the raising road, we walk alongside our child as compassionate, intelligent parents, and sometimes our acknowledgment of our past pain can help them. However, we repeat many of our former steps along the way. **As we travel through our days, we recycle our energy just like the sun does.** We recycle through many energy patterns that we have encountered before, either being consciously aware of them or perhaps unwittingly and unconsciously repeating patterns that we have ignored over and over in our lives.

NATURE-NURTURE CYCLICAL INTERACTION

We cannot blame genes for all of our behavior. As psychiatrist Dan Siegel points out, "Genes do not exist in a vacuum and may require experience for their expression."[6] Recent evidence suggests the importance of brain shaping that occurs though social experience. Educator Judith Rich Harris focuses on how frequently youth pick up attributes from others in their environments rather than from their parents (although she also views heredity as a strong contributor to the family stage). Harris and others argue that heredity likely furnishes 50 percent of a person's psychological makeup, leaving 50 percent to environmental factors.[7] Genes do carry temperament differences, but the environment grooms children in certain personality roles and energy outlets. **While genes may determine how our neurons link, our experiences trigger certain energy linkages.**

Instead of debating the percentages of influence "nature" versus "nurture" has, I view these influences as interactive. The complexity of our brain's circuitry makes it difficult to sort out any particular ratio of genetic versus environmental influence, anyhow: "The way the brain works [is through] electrical signals that cause chemical signals that cause electrical signals."[8] These electrical signals will become clearer in future research, but my 1960s textbook in child development and personality still seems relevant in terms of outlining the nature-nurture roadmap. Nature-nurture cyclical interactions cover at least five key components: (1) Genetically determined biological variables; (2) nongenetic biological factors (for example, birth trauma resulting from a lack of oxygen during birthing); (3) past learning history; (4) immediate social environment (including the people who live with you, peers, relatives, colleagues, and teachers); and (5) community/culture.[9] Nature and nurture are twin influences when it comes to our personality development. Therefore, both gene stories and environment stories get tossed into familial recycle bins.

MIRROR, MIRROR IN THE FAMILY

In this book, I primarily deal with powerful parental modeling in the personality development of children. The importance of caretakers cannot be overlooked. **As caretakers, we help shape the brain signaling underlying a child's personality.** Here is an example of how mammal parents can play a profound difference. A fascinating research study looks at "naturally shy" baby monkeys. When these shy monkeys are handed over to foster monkey mothers who are "confident," the previously shy monkeys quickly outgrow their shyness.[10]

Therefore, regardless of what we inherit from the mysterious gene pool, we must look to caretakers' modeling to understand our personality roles completely. One reason that family *interactions* are so powerful relates to the "mirror neurons" in our brains. Discovered in the 1990s, mirror neurons may explain our gut reactions to another person's behavior. These neurons respond with equal strength when we do something or when we watch someone else do the same action.[11] Thus, the emotional role guiding a parent's actions can reverberate in a child. Likewise, mirror neurons may allow caretakers to perceive some of a child's intentions.[12] Such mirroring is so powerful that psychiatrist Dan Siegel and parent educator Mary Hartzell advise that "adoptive parents should . . . also be called the biological parents because the family experiences they create shape the biological structure of their child's brain."[13]

On our good days, when we feel *up*, we approach the day and our children with vigor. On our difficult days, when we feel *down*, our energy level sputters, and we exhale exhaustedly. Our children often follow suit. Sometimes, though, children's actions energize the adults in their lives. One caring grandmother offers, "It is so easy to be with my grandchild. I'm not as tired when I deal with my four-year-old grandson's visits. He gives me energy!" In this extended family, it takes a child to raise *up* a grandparent to feel youthful and creative. However, as charming as her grandson is, this same grandparent admits that the main burden for his care does not land in her lap. She relishes what she calls "that degree of separation. . . . I don't have as much responsibility for my grandson's care as my daughter."

WHO OR WHAT ENGINEERS OUR ENERGY CYCLES?

How do we generate a satisfying amount of energy for every day? Who has enough energy available to raise children day in, day out? It's easy to suffer what I call an "energy breakdown." Just like the collective numbness that surrounded our country after the tragedy of September 11, 2001, when America and its people no longer felt safe, family members feel numb after a tragic fire, a robbery, a sudden death, or an act of violence. Their homes no longer feel like safe havens. We act as if we are in a fog after trauma, as if our energy train has gone off its track. Our sense of stability wavers, and all the fearful, insecure roles of our personality tumble out so fast that we wonder if we can catch our next breath. We think too of the negative things that could possibly happen next. If we suffer an energy breakdown like this from the negative events in our lives, we likely affect our children's energy levels adversely. Similarly, if we fuel ourselves with hope, it is probable that there is an advantageous effect on our children's energy levels.

Whatever the interactions of our personality roles are with those of our children, too often these seamless events are hidden from our awareness. We are unaware of our mirror neurons. We trudge through part of our day with our emotional eyes closed. As one beleaguered father says of his daily existence, "You stamp out fires as they occur." An exasperated mother blames her energy drain however, on her own mother: "You are just like a little kid," she tells her mother when she feels the squeeze between meeting her two-year-old son's needs and her cranky mother's needs. Like invisible parasites, personality roles from our ancestors can trail along with us, mostly without our conscious awareness. One caring mother loses energy every July, the month her father died. She sadly recalls how she lost her father when she was eight years old and how her mother never let her forget from then on that July was the worst month of the year.

Sometimes we come to believe that we have little control over our personality, because we do not consider causes and effects that occurred before our adolescence.[14] Yet, by our teen years, we have already experienced a considerable recycling of personality roles in our lives. It is likely that we unconsciously copy not only some of our parents' roles "but also [the roles] those grandparents, crazy cousins, and others played. . . . Examples are . . . mediator, manipulator, jester, saint, scapegoat, leader, crybaby, and follower."[15] Psychiatrist Mel Roman believes that such powerful personality roles remain with us the rest of our lives.

Each family personality role carries its energy in specific patterns, so our energy levels loop and recycle like the sun on an ongoing basis. Even being named for someone in the family sometimes leads us to mimic that person's personality roles and energy patterns. Many of us like our names, but others hate their names because of some weighty ancestral tie. In the novel *The Namesake*, writer Jhumpa Lahiri describes how naming a child in India carries a special connotation; Bengali families consider individual names sacred, and they resist inherited or shared naming.[16] Other cultures insist upon name sharing. In fact, the names parents bestow on their children (both formal and informal) often carry certain energy messages. For example, children can resent hearing that they are "just like" their parents or grandparents because of some negative energetic trait or personality role their ancestors had.

When we admonish children by swearing at them or calling them their names in rude tones, this behavior carries further negative energy information. Parents of adolescents often complain that their children are becoming "just like" a peer whom the parent perceives as a negative energy drain. The parent in training often uses a critical role when they sarcastically link the peer's name with that of their child. Behind their parents' backs, these adolescents then learn to play a sarcastic role, and they usually come up with crude names for their parents in return.

TRACKING THE ANCESTRAL ENERGY TRAIN

At the start of each day, we feel a certain amount of energy. Like the sun, our energy train runs along a very long track. Our surface "steam" may relate to the health of our family members, the amount and quality of sleep we had the previous night(s), and the daily habits of our family, both attitudinally and behaviorally. While our underlying energy issues have *connections* to our genetic makeup, the ways we are raised, and our daily experiences, ancestor history plays an important role in our personal levels of daily energy.

Doreen (37)

> One mother, Doreen, constantly complains about her "unpleasant" job and faults her coworkers for their indifference and laziness. She dreads dragging herself to another difficult day at the office and says, "Everyone at work is always negative." Yet as she explores her attitudes about work, Doreen suddenly realizes that her own negativity about her job might impact her children's energy at home negatively. When I ask if Doreen ever says anything positive about her job to her children, Doreen seems surprised by her own negative answer. Her voice softens and she sighs, letting out a low, wheezy whistle. She realizes that although she expects her children to be positive about their homework, she offers no constructive vibes about her own work to them. I ask about the patterns of energy that were released in her childhood. A sly smile forms as Doreen recalls her own parents "bitching and moaning all the time" about their jobs. As adults, we often sound just like our parents. Have intergenerational exhaust fumes lingered in our lungs?

DEVELOPMENT DIRECTIONS

> Even though our own parents did the best they could, given the circumstances of their own lives, we may not have had the early experiences that we would wish to pass on to our own children.
>
> —Daniel Siegel, psychiatrist, and Mary Hartzell,
> parent educator, *Parenting from the Inside Out*

Realizing how much exhaustion she tracks into her house upon arriving home, Doreen now makes sense of some of the negative energy in her household. Parents in training cannot expect children to embrace school or jobs with enthusiasm, and school friends as companions, when they perceive their own jobs as drudgery and their own colleagues as lazy gossips. Feeling perceptions are contagious. Caretakers model healthy or unhealthy energy equations for children, and parents in training need to choose wisely.

Tip for Raising Thirty-Seven-Year-Olds

Balance energy equations each day so that you can view your life with present awareness. "At midlife, if we are truly seeking a greater wisdom, a more authentic sense of whom we are . . . and are listening to the promptings of the Self, it is necessary to live in the moment in which we are existing."[17]

Energy Inhertiance

Upon greeting a rushing mother one day, I ask, "How are you?" She quickly chirps she is "fine." Within seconds though, her nonverbal body language takes over and extinguishes the real answer. Her eyes turn downward and her voice softens as another response erupts from another role in her personality. With a hanging head, she confesses to hitting one child and yelling at all three of her children that morning. "I don't know why I said 'fine' . . . it was a terrible morning." Most of us expect our children to go off to school happily and even enjoy school, yet we may role-play something very different than liking our own work, especially our "homework" from the office or our housework. **We must model for our children a sense of how to positively engineer our** own energy cycles, because we pass on to our children both a verbal and nonverbal *energy inheritance*.

Research shows that people who live with depressed family members are more likely to become depressed themselves.[18] The energy level of a depressed parent therefore greatly affects a child. Depressed parents have a bias toward negative events and situations; they tend to emphasize whatever goes wrong in their day. This negative cycle can become so ingrained in us that a parent in training becomes nearly immobilized or stuck in such thinking. **As well as having knots in your stomach, you can have "nots" filling your brain.**

Parental moodiness confuses our children. They may assume that our negativity relates to some incorrect or faulty behavior on their part. Parent-child cycles of negativity loop across each other just like the energy on the sun's surface. After a while, no one quite remembers where or when the upset loop that started it all began. An interplay of human cycles of emotional and behavioral energy exists from parent to parent, from adult to child, and from child to adult.

FEELINGS AS BODY-MIND ENERGY PERCEPTIONS

Neuroscientist Candace Pert writes a book that helps us understand our brain's chemistry cycles. Memory and emotion have strong *connections* in the brain. Proteins known as *peptides* (like opiates and serotonin) regulate behavior and mood. Pert suggests that peptides are the *biochemical correlate of emotions*; her team at the National Institute of Mental Health *maps* peptide receptors in the brain and have found dense groupings of these receptors in the areas most associated with emotion.

Peptide receptors actually reside throughout our body, even in white blood cells. Pert describes these cells as "bits of brain." This scientific description suggests that emotional memory stores itself all over our body. Pert's portrayal for this total body phenomenon, or one *body-mind*, includes the notion that the body holds our "unconscious mind."[19] Pert believes that we store past traumas in varying body parts, often without our conscious knowledge. The cycles of *bodymind* energy thus explain how physical aches and pains relate to our tense thoughts in stressful situations.

A further scientific description illustrates how our emotional energy operates. Our emotions alert us to outside influences. Neuroscientist Antonio Damasio's theory elaborates that all living creatures "from the humble amoeba to the human are born with devices designed to solve 'automatically,' no proper reasoning required, the basic problems of life . . . [by] finding sources of energy [and] incorporating the transforming energy."[20] Damasio also suggests that emotions consist of three layers: (1) *background emotions*, which are picked up by observing body language (as in detecting your child's energy level through their slumping shoulders and sad demeanor); (2) *primary emotions*, which make up the common list of personality roles, including the roles of fear, anger, disgust, surprise, sadness, and happiness; and (3) *social emotions*, which extend our personality role list to include the roles of sympathy, embarrassment, shame, guilt, pride, jealousy, envy, gratitude, admiration, indignation, and contempt in our lives.[21]

Emotions are exhibited in us and our children in similar bodymind ways. Our personality roles reveal our emotional body states, which frequently show up in habitual, nonverbal poses. The chemicals that cycle through our bodies change our muscles in special patterns; everything from our posture to the way our voice sounds can change depending upon our underlying emotional energy. The frequent changes in how we express ourselves can confuse us, and yet this happens to *all* of us in varying patterns: "Specific patterns of behavior . . . running, freezing, courting, or parenting . . . [are] all about transition and commotion, sometimes real bodily upheaval."[22] When we become aware of our transitioning energy signals, we are better able to make good choices in raising our child.

BODIES "TALK"

Feelings are complex thoughts, or energy perceptions, of our body, and they signal our distinctive body ways,[23] or poses. This neurological concept represents a reversal of how people usually think of their feelings and actions. **In other words, a child does not hyperventilate because he is feeling fearful—he becomes afraid because of the hyperventilating sensations that are cycling through the body. Body talk therefore cues personality roles.** Neuroscientist Damasio sees this process as a way to keep track of what happens to us and to maintain homeostasis, or a state of well-being. Similarly, we can maintain personality well-being when we learn to map our various opposite roles and to create a sense of balance in our personality. When caretakers learn to slow down their multitasking behaviors, they become better able to find this feeling of "balance" for relating one interaction at a time.

Damasio advocates a group goal of sharing and being cooperative. He explains an experiment in which monkeys abstain from pulling a chain delivering food if pulling the chain also delivers an electric shock to another monkey. When faced with the prospect of hurting another monkey, some monkeys do not eat for hours or even days. Apparently, these monkeys are using their "mirror neurons": they are able to anticipate the actions of others and have empathy for the plight of other monkeys. This research provides a hopeful experiment in group energy. Damasio proposes that humans who have personalities that include such sharing, cooperative roles "would be more likely to survive longer and leave more descendants."[24] Unfortunately, not all human personalities place a high value on thinking about what is best for another person. What happens inside a parent's bodymind when appropriate caring breaks down within the family?

MISPLACED SEXUAL ENERGY IN THE FAMILY

Ashley (17), Elena (42), and Warren (49)

> Ashley revisits a torturous early personality story-house. Both of her parents abused alcohol. Ashley recalls her early compensatory role. She functioned as the responsible backseat driver, trying to hold the family together. Her energy fluctuated dramatically on a daily basis. Some days she had so little sleep that she nearly fell off her chair in school. Her dreams were peppered with the recollections of fights between her parents, and these images disrupted her sleep. She recalled a time when her father shoved her mother through the kitchen doorway and locked her outside. Her uncle retaliated by punching Warren in the face.
>
> Ashley's parents' marriage dissolved, and as a nine-year-old, Ashley regularly traveled from her mother's home to her father's home.

One night, she awakened in her father's apartment to find her father lying on top of her. She recalls her father whispering that he wanted to "kiss her the real way." Ashley only knew how to "kiss on the cheek," and she felt confused. Another night, when she was twelve, Ashley awakened to find her uncle in her bed. He was trying to remove her underpants. A cousin who was staying overnight in the home walked into the bedroom and saved Ashley. Now, at seventeen, Ashley does not understand how to handle her sexual energy. While sexuality presents challenges for most preteens, Ashley has experienced sexual trust violations that leave her wary and angry. She experiences even more fitful sleep patterns, thus losing energy for the discipline to do her schoolwork.

DEVELOPMENT DIRECTIONS

Rather than focusing on changing children's brains, we should think more about changing parents' brains and improving their and their children's lives through job training, adult literacy programs, and appropriate continuing adult education.

—John T. Bruer, developmental consultant,
The Myth of the First Three Years

The complicated feelings Ashley has toward her parents make it difficult for her to find values she can copy from her story-house of memories. She vacillates between a sympathetic role for her mother's sixteen-hour workdays, which keep food on the table, and a rageful role whenever she imagines her mother not protecting her sexual innocence. Then Elena confides in Ashley that she, too, is a victim of sexual abuse. Ashley's image of a cooperative world dims further. Ashley learns in therapy what she did not glean at home: true intimacy only occurs when two consenting partners desire a mutually satisfying encounter. Coercion and sexual energy do not belong together. Ashley's confused and angry roles in her personality are normal reactions to incestuous behavior.

Tip for Raising Seventeen-Year-Olds

Shameful secrets obscure a child's energy for everyday activities. "[There are] . . . many problems with early sexual intercourse . . . it orients her sexual development toward what she believes a man wants. It cuts off her own process of development and redirects her to another's."[25]

Tip for Raising Forty-Two-Year-Olds

Every parent requires "downtime," or some chunks of time to replenish their own needs. "Parents who do too much do not do enough introspection. Are we afraid of what we might find if we look too deep?"[26]

Tip for Raising Forty-Nine-Year-Olds

Fathers are most likely to be successful at parenting when they consider how their child feels in any given situation. "Men's lives are less concerned with taking care of the way people feel and more concerned with simply solving problems, getting things done."[27]

THE FOOD-ENERGY CONNECTION

Our culture as a whole needs to revisit personal energy needs. We have to address our own energy, as well as our children's energy. Physicist Albert Einstein advocates forging an energy circle where we acknowledge all living beings with "understanding and compassion." British anthropologist Ashley Montagu refers to a similar energy source as the need for "compassionate intelligence."[28] **Some parents struggle every day to have enough compassion for themselves and for their children.** In fact, the wider culture frequently lacks compassion for children's needs. Children swallow enormous influences from TV, computer games, movies, and megabusinesses that are aimed at the child as a consumer. Nutritional biochemist William Dietz observes that children's unhealthy eating habits have a link to their TV habits; there is a link between obesity in children and TV watching.[29] Where are the compassionately intelligent and child-friendly agendas in our culture?

Ask any child what a Happy Meal is, and the child's answer likely includes the mention of a hamburger with fries. Many families today use fast-food restaurants as their home away from home; whether children love fast food or not, they are enticed by the fast-food restaurant's playgrounds and toys. As pointed out by journalist Eric Schlosser, more than 90 percent of the children in the United States eat at McDonald's at some point or another. According to Schlosser's research, Americans increased the amount of money they spent on fast food from six billion dollars in 1970 to over one hundred billion dollars in 2001. Americans spend more of their income on fast food than on higher education, personal computers, computer software, or new cars. In fact, more money goes into the coffers of fast-food restaurants than into the combined purchases of movie tickets, books, magazines, newspapers, videos, and recorded music. "On any given day in the US, about one-quarter of the adult population visits a fast food restaurant."[30]

As our quick-fix appetites escalate, our nation's nutritional bottom line is bottoming out in too many empty calories. Parents may not realize how many calories exist in French fries. Half of the five hundred calories dripping from one large order of fries comes from the fryer oil, and those calories come from a corn or soybean farm, not a potato farm.[31] A hamburger also contains corn, as it takes two pounds of corn fed to a cow to produce America's favorite fast food. (Eating corn delivers energy to our bodies, but when that corn is fed to cows or chicken, 90 percent of its energy is lost.)[32] If fast-food restaurants reduced the fat content of their offerings, there would be an immediate positive effect on children's nutritional energy,[33] as well as their parents' energy for relating one interaction at a time.

Parental values are what guide food and energy choices for a child. My own children did not visit fast-food chains very often. They wanted to, though; they knew from advertising, and from other children's visits, that toys come with food at certain restaurants. My solution to this nutrition issue was to make a game out of going to a fast-food restaurant a few times a year. When my children were least expecting a fast-food toy, we would engage in a fantasy. I would look skyward and say, "Look up in the sky—there is a blue moon tonight! Can you see it? What does it mean?" After the first time, my children learned that "once in a blue moon" in our household meant that we would go to a fast-food restaurant that evening for dinner. When they were older, they would gang up. The two of them would take me to the front porch and mischievously banter, "There's a blue moon, there's a blue moon," if it had been too many months since the last burger night. Most evenings, however, were home-cooking nights. Weekends were a good time to whip up big pots of stew that would last a while. Other nights were a blend of thoughtful, balanced meals, along with some furiously made dishes on harried days.

"PICKY" EATING AND "PICKY" PERSONALITY ROLES

Susan (infant) and Sandy (4)

Sandy expresses anger about her food choices daily, and she refuses to eat anything except chicken nuggets, bananas, and applesauce. When a certain brand of applesauce isn't available in their neighborhood grocery store, her loving parent drives to another store in search of "Sandy food." Sandy's mother admits that she babies her four-year-old daughter. Part of the food-energy connection for Sandy and her mother is because a new baby sister, Susan, has recently entered the family. Sandy also exerts her jealous role through secret pinches to the baby. At the same time, Sandy enjoys caressing her new sister and expresses pride in being the older and wiser sibling.

Sandy struggles to sort out her energy needs, and her conflicting feelings about having a sibling replace her special status in the family. While proud of her baby sister, Sandy also exercises competing needs for belongingness; she desperately tries to retain some of her babyhood status. Her food "pickiness" temporarily allows her some babying time, as she eats mostly a soft diet. She relishes the catering that she receives around her special meal requests. She is also not handling her toileting needs adequately, something her family wants but which she is putting off so she can continue to be "babied." In a puppet story, Sandy fantasizes how her toileting needs can be met: "This lamb has to poop. It's a magic lamb. The poop just wipes off magically and it never comes back."

DEVELOPMENT DIRECTIONS

Clinical and developmental psychology have historically focused on child development, with little attention paid to the lifelong relational development of mothers and children; even less attention is paid to the psychological development of mothers.

—Kathy Weingarten, Janet Surrey, Cynthia Garcia Coll, and Mary Watkins, psychologists, *Mothering Against the Odds*

Making the transition from only child to older sibling takes years for some children. Also in transition themselves, parents in training now have double escalators of needs; they move both up and down when the parents have two children in the family. As families continue to add members, needs escalate. It takes loving and patient parents to help a child ease into a big-sibling role in the family. One way Sandy's parents can help her is to look at Sandy's baby pictures with her and talk about all the big-girl things she can do at age four. This activity forges one step in the process of meeting four-year-old energy needs. Four-year-old children often have one foot on their tricycles and one foot in their baby strollers.

Tip for Raising Newborns

Savor the mystery of birth of your infant. "Attachment between parents and babies is virtually instinctual, but it gets complicated as soon as the child becomes more active and verbal."[34]

Tip for Raising Four-Year-Olds

Playing out your preschooler's conflicts with toys helps their transition to the next stage of growth. "Kids this age . . . still think they're the center of the universe."[35]

TEEN ENERGY DERAILED BY AN EATING DISORDER

Experiencing eating disturbances in a child is difficult for parents in training to encounter, because eating represents the very essence of health and energy. Four-year-old eating extremists present worrisome dilemmas, but adolescents with disturbed eating patterns conjure up more fearful images in parents' minds due to the imminent energy risks disorders like anorexia and bulimia create.

Daphne (14), Lena (44), and Jorge (48)

Daphne has loving parents who dote upon her. Lena and Jorge cannot imagine why Daphne feels so depressed much of the time, as she has many talents. Not only does she utilize her ability well to obtain excellent grades, but she has enormous creative talent as a dancer. However, Daphne does not see herself as having any particular skills. She exercises a critical role in her personality that denounces her dancing, her grades, her parents, and her peer group. Every time she perceives a peer to be criticizing her, she hides in the girls' bathroom and makes herself throw up. The waste of her body energy in this way begins to show on her face as dark under-eye circles. A boy at school tells Daphne that her hips are "too big," although Daphne's too-slender figure seems hip free. When I suggest that many freshman boys flirt by saying things to girls that are the opposite of the truth, Daphne rolls her eyes at me. Her sarcastic, nonverbal facial pose "screams," as if to say, "You had to be there—then you'd get it."

Her mother, Lena, wants Daphne to take belonging issues in stride, to realize that the other freshman students have similar struggles with their self-confidence and body image. Jorge has the idea that Daphne can "ignore the bastards" altogether; why doesn't she just stick to her dancing? Neither parent seems aware of Daphne's dangerous dance with food and energy. She has begun skipping breakfast every morning, and now this habit has escalated into her throwing up lunch nearly every school day. By the time Daphne goes to her after-school dance class, she feels light-headed. The roles of being shy, modest, self-deprecating, "dependent on men," and unassertive, as well as "not [having] enough friends," make up some of the rigid personality rules that Daphne blindly follows.

DEVELOPMENT DIRECTIONS

We are herd animals; we want to belong.

—Rita Mae Brown

Fourteen is such a pivotal age. The major transition from middle school to high school unsettles every teen for varying amounts of time. An even larger teen transition involves adapting to newly acquired adult bodies. Easing into their new sexual skin seems weird for most teens. Some teens have so much self-consciousness about their bodies that they have little energy for the rest of life. Some try to control their bodies and their physical shapes by controlling and limiting what they eat. After all, the cultural value of thinness for women defines nearly every female pictured on the covers of teen magazines. Dancers and gymnasts are especially vigilant about their thinness. Adolescent girls need realistic models of healthy female bodies. Parents in training need to express a caring role and talk openly with their daughters about bodily changes that occur in adolescence; for example, wider hips are one body part that defines a girl's femininity.

Tip for Raising Fourteen-Year-Olds

Be sensitive to the many issues that clothes shopping and food bring up for adolescent girls. "To treat eating disorders in America is to treat our culture. We need a revolution in our values and behavior. We need to define attractiveness with much broader parameters, so that most women, not an infinitesimal few, can feel good about their appearance."[36]

Tip for Raising Forty-Four-Year-Olds

Teen sexual innuendos raise a host of issues. "Watching our children develop sexually, we may be proud of their growth, anxious about their uncertainty and experimentation, sad at the reminder of our own 'lost youth,' jealous of their sexual blossoming—or some of each of these. . . . We are brought up against our own feelings about sexuality—for ourselves and for our children."[37]

Tip for Raising Forty-Eight-Year-Olds

Discussions of teen sexuality give you an opportunity to teach your family values. "No realistic parent believes he or she can be the only source of sexual information to a child . . . but parents with the right message and the right timing can preempt negative and harmful information."[38]

NEEDS ADD UP

Caretakers often do not appreciate the weighty struggles of their children. Skipping meals, vomiting vitamins, and substituting drugs for food are critical signs that ennui or exhaustion is threatening a teen. However, children do not appreciate the weighty struggles of their parents. One mother of a rebellious teenage son who engages in drinking parties every weekend says, "I wish Darnell would understand that all this parenting of a teenager is new to me too, and I do make mistakes." Another mother sighs after finding drug paraphernalia in the bedroom of her middle school daughter: "I'm the grown-up, and that's really scary. I can see that I'm projecting a lot of my issues onto her." Too many parents are exhausted themselves and feel like giving up. Instead of engineering their child's energy levels in a healthy direction, some parents struggle to get themselves and their youngsters out of bed every morning. All of us face competing needs every day. **Often we ignore both our own and our children's energy needs, pushing on to meet what we think are more important needs.**

The first step in overhauling a child's basic energy rests in opening communication channels between parent and child. Usually when this occurs, a plethora of personality roles rumble out. A child's anger, previously turned inward, can take an abrupt about-face, becoming anger turned outward in the parent's direction. Allowing a child a forum for their frustrations and an energy release begins with one interaction at a time. Sleep deprivation runs rampant in our families. One distraught mother divulges, "I can't sleep at night. All I can think of is paying back my credit card. I'm $29,000 into my card. I don't have money to buy anything. I don't know what to do."

Psychologist James Maas labels the lack of sleep among adults in America as a crisis, with most adults ranging from moderately to severely sleep deprived. When people do not sleep more than six hours a night, they miss out on rapid eye movement (REM) sleep. This REM phase, or dream-time sleep, occurs between the sixth and eighth hour of sleep. Our brain stores new information into its long-term memory during this critical dreaming time.[39] A 2012 survey of one thousand adults by the Better Sleep Council finds that 12 percent of the people in the study were so sleep deprived that they had fallen asleep at work.

Furthermore, "A whopping 79 percent of women would rather get a good night's sleep than have sex."[40]

NIGHT FEARS

Not getting enough sleep or rest every night takes on multiple meanings in our children. Night fears range from fear of the dark to traumatic events that have occurred in a child's life.

Victor (4)

> Victor comes to therapy after he experiences the traumatic event of a neighborhood house being hit by lightning and burning down one night. Victor hears a crushing sound as lightning strikes the home, and soon flames leap from windows. Although the neighbors are not injured, Victor later becomes paralyzed with fright whenever weather forecasts suggest even the possibility of stormy weather. If the sky appears gray, Victor anxiously asks his mother about lightning. Even mild storm reverberations are enough to send Victor into a fetal position with his hands over his ears. He has trouble sleeping; he stays awake at night, with his trauma thermometer registering in the exhausted range. His overall energy store is depleted. His warm and supportive parents watch Victor play out the fire with his toy fire truck ("Lightning struck the table . . . the fire truck put it out!"). Yet this creative play alone does not serve to diminish his terror.
>
> In the first therapy session, Victor complies with my request to draw a picture of a person and agreeably makes up a story about his drawing. "Well first . . . um . . . there was a king that wanted to share . . . and liked to do what all the other ones wanted to do. Then the tiger came and said, 'I am the jack.' And then a kangaroo, said, 'I'm the queen.' And then something else came . . . there was a big noise—a dinosaur was roaring. And he knew where they were . . . in his brain! And . . . um . . . they were playing together. The end." After Victor finishes his story, I ask a few questions. "Is the queen scared of the dinosaur?" "Yes." "Is the king scared?" "No." Victor quickly identifies himself with the king who apparently has a very brave role. He ends up saying, "Make it whatever the king said!" However, Victor coexists as opposites in his story, both comforter and comforted; he has both brave "king" and scared "queen" roles. He has

personality roles that experience fear of another catastrophic event and personality roles that make efforts to cope with the traumatic fire.

I ask Victor to set up a puppet story next. He gleefully surveys the pile of puppets barely hidden under a sofa table, and immediately he chooses the largest, scariest-looking, overstuffed puppet. His story pours out as the puppet goes to work. The monster immediately "attacks" a house; flames come out, and the monster acquires the offending label of "bad." As preschool teacher Vivian Gussin Paley points out, there are certain themes that frequent the play of three- and four-year-old children, and that of "bad guy" tops the list.[41]

Victor leaves the monster story midstream and begins to tell me about the real fire in his four-year-old logic: "Their house was up to the clouds, and the lightning could reach it." Young children understand the world based upon what they can see. Just like a preschooler examining the moon one clear night and saying, "The moon can't come in because the window is closed," Victor assesses storm behavior in the most salient perception he has about the sky. He sees clouds when he looks upward, and that is where the lightning appears to him.

Without missing a breath, Victor then weaves his real-life recollections back into his present puppet story. He focuses on putting out the fire; enthusiastically he tells of two fire trucks, two ambulances, and 103 police officers (it must have seemed that police were everywhere). Then Victor realizes that the puppet story lacks something. He once again picks up the protagonist puppet: "We have to go back to the 'fake life' story." This bit of reality shows Victor's considerable intelligence; he understands the separateness of his puppet story from his memory of the fire. In subsequent sessions, Victor and I soothe his trauma through play-therapy sessions as he "rebuilds" the burned house with blocks (along with rebuilding his confident role, or his ability to cope with his world). I coach his parents to keep encouraging Victor to talk about fires, both in imaginative play and through library books about fire fighters. Meanwhile, Victor's sleep disturbance goes away, and his energetic vigor for everyday life returns.

DEVELOPMENT DIRECTIONS

Each time I told my story, I lost a bit, the smallest drop of pain.

—Alice Sebold, *The Lovely Bones*

In the case of a young child like Victor, several different mediums help in externalizing details and contribute to resolving the trauma: drawing, having puppets (and the child) act out the story, playing out various scenes of both trauma and recovery, and verbalizing from the viewpoint of different personality roles. When we acknowledge fears and see them from various angles, we can accept them. **We do not attempt to erase a child's fear; in fact, we embrace children's fearful roles. In effect, we must say to a child, "Let me see if I can understand what *your* scared part feels like."**

After processing information in many different ways, parents in training can lead a child to find how personality roles can adapt to the fear-producing event. A key aspect in relating one interaction at a time rests upon helping a child locate a sense of self-territory, so that whatever the next day brings, the child can rely on an endless supply of resilience. This positive energy and resilience develops from learning to cope with yesterday's troubles. Coping with change remains the constant companion of childhood and adulthood.

As a therapist, I help a traumatized child face fearful events in their life by slowly getting their version of the scary event one interaction at a time. As a parent in training, you can use a similar approach, for we do not receive a child's "facts" all at once. **Traumatizing stories often take more than one telling for any individual to feel that the details are fully exposed or externalized.** When psychologists study children's feelings following a disaster, they find that the youngsters have fears that linger long after the event. After the Oklahoma City bombing in 1995, the surviving children experienced sleep disturbances, aggressiveness, and increased clinging behaviors. Children in Florida affected by Hurricane Andrew in 1992 continued to have post-traumatic symptoms five years afterward. Researchers find that children are often reluctant to talk about their own raw feelings because they are aware of their parents' emotional struggles.[42] Children are remarkably protective of their parents, although it remains more of our caretaking role to protect our child's fearful parts. One of the most important ways to restore a child's energy level after a crisis situation relies upon maintaining simple energy rituals for mealtimes, bedtimes, and exercise.

Tip for Raising Four-Year-Olds

Take your child's fears seriously, as they have great meaning. "The brain can be called an 'anticipation machine,' constantly scanning the environment and trying to determine what will come next." [43]

FANTASY IS AGELESS

Adults, like children, use up a lot of energy in floating between the worlds of reality and their own versions of internal storytelling, often called daydreaming. Daydreaming provides a stage for different roles of your personality to express their desires, needs, and grievances. **Children frequently play out fantasies about growing up, while parents in training internally fantasize about changing both their past and future lives.**

A variety of personality roles command parents to repair the past; another group of parts seemingly demand that parents fix the future. You may be reading a story to your child, and at the same time mulling over problems at work or home with a far different story line. Often we are not aware of how we are drifting into fantasies about the past or future. When we do, however, we are not free to relate to our child one interaction at a time. In fact, one mother confides that when she feels too preoccupied while reading a bedtime story, her three children never go to sleep easily. This wise mother has learned that it's when she focuses on just being *present* that her children go right to sleep at the end of the story.

Children also vary their personality roles that they use when they fantasize, sometimes moment by moment. In this conversation from a preschool classroom, the wee actors change roles at a dizzying pace: "I'm G. I. Joe. Who are you?" "I'm Superman," Christopher replies. "That means we're both good guys." Later, these same children grapple with goodness: "I'm the bad Superman. See if you can stop me, Christopher." "With poison or Kryptonite?" "Both. Try to change me into the good Superman."[44] This example reveals how even four-year-old children grapple with personality roles that are opposite in nature to one another.

ENERGY ENGINEERS

Community and school energy influences on a child are like inspirational sunshine energy—or enormous storm clouds capable of drenching a child. Because nine months in a year five-year-olds to eighteen-year-olds spend a major portion of their waking hours in school, teachers function as parent surrogates.[45] A teacher therefore chooses many times daily which student personality roles receive notice. These choices reflect the teacher's known and unknown "family" of genetic and environmental roles. Similarly, caretakers also make decisions on how to engineer energy in relating to children's personality roles. **We and society have the choice to rear our young through supportive and encouraging roles or critical and controlling roles.** Adult roles are powerful shapers in the energy equations of children's daily functioning.

We are an encouraging, inspiring model for raising our children when we can take care of ourselves and our own energy needs. But how do we raise and maintain adequate levels of energy within our bodies? We need to eat nutritious meals along with our young. We can make mealtimes special by initiating family rituals. One of my dinnertime rituals for a few years was to ask that each family member tell about the "best part" of their day and the "worst part" of their day. Both children and parents in training learn to show empathy and resiliency for the next day's issues in such discussions. We can put ourselves to bed to get the amount of sleep we need to engage in REM sleep. We are not adequate energy engineers if we harp on our children to do these things, but we do not make the time to replenish our own energy cycles. The developmental transition track requires constant recycling for both caretakers and children. Our energy level affects everything we do.

Our parent-in-training transitions take on many moves, sometimes careening like a train car without brakes around the energy-cycling curves of our day. **A state of ennui or listlessness is evident in far too many parents and their children. When we realize that we**

are running low on energy, we have to assess what we can do to recycle or replenish our energetic potential. For example, so many parent-child conflicts occur around the dinner hour, when both parents and children are running at low energy. One parent prevents disaster at dinner by having nutritious snacks in plastic baggies in her car when she picks up her son at his daycare preschool on workdays. The availability of nutritional food helps both parent and preschooler gain a bit of momentum until dinner time. Eliminating the whiny car ride helps this parent take a few deep breaths before reentering her home territory.

Even small changes in the amount of a family's exercise routine make a difference in the family's overall energy. Walk your child to school, or play with your child on a playground. We need regular exercise just as much as our children do. In fact, many parents and their children do not move enough of the time. Biologist and educator Carla Hannaford relates how simple movements enhance children's learning in the classroom.[46] I often suggest to parents and their children that they do a few yoga poses together every evening. Parents in training need to raise energy levels by putting some fun and relaxation into the energy equation. Whatever physical activities your family seeks, make fitness a regular habit for everyone. All work and no exercise spell U-N-H-E-A-L-T-H-Y Jacks and Jills.

ENERGY MAPPING

We are energetic beings. Some of our energy may relate to *temperament*, our inherited wiring. It is helpful to understand energy levels of others in our families, and perceive where patterns of energy originate. We also draw zest from our environment. Some believe that Druids, the priests of the Celtic religion of the Iron Age, sought energy through walking along "ley lines" at Stonehenge in England. These straight lines connect ancient sacred sites; one of two ley lines at Stonehenge runs through the Salisbury Cathedral and two Iron Age forts.[47] We need to understand both our genetic "ley lines" and the environmental pathways whereby we can enhance our energy.

- Describe the energy level(s) of your mother, stepmother, or primary caretaker.

- Describe the energy level(s) of your father, stepfather, or primary caretaker.
- What did your parent(s), stepparents(s), or primary caretaker(s) and grandparent(s) say about your energy level when you were ten years old?
- What do you believe to be true about your energy level today? What are the differences (if any) in your energy level from the age of ten until the present day?
- **If you feel that you had much more available energy when you were a ten-year-old child, what do you believe you can do to enliven your energy today?** If you have a good supply of energy day to day, what do you do to ensure that your vitality continues to work well for you?
- What are the environmental factors that you associate with your sense of energy today? What does your child's environment contribute in terms of a sense of zest for everyday living?
- What kind of energy level do you see in your child? What aspect or amount of that energy level seems inherited?

4

DISCIPLINE NEEDS: ARE YOU A DISCIPLE, OR ARE YOU DISORGANIZED IN DISORDER?

Our first baby changed me as a psychologist. . . . Having a second baby, and learning how profoundly different people are even before birth, made it impossible for me to think in terms of . . . the John B. Watson theory of 'give me two babies and I will make one into this and one into the other' . . . a parent cannot make his children into anything. Children make themselves into something.

—Abraham Maslow, psychologist, *The Farther Reaches of Human Nature*

On a family vacation in California, we see killer whales perform amazing tricks. A whale trainer in a "Window to the Sea" program explains the training process as follows: "We establish rapport, let the animals know what is expected of them. . . . We get to know them well." Positive reinforcement follows the rapport/expectation stages, as trainers use every available opportunity for praise. In talking with a whale trainer, I ask if some whales are easier to train, if some are more intelligent, and how trainers gear discipline to a particular whale. The wise trainer says, "All whales are trainable, but some are more conducive to training than others."

Just as it is with children, some whales take to training easily, while others require more time and attention. I ask whether trainers use any form of discipline other than positive reinforcement (the only form of discipline I noticed in the Shamu whale show). The trainer answers, "No, when the whales do not do what is expected, their behavior is simply ignored." Why do parents and teachers struggle so much in disciplining children? A partial answer includes the fact that most adults do not receive schooling to be trainers of children. The whale trainer tells of being a parent of two children. Later, I wonder if the whale trainer ever slips up at home, finding it easier to train killer whales than to rear his own children.

Contrast the discipline that the killer whales received with the non-verbal discipline of a child that I observed while waiting for several minutes for an elevator one day. A young family waits with me. The father talks animatedly to his wife in a language different from mine. A daughter, perhaps four years old, pummels her father's stomach as she attempts to get his attention. She then yammers to no avail in a high-pitched voice. Her father continues to ignore her screeching tantrum and nonverbal punches as he continues conversing with his wife. Suddenly, the mother delivers a sidelong kick to her daughter's legs. Immediately, the girl clams up. Her fists drop to her sides, and she casts plaintive eyes in several directions. A grim look hardens across her mouth. The parents finish their conversation, but neither one addresses this child, who is now taking her headband off and on repeatedly. The family and I enter the elevator somewhat robotically, all of us looking at the numbers lighting up above the elevator doors. **How many times do parents in training respond to their children in a negative and robotic manner, never listening to find out what need their child wants to communicate to them?**

WHO NEEDS MORE DISCIPLINE: THE PARENT OR THE CHILD?

Alisa (39)

> Alisa finds herself running behind schedule again. She leaves the house five minutes late because one child cannot find his instrument for his music lesson and another dawdles in putting on his shoes and coat. Alisa knows that yelling at them does not help; yet her unexpressed frustration role shows up in considerable muscle tension. The children snipe at each other as they begin their car journey, and

the traffic seems heavier than usual. Alisa finally blurts out, "Stop it . . . right now," as she sails through a yellow light trying to make up for lost time.

Alisa picks up a friend's child, shortly before an argument—who touched the other one first—burns Alisa's ears: "Did not!" "Did too!" "Did not!" "Did too!" Alisa raises her voice over the ruckus as she presses down on the accelerator: "If I told you once, I told you a hundred times—there is no arguing in the car." The children raise their bantering flags higher. Alisa retaliates. "When you get home, both of you are grounded," she screams, even though she does not know what they will be grounded from doing. Looking at the speedometer, Alisa finds she is going forty-five on a street with a twenty-five-mph speed limit. She also realizes that she has passed the intersection where she wanted to turn! Alisa just wishes she could leave the confinement of the car, stop carpooling, and go out to dinner with her friend, but the raising road of meeting everyone's needs goes on and on.

DEVELOPMENT DIRECTIONS

Some parents believe that love and good intentions are all we need to discipline our children. I believe that love isn't enough. . . . We need skills that help us find alternatives to punishment.

—Nancy Samalin, parent counselor, *Loving Your Child Is Not Enough*

Many day-to-day situations require some discipline to ensure a safe and rewarding journey for both parents in training and children. Many caretakers favor grounding and taking away of privileges for their brand of discipline choices. While such techniques may temporarily stop a particular undesirable action of a child, they rarely teach anything useful. Often parents punish a child for their misbehavior because the parents received similar punishments for their own childhood misbehaviors. But when asked what they learned when they received these childhood punishments, many parents have a startled look on their face when they reply, "I vowed that I would never do this to a child of mine, yet I just did it yesterday!" Effective discipline for children not only rests upon changing negative behavior to more positive behavior but also has the goal of teaching problem-solving skills so that a child knows *how* to behave in the future.

Tip for Raising Thirty-Nine-Year-Olds

Children's needs seldom stop flowing. You also are on call for meeting your own needs. But making plans to accommodate everyone's needs in the family takes discipline. "When we understand that our emotional system is automatic and hot-wired, we can start to make sense of the immediate—and even recurring—outbursts of energy, displays of anger, feelings of guilt."[1]

To discipline your child from the point of view of unconditional love, you need to address parental consistency, family values, simple rules for day-to-day living, and discipline dialogues that teach children problem-solving skills.

Parenting-Trip Tips

- Make sure all caretakers are consistent in their brands of discipline so that the discipline is clear to a given child.
- Gear the discipline to teaching the values you want your child to live by, such as respect, honesty, and fairness.
- Set a few house rules stating your expectations of what you want your child to do.
- Turn discipline into a time for values dialogues with your child. Realize that time-outs can offer "think it over" time for your child to consider alternative behaviors.

CONSISTENCY COUNTS

The word "discipline" comes from the same Latin word (*discipere*) as the word "disciple," yet we often attribute a negative connotation to "discipline" and a positive connotation to "disciple."

- *Discipere* means "to grasp."[2] When applied to "disciple," one thinks of a person grasping or understanding their leader. When applied to the word "discipline," we can similarly think of grasping something important, of following a good lead.
- In Tibetan, the word "discipline" is *tsul trim. Tsul* means "appropriate or just." *Trim* means "rule or way."[3]

If we combine an Eastern definition of "just or appropriate rule" with our Western idea of following a good lead, we have a concept of consistent discipline: grasping or understanding a leader with "just" rules.

Many caretakers face their most difficult challenges in parenting when they have to discipline a child. One struggling mother laments, "I don't have the structure, so how can I give my daughter the structure to go to bed by ten p.m.?" Parents have trouble modeling fair rules when they are consumed with meeting competing needs. The communication imparted to their children then does not resemble unconditional love, nor does it mirror the friendly reinforcement given by whale trainers. Not surprisingly, many children's responses consist of backtalk. One parenting consultant finds that adults consistently ignore 90 percent or more of their children's positive interactions. In the meantime, such parents give lots of attention to the aggressive, inappropriate behaviors.[4] In-your-face, boisterous behavior is what all too often commands a parent's attention.

Additionally, mothers and fathers often exhibit two completely different parenting styles as they strive to deal with their child's behavior. One father demanded that his daughter finish out the soccer season when she wanted to quit and begin a second sport; a verbal tug-of-war ensued because the mother supported her daughter's position. And if parents bring their children in for therapy, they have a combined list of child behaviors that are irksome, bothersome, puzzling, disrespectful, destructive, worrisome, or embarrassing. **Parents do not recognize, however, that they themselves have personality roles that are irksome, bothersome, puzzling, disrespectful, destructive, worrisome, or perhaps embarrassing to their child.** Interestingly, children often have a wish list for adult change that dovetails nicely with their caretakers' change list for them.

OUT-OF-SYNC CARETAKERS

Mike (8), Diane (36), and Damen (42)

> Mike speeds into the therapy office tailgating his mother, Diane. He
> has received an anxiety "ticket" from his pediatrician. Mike had been

whisked to the emergency room of the local hospital for a panic attack, but there were no indications of an underlying medical condition. When asked what changes she wishes for in her family, Diane wants her husband to abandon roughhousing with his children. Damen scowls critically at his wife as she speaks; what he wants is for her to stop "babying" Mike. Both parents want their son to follow school rules and succeed in learning tasks.

While it is clear that both Diane and Damen love Mike, they are at different speeds in raising him. Diane is the avowed enforcer of rules, while Damen models a rough-and-tumble, pal-like role. When Mike misbehaves, both parents respond to the misbehavior by hurling obscenities. Diane and Damen tell Mike to listen to them and refrain from yelling at them. Mike, in turn, wishes for changes from his parents' emotional poses that resonate with their desired changes. "Don't yell at me!" he exclaims. What would happen if killer whales received such constant criticism? Would they learn to jump through their hoops, or would they end up lost at the "wrong" end of the pool?

In front of his parents, Mike cannot fully reveal how scared he feels. When Mike is alone with me in the therapy room, he draws a picture, telling an accompanying story of an imaginary boy: "Once upon a time my friend and I were walking by an old house. Can it be a scary story?" "It can be any kind of story you want," I say. "We had to watch out for broken glass. And then we heard a big bump against one of the windows . . . the house was tilted to one side . . . at night we heard something bump into the door. It was a walking tombstone, and it was saying, 'Give me back my flower.' And then I realized there was a flower on the bottom of my shoe. Then I fluffed the flower up, took it off my shoe, and gave it back to the tombstone. The tombstone ran away making big thumping noises."

Next, Mike draws a map of his personality so we can visualize the roles that take up residence in his mind's theater. Asked to draw a peaceful self, Mike pictures a CD: "It would play all the songs in the world." When prompted to draw one part of him that happens a lot of the time, Mike begins scribbling furiously with a red marker: "It would take up the whole piece of paper. When I'm playing with a toy and I get really, really mad, I start throwing things around." Just as intensely, he switches to a black marker for scribbling hard on the lower half of the page: "For when I get really, really frustrated and I start to cry." His stark art, resembling a work by modern artist Mark

Rothko, depicts a rendition of red anger and black tears. When asked how he calms himself after such feelings, Mike replies matter-of-factly, "Drink some water and sit down, listen to my CDs; then I go back to whatever I was doing and try it again." I compliment Mike on knowing how to find self-territory so that he can feel relaxed or calm. Asked about what happens to the fierce red and black colors when he relaxes, Mike says, "Then it turns blue and into a CD."

DEVELOPMENT DIRECTIONS

Children tasted what their parents swallowed.

—Rosellen Brown, *Before and After*

Children cope with feelings of fear and sadness much more than parents recognize. Parents set different limits for their children, because they use different personality roles in meeting their own basic needs. One parent focuses continuously on establishing basic discipline in the home, while another emphasizes belonging, assuming their child "already knows what he is supposed to do." Diane wants to coerce, crackdown, and impose limits for Mike, because she wishes that her parents had held higher standards for her as a youngster. Damen takes an opposite discipline approach, trying hard to undo some of his own childhood upbringing. He backs up, approves of, and vouches for his son, as these behaviors represent the treatment that Damen always wanted from his own father. An open discussion about unmet needs refocuses a family's energy in a more positive direction.

Tip for Raising Eight-Year-Olds

Work toward setting a discipline tone in the home that models what you want your child to do. Consider this: "The eight-year-old listens closely when adults talk among themselves. He watches their facial expressions; he keeps looking and listening for cues. . . . His feelings are easily hurt."[5]

Tip for Raising Thirty-Six-Year-Olds

Acknowledge differences in parenting styles openly, as they reflect important roles each partner plays out in all of their relationships. "Even when parents notice a problem in the family system, they are likely to bring the child in as the designated patient, while their marital pain stays unacknowledged."[6]

Tip for Raising Forty-Two-Year-Olds

Masculinity and femininity definitions need discussion in our families. "The ordinary man is no fool: he knows he can't be Arnold Schwarzenegger. Nonetheless, the culture . . . [promotes the notion] that masculinity is something to drape over the body, not draw from inner resources."[7]

ENDORSE AND ENFORCE

Often parents in training do not appreciate how important it is for parents to agree on discipline when it comes to having a peaceful home life. Also, establishing parental consistency in raising children can relate to a family's energy levels, with unresolved energy needs paving the way to disorganized discipline. **Attaching your own personality story-house memories to your current discipline methods helps you connect the dots during everyday household arguments and become more objective.**

Consistent parenting in your family develops around establishing key agreements about such things as children's eating or bedtime rituals; both parents must choose to endorse and enforce them. When such agreements are in place, the family energy step glides more smoothly into the family discipline step. If one parent loves junk food and the other parent espouses a health-conscious diet, they need to negotiate on what they will endorse in food choices for their child. Rather than being at odds, parents who join together in cohesive plans around eating and sleeping for their children are endorsing a set of similar values. Each parent has the right to choose how to self-feed. Feeding offspring takes negotiation and a few rules. I watch adult robins on my front porch and take note of the consistency in their nest patterns. Bird parents seem to have fewer family food fights; worms work for all concerned.

FOOD INFLUENCES DISCIPLINE

Fortunately, today's busy parents and teachers are taking note of the effects of fast food on youngsters. One cutting-edge teacher, Sandy Noel, runs a nutrition campaign in an elementary school, which includes serving an evening meal with all the food groups to her students and their families. Noel tells caretakers about a Wisconsin alternative school where the number of child behavior problems dropped off after it removed junk-food vending machines and improved the quality of school lunches. Not only do well-fed youth have fewer disciplinary referrals, but they increase their attendance, concentration, and cognitive development in school.[8] Unfortunately, teachers from a middle school find that numerous students do not eat their lunches; many students toss noontime nutrition into the lunchroom garbage bin. Some trashed lunches represent a student's first opportunity for food energy in the day so far, as many children rush off to school without breakfast. **How can family discipline influence kids to eat well? Youth (and likely their caretakers) eat more of a balanced diet when they eat meals *with* their families.** The importance of family mealtimes together endorses family values as well as reinforces the energy and discipline in the family.

Some families benefit from the simple food rule of "pleasant talk—no arguing" during family dinners. Loving conversation at the breakfast and dinner table can go a long way toward steering success in a child's day. Unfortunately, some children develop poor eating habits because the tabletop holds more negative emotion than nutritious food. Other children have to fend for themselves when their parents are too busy to make time for togetherness. Psychologist Mary Pipher's astute understanding of family life includes her belief that important family metaphors often relate to food.[9] Basic energy and discipline for our children derive not only from the directions we give them but from the love that accompanies those practices.

Consider the different needs of a wailing toddler and a hassled mother sitting at a restaurant table at lunchtime. The mother becomes more and more agitated: "Do I have to tell you one more time? You aren't getting a treat. . . . Do you want a time out? If you keep this up, you aren't getting anything. I can't believe this. Now you are hurting my ears." Does the toddler need a nap instead of food just now? Is the mother happy with the ways she is meeting her needs for creativity, belonging, and ability in her present life? Juggling needs seems to take more than two hands on some days, but trying to "control" a child seldom works. "Anxious parents are rewriting child development as a business plan. Doing so provides the illusion of control over a process that is more like sleep and sexual arousal: it can only be allowed, not willed."[10]

Plenty of opportunities exist for parents to have their limits tested. Most caregivers think of discipline as a form of limiting behavior, a way to punish a child for some wrongdoing. A more useful approach realizes that many of children's conflicts stem from their feeble attempts to satisfy their basic needs. All of our needs keep recycling throughout our lives. We do not master our needs; they simply are part of our existence and require our attention on a rotating basis. By eating and sleeping well on one day, we have a better chance of meeting that day's many needs. The next day requires more of the same attention to basic energy needs. Similarly, we require some basic discipline in our lives to become proficient in meeting new needs. However, we do not "master" discipline either, as we will face the need to have simple organization in our life again tomorrow, and the tomorrow after that.

PROACTIVE DISCIPLINE

Discipline that fosters learning from our mistakes and becoming stronger for the next situation seems like such a practical approach. Yet, one teenager looks at me in surprise, after I describe this manner of discipline to him and his parents: "Oh, I thought discipline was something bad!" The reason this adolescent thinks of discipline as "bad" relates to his experiences at home; something "bad" usually happens to him whenever he displeases his parents. The punishment theme of discipline has many flaws. The most important issues in proactive discipline are that your child is "safe"[11] and learns what *to do* the next time. Parents position themselves as the discipline leaders of their families by modeling how to handle conflicts. Every day brings many opportunities for parental leadership and for children learning to follow a good lead.

When my own children were in elementary school, I talked with them frequently about the qualities of leadership I would see in people. In my desk drawer, I kept a child's noisemaker, which made the sound of a bleating lamb. Whenever either of my children came home from school with yet another tale of one's child injustice to another, I would explain "sheep" behavior with the noisy bleating of the noisemaker. I told my children that someone had engaged in "sheep" behavior rather than "shepherd" behavior. Perhaps the perpetrator instigated the sheep crowd by teasing, tormenting, or otherwise hurting a child at recess. Perhaps the sheep crowd spread cruel gossip, offering vicious rumors with relish. I told my children how the sheep crowd made a choice to follow the wrong leader, how they were not thinking from *self-territory*. Then I would give my children examples of how to be a shepherd instead of a sheep. This lesson became a small ritual for a few years, until my children outgrew the pathetic bleating of the noise-maker.

VALUES UNDERLYING DISCIPLINE

Many adults question the values of our youth today. Consumerism and consumption, especially the consumption of entertainment, have largely supplanted parents' influence upon their youth: "[Teens] live a practically tribal life, virtually undisturbed, according to their own rules and appetites."[12] We might also question the values of adults today. I overheard two men on a train commiserating with each other: "I was upset because she lied. She told me she had stopped messing around, but later I found out she didn't stop messing around." On the radio, an interviewer asks a man about his expectations for his bride-to-be in an arranged marriage, as he has not met this woman. The man pauses briefly and then tells his most important expectation for his future partner: he wants an intelligent spouse who knows "what is right in a moral sense." I wonder if all these men value commitment for themselves as much as they desire their mates to value commitment. I wonder how often couples openly discuss commitment values with each other. I wonder if caretakers consider that their underlying values shape the discipline for all of family life. As parents in training, we need to look into our own personality roles and determine which values we live by in our personality *story-houses*.

Psychologist Lynda Madison found four ingredients for raising well-behaved, responsible children: commitment, trust, respect, and good technique. Her discipline model illustrates a good example of positive parental leadership. She stresses the goals of effective discipline in terms of teaching, not punishing, and suggests we guard against providing children with overdirection; when we truly respect a child, we are not intrusive.[13] Notice that Madison states the values of commitment, trust, and respect *before* she comes to her final ingredient of "good technique." Also notice that **core values for the family and community life are the underpinnings for our discipline.**

One version of ten basic values worth teaching in the home is Rabbi Wayne Dosick's *Golden Rules*, which lists some of the values to be employed to raise children well: respect, honesty, fairness, responsibility, compassion, gratitude, friendship, peace, maturity (or wisdom), and faith are important building blocks of a family's character.[14] Every family's challenge is to reinforce such values by creating their own traditions. Some common family activities that promote desirable values include the following: going on regular weekend outings as a family; pairing up for an activity with each child and each parent; partaking in special holiday or seasonal activities; developing skills together in music, sports, or a shared hobby like photography, for example; practicing religious traditions; attending family reunions and family outings with extended family; reading and discussing books together; finding discussion topics that interest both generations; or subscribing to magazines that interest several people in the family.[15]

VALUES EMBEDDED WITHIN SELF-TERRITORY

Imagine the steps of our basic needs escalator are stripped away, and just the internal parts remain. The internal space represents our inner self-territory; our values are the gears underlying each step. Our values are embedded within self-territory. When we

operate from a sense of our self-sphere, we are connected to a moral sensibility that considers not just what is good for ourselves but also what is good for another person. For example, being honest aids our own development, but truth telling also supports a child's healthy development. When you decide to make a significant change in your behavior, do you consider your underlying values first?

Psychologist Eugene Gendlin suggests that people usually make changes in life based upon their values.[16] But do you know what you value? Does your child know your family's value system? As parents in training, we constantly act upon our values, although sometimes we teach values to a child without our conscious realization. Yet our children are exposed to values that differ from our own. Their peers often preach a variable line of "shoulds" with little recognition of the values behind them. The media sells yet a third brand of what one might value, such as fame or wealth. Thus children are confused in knowing whose values to follow in an ever-changing world.

My children's elementary principal, Paula O'Malley, taught the values of fairness, respect, and friendship through a simple saying: "No hurts, stick together, and have fun." She did not use out-of-school suspensions, as she believed that "suspensions give kids the refrigerator and the street"; instead, she modeled problem solving through consulta-

SELF Escalator

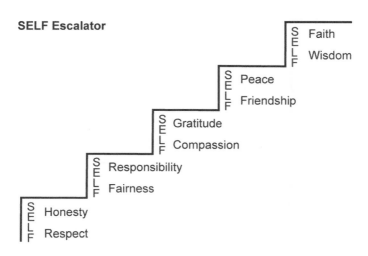

Figure 4.1.

tions with students in trouble, telling them wisely, "Reflect and adjust." We reach children best with a few simple phrases that are repeated frequently. One child reports on her father's speeding ticket with the concrete description he explained to her: "My Daddy got stopped by the police—he had to go to the police station. He had Big Boy timeout." Notice how this caring father does not lie about this story. He values honesty and wants his daughter to grow up with the value of honesty.

Robert Coles, a child psychiatrist, recalled hearing theologian Paul Tillich speak. Tillich said, "Morality is not a subject—it is a life put to the test in dozens of moments."[17] These daily dozens characterize the numbers of times that family values surface, often with little awareness on our part. Coles viewed morality for children as encompassing those values that characterize the "best side of our parents."[18] However, he recognized that parents have multiple sides to their personalities. Caretakers may act from a stingy role. Or they may immerse themselves so thoroughly in meeting their own needs that they treat their child in rude or even abusive ways.[19] Adults switch parts of their personalities and accompanying values so many times throughout the course of one day that even Shakespeare would have difficulty putting the many character roles into a cohesive five-act play!

"HAND-ME-DOWN" VALUES

Values are hand-me-downs, just as family heirlooms get handed down. Educators Sidney Simon, Leland Howe, and Howard Kirschenbaum believed that adults utilize several different ways of handing down values to the next generation. Realistically, most parents use some combination of these approaches. *Moralizing* involves heavy-handed discipline whereby the parent wants a child to avoid any pain by just hearing and accepting parental values. At the other end of the continuum, some parents have a *laissez-faire* manner toward values; youth choose whatever set of values they want, and the parents hope that "things" work out. Still another approach relies upon the parent modeling family values, as in the popular saying, "Walk the talk."

Finally, there is the *values-clarification* method, whereby adult modeling accompanies teaching a child to evaluate roles, to come to a *"process of valuing."*[20] Students who were taught a values-clarification curriculum at school were less apathetic, less flighty, and less conform-ing.[21] Yet forty years after the publication of educator Louis Edward Raths's 1970s bestseller, *Values and Teaching,* [22] [23] many value-laden issues remain. Both teachers and parents in training can help youth by actively emphasizing in their everyday acts which values they cherish and wish to pass onto the next generations.

In our great-grandparents' day, young girls sewed the family values to walls by learning to cross-stitch samplers. They had sayings like, "A stitch in time saves nine," and "A penny saved is a penny earned." The "classroom family"[24] of yesterday etched its values—or what *to do*—on blackboards, but today's classroom blackboards more often tally the names of children who do not follow the rules and have to stay after class for detention. What does this change tell us about what adults value in child development? Compliance with class rules may or may not reflect the values of respect and responsibility. **In our new millennium, we need to offer children more chances to do mental cross-stitching of values both at home and at school.**

CAN YOU "SPANK" VALUES INTO A CHILD?

A mother and her toddler are in the bathroom stall next to me: "Don't touch the toilet! That's gross! Do you want a spanking on your bare bottom?" A tiny voice utters, "No." One of our most obvious clues that families and schools are in dire need of creativity relates to the simple fact that some family and school discipline still includes spanking. Twenty-two states permit paddling in schools: "Schools continue to paddle children despite [the fact that] . . . numerous prestigious institutions, as well as legions of respected pediatricians, authors of child-rearing manuals, and child advocates have taken forceful positions against physical punishment."[25] As Rick Lyman noted in a *New York Times* article on September 30, 2006, in one school, 150 students out of the school population of 685 receive a paddling in the course of one academic year.

Drawing upon twenty years of research, psychologist Irwin Hyman studied discipline and the effects of school paddling. Hyman found that schools do not only resort to spanking as a last step. Sadly, minority children get hit four to five times more frequently than middle- and upper-class white children; poorer students are more likely to receive a paddling. Schools have an obligation to report incidences of suspected familial abuse in children, but ironically, they have no similar legal edict to report any of their own abusive actions.[26] How much spanking does it take to teach values to schoolchildren? What will the spanking actively teach our youth?

Just as many schools sanction spanking, there also are many families who endorse spanking policies. I have met quite a few of them. One father whips off his belt to convey to his son that some behavior crosses a line. The son's scared role of his personality clutches onto the painful memory of the last whack from Dad's metal buckle. When this father realized that his own father used the same discipline tactics without success, he acknowledged his unwittingly copycat behavior. Without meaning to copy his dad's angry outbursts, he fell into this behavior when he became "all fired up."

We are among the mammals gifted with insightful communication. We can figure out how to set "just" rules in our caretaking of children, both at home and school. Hitting down on a child seems like the opposite of raising *up* a child who comprehends and carries out our core values. When adults whip children with words or paddling, it hardens a portion of their personalities. **How many parents and principals attempt to spank values into the youth in their care, thereby cloning threats they heard and hated from their own childhoods?** What parent would continue spanking their child if they first thought of the value they most wanted to teach their child in a conflict?

THE YELLING-HITTING-FEELING-GUILTY PARENTAL POSE

Trina (5), Erica (41), Lucy (66), and Elena (deceased)

> Erica fondly recalls her childhood alongside a loving grandmother, Elena, who spent many hours of patient play with her. "She listened and was very patient—no yelling," reminisced Erica. A frown flashes across her face as Erica contrasts childhood memories of her mother, Lucy, with those of her grandmother. Erica relayed one story after another about times when her mother, Lucy, yelled at her or spanked her. A variation on this discipline theme involved her father.

Some behaviors could "wait till Dad comes home," and the end of his workday resulted in the same approach: yelling first, followed by a spanking.

Trying hard not to re-create her parents' mistakes, Erica now struggles with teaching values when her daughter misbehaves. Spanking hurts Erica's caring role more than it does little Trina's bottom. Acting as if her sole purpose in life is to test her mother's resolve, Trina turns out to have a spirited, flamboyant main role. From exuberance to exhaustion, Trina flits across the family stage as temptress, tyrant, teaser, and turncoat; one moment she taunts, but the very next interaction brings tenderness. This saucy repertoire stretches from home to school. Trina exists as either the life of the party or the havoc wreaker.

One day, Trina flops into Erica's surprised arms at the end of a kindergarten morning. Between sobs, Trina tells about a classmate who cruelly said to her, "I wish you had never been born." Erica juggles a multitude of responses in her mind as she rocks her daughter close to her heart. Erica then takes a deep breath, thinks of what grandmother Elena might say, and softy begins to tell Trina about how the child at school forgot about the Golden Rule, or treating others the way you like to be treated. As she speaks softly to Trina, she promises to start reflecting the Golden Rule more in her own discipline and actions.

DEVELOPMENT DIRECTIONS

She simply stoppered a part of herself and turned to new directions.

—Deirdre McNamer, *My Russian*

When parents lose their ability to problem solve, they sometimes resort to spanking, pinching, grabbing, and even throwing their child. Most parents feel a guilty role in their personality whenever they lose touch with their discipline values of respect and fairness. Many start to remember important values when they consider their grandparents. Many grandparents enjoy mentoring their family's youngsters. Telling grandchildren about family values, and backing up those values with examples from a grandparent's story-house of memories, provides valuable instruction for the next generations and their tough transitions.

Tip for Raising Five-Year-Olds

Conversations with a five-year-old teach a caretaker about the budding social world a child faces at school. "Five is a great talker. . . . He can tell a tale . . . he is using words to clarify the multitudinous world in which he lives."[27]

Tip for Raising Forty-One-Year-Olds

Caring for a young child and caring for a career make juggling basic needs every day a challenge; consider family needs in a context of your values. "The forties are a time for inward reflection, reevaluation . . . and deepening of the human journey."[28]

Tip for Raising Sixty-Six-Year-Olds

Life transitions among family members may turn out to be different from your expectations; find some new learning in these transitions. "The fountain of age opens possibilities of change. . . . There is a pattern that becomes more and more clearly one's own, integrating previously unrealized parts of oneself, moving, even in the face of physical decline, toward a wholeness of spirit, realizing the mysterious self."[29]

TREAT OTHERS WELL

The so-called Golden Rule, or treating others in a manner we would like to be treated, is an ancient hand-me-down value mentioned in all of the world's major religions. Some of our family values follow from those of the ancient Greeks, who pursued values of knowledge, courage, loyalty, physical strength, and beauty. From early times, beauty and goodness paired up as twin goals; having moral integrity carried equal weight with beauty.[30] In a similar time frame to early Greek philosophy, the venerable followers of Confucius expected a youth to have skills in the arts; show loyalty to family and the state; exemplify humility, graciousness, kindness, and justice; and exhibit courteous behavior with everyone.

Our current culture appears to overemphasize the value of surface beauty and underemphasize other values. Have we misplaced ancient parental values that modeled the most important ones for raising children? Time-tested values need caretaker repetition on a regular basis. Psychologist Howard Gardner states that the two major goals of education across time and space are the modeling of adult roles and the teaching of cultural values. "Every society must ensure that the most important adult roles—leader, teacher, parent, priest—are properly filled by members of the next generation."[31] Yet in today's corporate-business mentality, it seems increasingly difficult for parents to sift through the conflicting values and roles they play at the workplace and then relate those to everyday actions they want to teach children.

TELL YOUR CHILD WHAT *TO DO*

Much parental discipline tells children what not to do. In a crowded museum, I overhear a father who is intent upon keeping his two children close to his side: "A couple of rules. You cannot get out of my sight." The youngsters (and I) await rule number two, but even the dad seems to wonder what else he might say at this point. He stares off into space. Meanwhile, his children continue to listen, waiting patiently for him to bring his gaze back to them. When he apparently can think of no other rules, he takes each child by the hand, and they disappear into the crowd. His nonverbal hand-holding pose actually conveys his intended message best, because the most powerful discipline for any child is to demonstrate to them what *to do*.

Often, when parents give specific directions as to what a child is expected *to do*, the directions fail to take the child's needs into consideration. At another museum, a young child asked his mother a reasonable question: "Can I get a drink of water?" I am surprised when I hear her respond angrily, "No, I want you to stand right here." The two of them are standing very close to a drinking fountain. I cannot decipher what her need might be in this moment, although the child's need seems clear. I wonder if the child thinks about sneaking a quick drink while his preoccupied mother has her attention elsewhere. Children often use sneaky actions to meet some need, and parents in training sometimes sneak around to meet their unmet needs as well.

SNEAKY BEHAVIOR

Ben (8) and Rob (37)

In my office, eight-year-old Ben pops out a question for his father, "If I listen, will you stop yelling?" Rob's response comes quickly; a resounding, definitive "yes" bounds into the air. Discussing what changes each person wants in other family members leads the way to understanding some simple rules for everyone. When we continue the dialogue about other changes desired in their family, Rob sighs loudly. He then takes Ben's hand. Rob believes that Ben has a sneaky part, as there are several objects missing from the home. Initially, when Rob confronts Ben about the lost items, Ben denies knowing anything about them. Later, the items turn up in Ben's room. A discussion about personality roles in the household brings out the detail that this caring father carries home an anger role. After working sixty hours a week at a demanding job, with his time seeming overscheduled and the amounts of paperwork overwhelming, Rob often feels and breathes exhaustion. Ben then confides his own exhaustion from being a student. The two guys make a pact to tell each other about their anger without sneaky behavior. When I ask this caring father whether he ever had sneaky behavior when he was a boy, a wide grin breaks out across his face. He then turns to his son and asks, "Wanna go for a burger?"

DEVELOPMENT DIRECTIONS

I find that principles have no real force except when one is well fed.

—Mark Twain

Unresolved energy needs often get tangled up in a parent's attempts to be a model of appropriate discipline. For example, what ensues after a lack of sleep more often resembles some disorganized kind of discipline rather than parents' ideal brand of discipline. When caretakers feel rushed and stressed most of the time, children pick up rushed and stressed values. Lost in between the pages of the crammed family calendar, many interactions between father and son do not ever take place. What do you say when your child asks, "If I listen, will you stop yelling?" First, you want to take a few deep breaths and allow *space* for your unconditional love to well up inside you. Remember, we grow *up* a little, or a lot, every single day of our lives.

Tip for Raising Eight-Year-Olds

Children crave attention from their fathers; they can sense when work seems more important to Dad than family. "People often see in boys signs of strength when there are none, and they ignore often mountainous evidence that they are hurting."[32]

Tip for Raising Thirty-Seven-Year-Olds

Juggling the needs of your child with your own needs takes planning; if necessary, write into your appointment book some times during the week to bond with each child. "It takes a lot more time and effort to spend the hour with your son that he needs than it does to yell at him and then go do your own thing, whether it's work or a . . . rerun on television."[33]

PROBLEM-SOLVING VALUES

Which comes first: a child not *listening* to a parent or a parent not *listening* to a child in a manner where relating can occur? **Caretakers may consider their own value-laden issues as those that are the most pressing. However, their children face a host of value-laden choices during and after school.** For example, middle school students report being asked to buy drugs on the playground. High school youth face sexual pressures. College students routinely encounter other students cheating on exams. Many caretakers are oblivious to their child's distress over these values dilemmas and morality manners. Psychologist William Damon suggests that parents focus on adult moral issues that are not too different from their children's lives; parents in training sometimes overlook the moral choices a child regularly encounters because they have their own moral dilemmas.[34]

Morality manners matter, especially when teaching children about friendship mistakes. At elementary schools, excluding some child from group play runs rampant. Every household needs to address having respect for others. Additionally, the underlying value of respect needs to accompany every parent-child dialogue. Parents in training need to model respect through practicing *one interaction at a time* with a child, and they need to use creativity in problem solving any discipline issues that surface in the home or at school. The SCANNER Problem SOLV-ING (SPS) model in the next chapter provides details for respectful and creative problem solving with your child.

Caretakers can ensure that children act on the value of respect by making a small list of house rules. Remember that the most successful rule lists are stated in affirmative wording. For example, "At bedtime, choose your clothes for school for tomorrow," and "Have your room clean by noon on Saturdays." Caretakers seldom are clear enough in their expectations when they tell a child what *not* to do: "Don't hit your sister. Don't you ever listen to me?" Too often parents tell children, "Do *not* do it," or some variation of negative wording. For example, in the first eighteen years of life, the average individual is told "no," or what *not* to do, approximately 148,000 times.[35] Admonishing a child with *nots* rarely ensures compliance. Children simply are not listening; they have heard too many *nots* already. The killer whales receive train-ing without *nots*.

As caretakers we must look ahead, set discipline expectations for our children and ourselves, and then enforce a few simple rules; then we will all have a greater chance of reaching those expectations. One family restates their rule for respecting siblings in this manner: "Hands are for hugging." We elaborate on this theme by having a lot of alternatives for hands: "Hands are for holding, building, drawing, eating, playing and sharing." Siblings in this family receive a concrete rule to guide them away from shoving and instead grab hands in bids for attention.

Having a child jot down the household rules in his or her own hand-writing or type them on the family computer places ownership and expectations on that child. Just as teachers could have a different child everyday write their classroom rules on the blackboard, parents need to post a copy of the family rules in a place where all members can see them. The refrigerator, a family bulletin board in the kitchen, a bath-room mirror, or any other common area can serve as a values display.

Once a rule establishes good manners, it requires frequent rein-forcement. Parents in training can follow up good behavior with non-verbal reminders, as in praising children when they follow a house rule by flashing a thumbs-up. Another way to endorse a rule is through linking the desired behavior to family values. One parent elaborates: "'Hands are for hugging' tells us a rule about fairness." For an older child who studied the Declaration of Independence in social studies, a parent used these words: "'Hands are for hugging' explains our family's Declaration of Independence." Reinforcement included, "Remember the Declaration!" Notice how such reinforcement tells a child what *to do* and makes no mention of the misbehavior.

When children grow into adolescence, most teens require a few house rules about Internet use: keep personal information (such as home address and phone numbers) off the net; any online subscriptions require a parent's permission.[36] Remember, caretakers are the ones with greater cause-effect thinking skills; teens do not always think about the effects of their behavior and often believe that they are immune to danger.

TEENS AND RISKY BEHAVIOR

Marissa (15) and Maria (34)

Marissa dances with energy. A pretty teen who likes parties and talking endlessly with her friends on the phone, she dates twenty-year-old guys. When her school progress report arrives in the mail, she finds she has three Fs, so she hides the evidence in her bedroom closet. School cannot compare to her exciting social life. One week-end Marissa waltzes out with alcohol and a group of friends. The last dance is with the police. When they question her, she vehemently denies any wrongdoing in the situation, although she has stayed out past curfew. She then talks back to one officer and takes a swing at another. She is charged with disorderly conduct and aggravated assault. When Maria arrives at the police station, she encounters a policeman who labels Marissa "a bitch." Maria delivers a spanking for Marissa's discipline. But the spanking does not stop Marissa's dangerous dance.

Like many adolescent girls her age, Marissa's ability goals require fame and fortune; she fancies becoming a model. Secretly, she fears failure. In drawing a map of her personality, Marissa draws a heart with dancing waves inside for self territory. Roles of her personality then tumble out in written words: "Timberlands, they are in style. . . .

I need some boots soon. . . . Good progress report and new boots, right? . . . I can be a loving person when I am not mad or angry. . . . Good-bye, we'll miss you World Trade Center. . . . Kill them." Near this last phrase, Marissa draws the twin towers of New York's 9/11 tragedy; the phrase about killing refers to the terrorists.

She flips her map over and keeps her personality roles flowing in a singsong manner: "Athletic . . . $ . . . famous, nice house, nice clothes . . . model." A tall stick figure appears under "model," and a tiny stick figure appears next, with the label "me." The height under each figure defines Marissa's fear of failure, as the model is 5'8" and "me" has the following derogatory labels: "Short height . . . can't model . . . 5'6"." Her underlying frustration spills out more words: "Crazy acting . . . energetic . . . young . . . can't drive, can't go clubbin'." This young woman perceives a continuous stream of *not* words in her environment.

In spite of insisting to her parents that she intends to hang on to her virginity in high school, Marissa becomes pregnant. She drops out of high school and relies on family support to raise her son. The father of her child has another son with another woman. He does not pay any child support to Marissa. New grandmother Maria feels the aftershock of plans gone awry. The complexities of her daughter's situation bring up old, unresolved issues from her own adolescence. With a sad gaze toward her daughter, she suffers her anger slowly. Marissa is a ballerina who cannot take center stage anymore.

DEVELOPMENT DIRECTIONS

I looked on child rearing not only as a work of love and duty but as a profession that was fully as interesting and challenging as any honorable profession in the world and one that demanded the best I could bring to it.

—Rose Kennedy, mother of a president and a senator

All children make mistakes; some errors result in greater consequences. All parents make mistakes as well. If parents use punitive discipline, adolescents may respond with retaliation or rebellious acts. Making demands and threats are not "just" discipline. Understand too that any adolescent disagreements with your adolescent may not apply to the subject at hand but to something they are concealing. Parents need to think of resolving adolescent issues through reaching agreements instead of having arguments. Ask lots of questions, including what *changes* are desired at this time. Keep the focus of the discussion on what *to do* next time, instead of refocusing on what went wrong in the past.

Tip for Raising Fifteen-Year-Olds

Discuss sexuality with your teen; watch a current movie with (or separate from) your teenager, and discuss how screen sex never addresses contraception, sexually transmitted disease, or the adult responsibilities of intercourse. "Ask if you can read [your teen's] health book about sex and social diseases . . . so you have a basis for more direct conversation."[37]

Tip for Raising Thirty-Four-Year-Olds

Dealing with a daughter's precocious sexuality raises not only sexual issues for caretakers but also brings up power issues. "In adulthood, many women yield power to others by depending on [another's] gaze and evaluation for self-worth. . . . When girls dress up and dance in front of a mirror . . . they become the looker, the one with the eyes, the one desiring and approving of themselves."[38]

DISCIPLINE THROUGH *VALUES DIALOGUES*

The word "dialogue" comes to us by way of Sicilian mime or puppet plays, but it was introduced to the wider culture through the teachings of the Greek sage Socrates. Prior to Socrates's time, much of speech consisted of monologues, or one-sided speeches. However, Socrates decided to take his own confusion about what to believe about science to the commoner on the street. He wandered the streets of Athens, questioning everyone about their work and opinions. Socrates operated from the position that if two uncertain people are discussing their beliefs, they can discover a truth not found possible when solo. Without insulting or attacking but through asking questions and breaking down the many parts of one's position, Socrates maintained that each person finds small steps of agreement and clarity.[39] When a caretaker desires to understand a child's position, Socrates' searching-for-truth mentality fully opens the door to *values dialogues*. The SCANNER Problem SOLVING (SPS) model offers sample questions in the next chapter.

Children generally know if they are following your home rules. Psychiatrist William Glasser advocates straight-forwardness in questioning children's moral choices: "Are you doing right or wrong? Are you taking the responsible course?"[40] If a child's response gives little information, follow up with more open-ended dialogue. Some questions a caretaker can use to clarify the value of responsibility are the following: "What were you thinking of when you threw the rock? So you were a scientist without even meaning to be. . . . What did you learn from your experiment? What will you do next time? What do you need to do about the window [now]?"[41]

Helping a youngster see that manners still matter after a mistake presents a challenge. Long explanations fall on deaf ears, and a caretaker's angry role can distort the idea of clarifying values. Sometimes a productive values dialogue follows the simple question, "What did you do today that you are proud of?" If no proud roles emerge, remind your child that there are some hours left in the day to locate something. If you stay curious about a child's perceptions and help the dialogue proceed to some positive plan of action, you will see it leaves both child and parent feeling hope at the end of a day, however difficult it may have been. **The goal of discipline is to rehearse creative alternative behaviors with children, enabling them to learn how best to meet their basic needs.**

BROKEN RULES

Parents must prepare for occasions when rules are broken. Because both children and parents often handle frustration roles with angry roles, they must practice to change these old patterns. Both can benefit from a new structure to help make the changeover.

Winona (9), Laura (6), and Sheila (26)

Winona struggles with her headstrong sister, Laura. Winona views

Laura as trying to upstage her in every way possible, and she believes her parents hold her solely responsible when the two girls catapult into a noisy battle. Winona illustrates a need for different discipline rules in her pretend puppet story in the therapy office. Winona has the witch puppet severely scold a girl who is "very, very messy." Sheila later acknowledges that she often scolds her daughters to no avail; they still leave toy messes all over. The sisters nosily blame each other, accusing each other of getting out more toys and making the bigger mess.

Just placing rules on the refrigerator door does not enforce respect and fairness values in this family. To back up parental rules, I suggest that Sheila add extra instructions. Sheila will calmly count to three when announcing cleanup time; if no movement toward pickup begins in this three-second interaction, Sheila will walk the girls to the toy area and model the beginning of the shared task. When the girls begin picking up their toys, Sheila praises their cooperation. If one child begins, Sheila commends that child for cooperating. However, if one or both girls fail to comply with the rule, the uncooperative child receives a time-out for the number of minutes of her age. Each girl must serve her time alone.

Instead of using time-out for a punishment, my instructions suggest using time-outs as "think it over" time. At the end of the brief "think it over" time, Sheila asks Winona and Laura what might have been a better choice when she announces time for shared cleanup. If there are no adaptive responses, Sheila offers alternatives: "Instead of telling your sister she has to clean up everything, you pick up the toys that you keep in your room, and she can pick up the toys that she keeps in her room." Or, "You can make a deal with your sister that you will take turns cleaning up everything; we will flip a coin to see who gets odd days and who gets even days. We can mark it on our kitchen calendar to make sure it stays fair."

DEVELOPMENT DIRECTIONS

In the old days [in Scotland], if there were any arguments or quarrels, the parties were put on the Island of Discussion with cheese and whiskey and oat cakes, and they were left there until they could sort their problems out.

—Rick Steves, *Europe Through the Back Door*

Teaching problem solving as part of the discipline dialogue not only reinforces many family values but also models how children can resolve *any* kind of problem. Punishment methods of discipline all too often unleash a parent's frustration role instead of teaching what *to do*. What a child learns from a parent's smoldering anger role usually has nothing to do with a good alternative to their misbehavior. In fact, the parent just mirrors a child's anger role in many situations. When parents realize that punitive techniques waste their breath, they embrace a problem-solving model of discipline.

Numerous books on child discipline use forms of behavior modification that are instrumental in getting a child to do more of a particular task. But mere compliance when it comes to chores does not ensure that a child learns a lesson. Realistically, most parents want *more* from their child than simple chore compliance. The family values of respect for each other and cooperation in fulfilling home responsibilities are the underlying goals. **The most essential discipline training involves ensuring that children comprehend basic values, learn how to negotiate their own solutions to sticky situations, and build up a reservoir of resilience for handling interpersonal conflict the next time around.** "Think it over" time-outs, combining discipline values dialogues and problem solving, work well for many childhood incidents. If a child's behavior includes stealing, use action consequences as an additional measure.

Tip for Raising Nine-Year-Olds

Problem-solving training does not end with one sibling squabble; each new skirmish allows for more practice. "Framing the problem as a conflict of needs prevents each person from blaming the other for 'causing' the problem. If you're focused on blaming, you can't focus on resolving the problem."[42]

Tip for Raising Six-Year-Olds

Patience, patience, patience comes with taking three deep breaths. "Six is an active age. The child is in almost constant activity. . . . Six is the center of [her] own universe. . . . [She] believes that [her] way of doing things is right. . . . [Six] is bossy."[43]

Tip for Raising Twenty-Six-Year-Olds

Children's needs are only one piece of the daily agenda; parents in their twenties have major job and education decisions to make for them-selves. "We . . . are going through our own developmental changes, some of which are influenced and affected by what's happening with our children."[44]

ACTION CONSEQUENCES FOR STEALING

Vance (12), Linda (32), and Vincent (35)

Vance steals. His mother, Linda, uncovers the evidence while doing the laundry. There are bunches of candy wrappers and baseball-card wrappers stuffed in his jean pockets. When confronted, Vance initial-ly lies, making up one excuse after another as to how somebody else put wrappers in his pockets. Finally, he confesses that he shoplifted after school. He says simply, "I was hungry." After a recommended mother-son trip to the store to meet with the store manager and pay for the stolen items, the real needs surface. While energy or snack issues exist, the crux of the situation is that Vance does not believe that his parents love him enough.

Linda, Vincent, and Vance explore love themes in our therapy session, and we uncover an unmet belonging need spanning (at least) two generations. Both parents are asked about feeling loved by their own parents. Vincent believes that his father was always too busy to spend any time with him and therefore figures that his father must not have loved him very much. Linda recalls experiencing closeness with her father but believes that her mother preferred her sisters; she concludes she too was not loved enough. This information en-lightens Vance, who has the impression that his younger siblings are Mom's favorites. As the generational story-house memories are re-vealed, all three family members find they possess some of the *same* basic needs; each person struggles to soothe the belonging feelings of being unlovable. While honesty rises in importance as a family value, Vance also renegotiates his place in his family. His face lights up upon being reassured about his parents' love and commitment to him.

Meanwhile, Vance also has taken peers' belongings at school. I consult with Vance's teacher, who agrees that the usual school disciplinary measures of suspension are not very helpful in most instances of petty theft in the classroom. She accepts my idea of trying something new. Because the stealing occurs during the class-changing times between specialist classes (art, music, and physical education), I suggest that the teacher engage Vance in a responsibility during these time frames. Vance plays the role of classroom engineer as his class moves between rooms; he follows his teacher's direction in rearranging some furniture in the class and helps pass out papers for the next classroom assignment. Vance thrives in his newfound belongingness at school. The stealing stops.

DEVELOPMENT DIRECTIONS

> I was a wonderful parent before I had children. I was an expert on why everyone else was having problems with theirs. Then I had three of my own.
>
> —Adele Faber and Elaine Mazlish, parent trainers, *How to Talk So Kids Will Listen and Listen So Kids Will Talk*

Parents need to put themselves in a child's shoes when they consider their offspring's stealing behaviors. Since knee-jerk first reactions usually bring forth shameful and embarrassed parts from both child and parent, this feeling-as-my-child-feels-right-now approach does not come easily to parents in training. When parents get heavy-handed on the side of punishment, they forget to address important values and to look for a child's unmet needs. Additionally, many preteens are surprised to learn that people have to pay more for items at stores because of all the theft that takes place. Preteens usually do not grasp the big picture when it comes to their actions, nor do they consider anyone else's needs. Values dialogues prove useful in enlarging a preteen's perceptual world.

Tip for Raising Twelve-Year-Olds

Parents can prepare preteens for greater spending independence, including going into stores by themselves and buying their own clothes. They can do this by asking questions about what clothes and special items a child "needs." "When parents turn statements into questions, kids turn problems into problems to be solved."[45]

Tip for Raising Thirty-Two-Year-Olds

Review your own preteen years; what stories from your story-house of earlier memories help you understand the insecurity that most preteens experience? "What do you remember of your first childhood relations? What did they teach you about love? About discipline? . . . What did you learn to feel guilty about?"[46]

Tip for Raising Thirty-Five-Year-Olds

Consider what your family goals consist of and how they mix with your personal goals. "Thirtysomethings want their piece of the rock, and they feel an urgency about reaching their goals. Forty is an approximate deadline that many young adults unconsciously set for reaching the goals that so often constitute 'making it': career recognition, financial attainment, marriage and having babies . . ."[47]

LIES AND MORE LIES

Around four years of age, a child begins to distinguish right from wrong. The bad-news portion of this fact involves the realization that children may begin lying around their fourth year. Usually, little sophistication exists at four, so a child claims not to eat a cookie before lunch and yet has cookie crumbs all over her face. At ages five and six, children often exaggerate or misrepresent reality to appease parents; for example, they claim they brushed their teeth, but a parent can see there is no water in the sink. A common early lie occurs too when a child has lost something—a coat, a backpack, a watch. Some children fear their parents will not forgive them. **Children sometimes misrepresent reality to duck anticipated punishments or to get out of possible work.**

Progressively, it becomes more difficult to detect untruths when an older child lies. Many middle school and high school age children erroneously tell their parents that they have no homework or that they have finished their homework when they have not even begun their assignments. Teens and college age youth often continue telling lies. When leaving home, there are fewer structures for the young adult. Many college-age children lie to their parents about substance abuse just when the responsibility for their health rests predominantly upon their shoulders. More than one hundred fifty thousand college students develop an alcohol-related health problem.[48]

Under the influence of alcohol, a fourteen-year-old can seem a lot like a five- or six-year-old. Parents often have no idea about the extent of their teenager's drug usage. Young teens usually get their drugs from older teens. Some teens hang out on the corner by the liquor store and have any willing adult make purchases for them. Others lurk in the dark at prearranged meeting places to buy weed or marijuana, while others more brazen trade cash for a stash in school bathrooms. Some junior high youth smoke pot or marijuana along with their older cousins or siblings. Very often, teens even obtain alcohol from their family's home supply.

Bernie (14) and Sam (48)

Bernie reeks of alcohol when he returns home after spending time with peers. Confronted by his father, Sam, Bernie denies having any alcohol, saying he must smell like beer because "other people were drinking." Since this argument works for smelling like cigarettes but not for having alcohol on one's breath, Sam launches into a yelling lecture. Then he catches himself. He had a few drinks himself in the evening. Also, he realizes that Bernie's drunken state precludes any ability to have a meaningful values dialogue. Sam carries his son to bed as if he were only five years of age and crafts his speech in his head to use later. When Sam discovers that his home liquor cabinet has been tapped, he decides to take all alcohol out of the house. He does not know if Bernie, at the age of fourteen, can resist the temptation to take free booze. He prefers not to banish Bernie and his friends from hanging out in his home.

DEVELOPMENT DIRECTIONS

Possible addiction is not the only troubling aspect [of an adolescent]. . . . At a time of life when he should be building a unified self, he has found a way to choose from a wardrobe of selves according to the occasion.

—Stanley I. Greenspan, psychiatrist, *The Growth of the Mind and the Endangered Origins of Intelligence*

Youth lies about using marijuana, alcohol, and other drugs run rampant today. Many teens try on drugs as if they were articles of clothing, with some drugs becoming "keepers" for a period of time and others getting discarded after one fashion show. The peer culture fosters fast experimentation, while parental discipline favors abstinence. The upside of all this is that teenagers have a tendency in this stage of life to be philosophical. They want to experience the world in their own terms. Parents can exert a strong influence in a teenager's philosophical phase. Looking forward for solutions, instead of looking backward at "the problem," helps launch a dialogue that can be productive. Parents in training can best help a teen struggling with lies, alcohol, and drugs by remembering the awkward adolescent belonging snafus of their own high school years. The rush of hormones, the mood swings, and the inconsistencies of teen logic all have sway in a teen's desire to self-medicate with drugs. Many teens, as well as adults, have the persistent illusion that alcohol makes them more extroverted. However, researchers show that the gregarious behavior at drinking parties actually comes from the participants' *expectations* that they will be less inhibited, rather than from the effects of alcohol itself.[49]

Parents can say to their children that they too have made their own share of mistakes. One father truthfully says, "It's not that I have never lied, but today I am not proud of the times that I have lied." When parents in training own up to past mistakes, they create an atmosphere for a child to own up to present mistakes. Remember, adults have their share of values-challenged moments, too; no one in a family escapes such challenges. One young mother breathes a sigh of relief when I tell her that she does not have to be perfect, that there are no perfect parents. Sheepishly, she looks at me and says, "You don't know what a relief it is to hear you say that; I thought I was the only parent who made so many mistakes." Children also benefit from hearing that they are not expected to be perfect.

Tip for Raising Fourteen-Year-Olds

Keep your teen talking to you about their needs and desires in life. "The teenage years require special parental attention to help the growing boy achieve balance between his inner urge to reflect on the puzzles of life, and the outer drive toward action."[50]

Tip for Raising Forty-Eight-Year-Olds

Spending time with your teen in *some* kind of shared activity goes a long way toward keeping the belongingness fires tended in the family unit. "Boys this age desperately need love and affirmation from their fathers."[51]

EFFECTIVE DISCIPLINE FOSTERS PARTNERSHIP

Disciplining children effectively takes courage and many deep breaths. When a teenager blossoms into an adult body, has the tall gene that makes them tower over a parent, and screams at the top volume possible in their newly developed bass voice, caretakers feel threatened. The typical parental pose in defending against this perceived danger looks like an irate tiger with a ready roar. **However, most of the rage-filled arguments in parent-teen conflicts arise from grave misunderstandings.** Often, one person's insecure role in their personality triggers the next person's miscommunication. As research points out, family processes are "co-constructed by parents and children."[52]

As caretakers, we want our children to experience safety and to follow basic family values. Our message cannot get through, though, if the messenger roars in loud, disorganized bursts. Youths receive loud messages as authoritarian, or coming from a parent trying to dominate them. And teens perceive parental control as symbolic of *all* authority trying to impinge on their budding independence. When parents comprehend how such domineering messages are received by their child, they stand a better chance of communicating respect in their discipline.

When researchers asked both parents and their children how they might improve parent-child relationships, the parents imagined that their children would choose to spend more time with them. The children, however, had a different response: "We want our parents to come home less stressed."[53] Parental stress often trumps child stress in terms of the amount of time spent processing their own stressful days. Some parents are simply too busy running their adult jobs and the housework at home. Stressed-out partners in the business world frequently take too few deep breaths, feel too immersed in work issues, and simply are not available to relate in family partnerships one interaction at a time.

Cultural historian Riane Eisler advocates partnership parenting, in which gender equality and cooperation raise the bar for more democracy in families.[54] Each parent can make a critical difference in their child's life through discipline that teaches family values and problem solving alternative solutions to conflicts. When parents view their offspring as personality partners, capable of connecting the dots in family values dialogues, there exists equality within the home and one-interaction-at-a-time relating.

When equality reigns in our families, it creates healthy alternatives for raising our children. Psychologists Dan Kindlon and Michael Thompson believe that the single missing ingredient in most boys' emotional development is flexibility, or the ability to adapt and consider alternative behaviors. They go one step further, saying that flexibility rates as the most important element for growth during the rapid change period of a young man's adolescence.[55] When parents in training promote flexibility, creativity, and belonging teamwork, they move away from controlling children through punishment and endorse caretaking through the discipline of values dialogues. Both whales and children thrive best in partnership interactions.

DISCIPLINE MAPPING

Everyone's family has scripts, especially when it comes to our discipline efforts. We hear them so often that we come to take them for granted. The sad fact is that many home scripts could make B movies look good. Be on the lookout for the repetitive scripts you use with your children. Some wording may be different, but you often pick up scraps of scripts you heard as a child. Also, children copy what they hear or see in our culture. Often weaned on television and groomed by electronics, many of our children currently are under the dictatorship of TV teachers and computer coaches more than we realize. **Parents need to *choose* the "basics" they endorse, instead of allowing the culture to wield this kind of influence on their children. What are your "basics?"**

- What discipline words did your parent or caretaker say repetitively to you? Make a list (example: "If I've told you once, I've told you 100 times"). Then consider: What value does this script espouse? What was your reaction to the words of each script? What part or role of your personality responds now?

SCRIPT   VALUE   YOUR ROLE   YOUR CHILD'S
                                                  ROLE

- What are the replayed words you use with your child? What value lies behind each message? When you say these words or phrases, what role of you is speaking? What role of your child hears the words?

SCRIPT   VALUE   YOUR ROLE   YOUR CHILD'S
                                                  ROLE

- What changes can you make in your discipline scripts to promote the values you cherish? What happens if you step away from the chatter of all your personality roles and, functioning one interaction at a time, simply speak to your child from self-territory?

5

CREATIVITY NEEDS: ARE YOU A COMPOSER, OR ARE YOU A CLONE TO CONFORMITY?

Be brave enough to live creatively. . . . You have to leave the city of your comfort and go into the wilderness of your intuition. . . . Only by hard work, risking and by not quite knowing what you are doing . . . you'll discover . . . yourself.

—Alan Alda, actor

It takes a lot of imagination to raise children well. Often, our children lead us by their own inventiveness as much as we lead them. Watch the dancing eyes of any toddler. Soon the infectious inspiration of pretend play overtakes almost all adults. A grinning dad writhes on the floor as a pretend snake that his child conjures up after a visit to the zoo. A playful mom lays toy construction bricks according to her toddling architect. A laughing grandpa trots a bucking bronco grandchild up and down on his knee, delighting in the chortled words, "Papa, do horsey! Papa, do horsey!" When we can go with the flow of child play, intergenerational differences disappear for a few significant minutes.

Creative parenting follows a child's needs one interaction at a time. Initially, children use their play language to enact scenarios with their toys. Many of my parenting memories are dear ones. My son played with Lego blocks around the clock. He never showed any interest in copying the designated space shuttle design from the Lego box instructions—he preferred his own creations and his own stories. Each of his space ships held several "astronauts," with each of the tiny figures standing or sitting at Lego computer terminals. It was in the early 1980s that my husband and I chuckled over our son's myriad possibilities for computer usage. We marveled at the creativity of our son as he chattered on and on about each computer's mission. At the time, neither of us adults could imagine the computer explosion that was about to take place in our world. Unfortunately, we did not write down any of our son's precious imaginings. Fortunately, we did enjoy our son's creativity one interaction at a time.

Our own creativity and unconditional love soars for our child when we encourage: original thinking skills, brainstorming of many solutions to problems, imaginative moral lessons, and inventive parent-child playtime.

Parenting-Trip Tips

- Build creative-thinking skills in your child by asking open-ended questions.
- Use creative alternatives in your discipline; encourage your child to imagine morals or lessons for common situations.
- Model creative problem solving by thinking of several alternatives to negative behaviors, expecting your child to join in generating alternatives.
- Turn off the electronic toys, and spend time playing with your child.

THREE, GLEE, AND CREATIVITY

Many parents find fun in the preschool stage. During this time, early language attempts offer humorous material, and a young child's pretend play emerges effortlessly. Children love pretending, especially when a parent joins in the activity. Important bonding opportunities occur when parents engage in playful stories with their youngsters and build a common story-house together. Shared creativity is fun!

Daniel (3) and David (25)

Three-year-old Daniel uses his best approximations for words when he engages in pretend play: "I betend I go poo-poo!" exclaims Daniel. "Yes," says his father, being helpful, "you pretend to go poo-poo, and when you really have to go poo-poo, you go in the potty just like Daddy." Later, when drawing lots of lumpy zigzags on a page, Daniel startles his father with his insight: "Mountains are Ms!" David appreciates his young artist-son's creativity: "Yes! You have drawn many Ms, and they look just like mountains! What else can they look like?" This simple practice of asking open-ended questions keeps children's creativity flowing.

DEVELOPMENT DIRECTIONS

We don't stop playing because we grow old: we grow old because we stop playing.

—George Bernard Shaw, playwright

Parents get lots of training from three-year-olds on how to be in the present moment for one interaction at a time. There is a here-and-now exuberance to most preschoolers that captivates our imaginations. Their endearing vocabulary, increasing motor skills, and general antics help engage adults in playtime. Almost everything turns into play for this age group, which has an accompanying high energy level that most adults wish for themselves.

Tip for Raising Three-Year-Olds

Play, play, and play some more with your three-year-old child. "Typically, three-, four-, and five-year-olds are full of energy, eagerness, and curiosity. They seem to be constantly on the move as they engross themselves totally in whatever captures their interest at the moment. . . . Creativity and imagination come into everything, from dramatic play to artwork to storytelling."[1]

Tip for Raising Twenty-five-Year-Olds

Enjoying child creativity balances the work of parenting. "Creation is half sweat and hard work . . . sticking with it through thick and thin. But the other half is play and levity."[2]

COMPOSING CREATIVE THINKING

All people exercise spontaneous or creative thinking at some points in their lives. However, the opposite thinking of checking our spontaneity through an inhibiting role occurs in most of us as well. Why is youthful ingenuity choked off as children travel the raising road? In one study, fifth-grade students asked elders what children of today might be missing that the elders had as children. Many of these senior citizens responded that today's child is missing creativity or imagination. These elders reported having fewer toys, or things, when they were children; in the absence of having so much, they recalled being outside in nature a lot. They turned to their imaginations to make up their fun, and they still chuckled when they recalled their antics, such as pretend spaceships to the moon. Later, in adulthood, they witnessed their creative fantasies come true. Glued to their TV sets, they shook their heads in astonishment while watching U.S. astronauts land on the moon.

What has happened to childhood creativity today? As creativity researcher Mihaly Csikszentmihalyi suggests, our culture trains children in the ways of consumerism (buying toys and videos), rather than instructing them to think creatively and independently for themselves.[3] Some people blame schools for a lack of childhood creativity; education's lock-step curriculum with the three Rs (reading, 'riting, and 'rithmetic) reigns supreme. Others indict television for encouraging too much passivity. While these systemic factors impact children's creativity, parents in training have the power to weave originality into family personality story-houses. **Many see creativity as the birthright of a select few. However, creativity underlies all innovative problem solving.** Our present culture cannot afford to limit visionary endeavors to a small minority of our population. We need homes and schools to value the imaginative roles in each of our children's personalities.

CAJOLE, NOT CONTROL

Many children skip out the door to attend their early days of school; years later, their parents cannot drag them out of bed to go to high school. What changes between preschool and later-school years? One preteen reports feeling bored in school and at home. She draws the bored role in her personality as a "smiley face that isn't smiling." She elaborates: "Whatever I'm doing, I want it to end," as if this explanation provides answers to all questions about her boredom. In therapy, she tolerates only small chunks of projects, as if she needs commercials to break up the program content. She finds school especially tedious: "Kids aren't supposed to like school." So how can parents bring creativity to the forefront of raising children to ensure that we are not producing conformity clones?

Fred (4) and Eve (34)

Fred flaunts his typical four-year-old nature, relishing all acts of independence. He orders his parents to "go upstairs and get my blocks." He puts his feet on the sofa whenever he hears the rule that feet stay on the floor. Some dinners revolve around Fred's insistence that he wants something different to eat than the nutritious meal on his plate. His mother demonstrates patient poses until her stamina fails, and she suddenly screams out in response to Fred's demanding poses. When Eve reviews her own childhood, she finds a "high-strung" role similar to that of her demanding son. Eve admits that she "loses it," when her initially calm attempts to channel Fred's actions backfire. Her jaw clenches. She slips into a vicious pose where she fears the words that she hisses. She realizes that her discipline echoes that expressed by a previous generation. Obscenities, unrealistic threats, and tears fill the airwaves.

A family session in my office begins innocently enough. Fred shows curiosity about nearly every item in the room. Finally, he settles his attention on a couple of stuffed toy snakes and begins to fly them around in frantic circles. All at once, a snake ends up in Eve's face, with Fred shaking it over her with enthusiasm: "He's throwing up on you!" Disgust flashes across Eve's face. Before Eve's impending criticism role leaks out, I try out a compassionate pose to see how Fred can respond: "Oh, Fred, you need to help that poor snake. He looks so sick. Can you be Dr. Fred and help him?" Fred immediately changes gears; looking concerned, he mimics my compassionate pose. He becomes thoughtful and patient in his snake doctoring. He takes a small flashlight key chain from my end table and inspects several snake eyes. My stopwatch becomes a stethoscope, and he listens attentively to the snake's heart. Meanwhile, I comment on how Fred knows just what to do to take care of sick snakes.

Eve catches the drift of the creative play scene, and she weaves her own imaginative comments of snake doctoring into the play scene. Her pose changes, from expecting disobedience and delivering criticism, to a more relaxed, playful pose of exploring creativity and finding new options for dialoguing with her very bright boy.

DEVELOPMENT DIRECTIONS

The child . . . tends to have a wild imagination and seems suddenly to realize that he can say anything he wants to. Some four-year-olds seem to make very little distinction between fact and fiction. Others, perhaps the brighter ones, really enjoy telling untrue things.

—Louise Bates Ames, psychologist, *Child Care and Development*

Preschoolers are incredibly creative; spontaneity oozes from their pores. They receive plenty of latitude to fantasize in free play in nursery school, and their teachers joyously brag about preschool inventiveness in the classroom. Kindergarteners enjoy a modicum amount of imagination time; teachers praise their resourcefulness. Then our youth finish off their childhood by going to elementary, middle, and high schools. Innovative children thrive in some schools, but there are many creative children who gather predominantly critical teacher commentary: "He is always looking out the window." "She marches to the beat of a different drummer." "He has the messiest desk." "He's not motivated." "His mind is elsewhere." "She's not interested in her work." As caretakers of creativity, we need to ensure that our children receive opportunities throughout their lives that foster their incredible imaginative ability.

Tip for Raising Four-Year-Olds

A four-year-old reaches toward independence; a sense of humor coupled with creative drama helps caretakers ease youngsters into positive actions. "Bouts of stubbornness and arguments between child and parent or caregiver may be frequent [at four]. Children test limits, practice self-confidence and firm up a growing need for independence; many are loud, boisterous, even belligerent."[4]

Tip for Raising Thirty-Four-Year-Olds

All parents grapple with the opposites of dependence-independence roles. "[We] sometimes still miss that bliss of early parenting, of being . . . the One and Only Indispensable Mommy. The Mommy who put on the Band-aids . . . while all of that need and dependence were often encroaching and sometimes oppressive, there were, in exchange, some exceedingly sweet payoffs."[5]

CLASSROOM CLONING

Our culture expects creativity from preschoolers. However, when our children reach upper elementary school, their creativity quotient seems less desirable. The truly creative child may not "fit" in the average school classroom.

Stacey (10) and Kathleen (42)

> One insightful parent observes her fourth-grade daughter's classroom after the teacher disparages her daughter's academic progress at parent-teacher conference time. Kathleen feels the teacher does not understand her creative child; however, the teacher perceives Kathleen as the one who lacks understanding. During the mother's class observation, Stacey gets called upon to answer a question. A collective groan emanates from her classmates. The perceptive girl crafts a creative response, long and circuitous, quite unlike the usual quick answers the busy teacher and impolite students expect. The silent mom in the back of the room knows that her daughter has

brilliance in her unusual response; she also grasps that no one else in that classroom can detect it.

DEVELOPMENT DIRECTIONS

> Every child is an artist. The problem is how to remain an artist once he grows up.
>
> —Pablo Picasso

Parents need to be advocates for their child's brand of creativity. Who knows a child better than the child's primary caretaker(s)? Perhaps as parents in training, we expect too much of our child's teachers. Instead of going to teacher conferences and expecting teachers to tell us about our child, we need to partner with teachers. We can share as much about our child's personal needs with teachers as the teachers share about our child's ability needs.

Tip for Raising Ten-Year-Olds

Ten-year-olds show perceptive insights; take the time to get your child's angle on what happens at school. "A typical ten-year-old . . . is so adaptively and diversely in touch with the adult environment that [she] seems rather to be an adult in the making, or at least a preadolescent. . . . Parents often fail to sense the social intelligence of the ten-year-old child. Sometimes they treat [her] as though [she] were less aware than [she] actually is."[6]

Tip for Raising Forty-Two-Year-Olds

You know your elementary-age child better than anyone else; when you have a hunch that a school problem exists for your child, follow your intuition and visit the school. "Pretend you have the lead role in a play . . . this is how your child sees you. Recognize that this is the most important role you will ever play."[7]

CREATIVE ALTERNATIVES

What has happened in our schools when state test results rate higher than childhood creativity? Why do the arts get slashed first when budget butchering cuts education costs? As creativity researcher Mihaly Csikszentmihalyi points out, this situation would not be so disastrous if basic teaching included originality and creative thinking in every subject; unfortunately, classroom innovation happens more as the exception than as the standard.[8] Some say the same thing about familial innovation; one veteran teacher blames parents for the problems in schools today. Noting the lack of respect shown to teachers in many public school classrooms, he states categorically, "Parents don't raise their children anymore," meaning that his students are not paying attention and are not making use of their schooling.

However, blame does not fix problems. We need inspired homes, as well as resourceful schools along the raising road. One mother in training fosters originality and creativity in her shy child, who appears to be a loner, through projects; she provides stimulating family field trips on weekends. A classic example of a visionary teacher is one of artist Pablo Picasso's. The teacher notices his inability to pay attention as a young schoolboy in Spain. When she gives Pablo the same work as the other children, it remains unfinished. Pablo's teacher decides to allow him to doodle on his school papers, as he appeared to have a flair for drawing. This caring and creative teacher was observing her precocious young student one interaction at a time.

Rules provide guidelines, and families function best when they establish a few household rules to fit the ages and stages of children. However, if we are to raise our children one interaction at a time, there are times when we need to relax certain rules. Creative discipline makes space for breaking "out of the box" on occasion. Relaxing rules allows for creativity opportunities. Sometimes a child can think of a more age-appropriate consequence to a mistake than a parent. We need to allow our children to do some of their own problem solving and some of their own consequence setting.

We construct aspects of a child's reality, and our children help to construct aspects of our reality, too. Psychologist Robert Kegan emphasizes that we need to think about meaningful interactions between human beings as "activities": "The activity of being a person is the activity of meaning-making."[9] Our young children constantly make or invent creative meanings at their concrete level of thinking every day. We can either contribute a creative role to their innovative meanings, along with their siblings, teachers, and peers, or we can exercise a critical role that may crush their budding creativity.

Computer expert Roger Schank suggests that we use Socrates as a creative example in our parental teachings. We can deliver slivers of information so that our children can further their thinking of an issue: "Whatever you do, don't answer [all] their questions directly. In fact, you don't have to know the answer. . . . Find a gnarled old tree, and speculate on how it became so hunched and crooked."[10] Speculations, or "I wonder what if . . ." comments, offered in daily spur-of-the-moment discussions with our children, foster creativity. And remember, caretakers do not have to have all the answers. In fact, no parent has all the answers.

Children are very capable of creative problem solving. Many times, though, they find a creative solution only after they stumble through some predicament. A teen agonizes over her poor choice of attending a peer's beer blast: "I should have made my own choice when my friends decided to get wasted." I listen carefully to her alternatives for her next encounter with her drinking peer group; she makes the decision to accept babysitting jobs on Friday evenings. Knowing how to research questions and then in turn teaching children how to search for answers on their own fosters how-to-think skills for every kind of problem. But devoted listening comes first, before any suggestions.

PROMOTING CREATIVE POTENTIAL

Adults can enhance a child's creative potential through fostering a "resilient mindset,"[11] which helps her cope with family and school stress. Resiliency includes fostering a child's problem-solving skills so she can more easily rebound from disappointment.

Fran (11) and Sally (38)

> Sally worries that Fran seems lost, both ability-wise and belonging-wise. School assignments receive only a half-hearted attempt, and

Fran's teacher pronounces that Fran "is not living up to her potential." Playground issues echo world politics; just like countries, the
fourth-grade girls are wary friends one day, warring enemies the next
day. Fran's friendships lack creativity. Fran tires of hearing recycled
gossip. She has little patience for her friends or her younger brother.

In one therapy session's puppet miniseries, Fran's issues tumble
onto the therapy-office floor. The first puppet segment features
dogs. The mother dog always takes the side of the older-sister dog,
"Trickster," and ignores the younger-brother dog, "Chatty." Then,
one day, Mom Dog hides to watch what really happens between the
dog siblings; she catches Trickster grabbing a toy from younger Chatty. Trickster lies to Mom Dog, saying that she had the toy first, but
Mom Dog knows the truth. In a second scene, the action switches to
my turn at storytelling. I follow Fran's lead; the dogs remain onstage.
Trickster and Chatty receive name changes. Now known as "Tricia,"
the older pup becomes a coach to a younger "Chanel," who has
trouble making dog friends on the dog playground. Fran nods her
head in approval, indicating that she is digesting a different kind of
dog day.

In the third and final puppet act, Fran eagerly directs the play
again. She is done with dogs; a duck family waddles its way into
primetime. There are two ducklings who fight constantly. Meanwhile, the parent ducks talk calmly to one another about how to raise
their brood. They take turns watching the baby ducks so that one of
them at a time can go to meet with other animals. They try to figure
out how best to teach discipline to their ducklings. Each animal
puppet gets asked the same question by Mom Duck or Dad Duck:
"What can you do to punish the ducklings so they won't fight anymore? The eagle says, 'I'll fly them above the clouds and scare them.'
The chipmunk says, 'I'll make them say, "How much wood would a
woodchuck chuck if a woodchuck could chuck wood," one thousand
fifty-eight times!' The hummingbird says, 'I'll get bees to sting them.'
The iguana says, 'Spank them, and if they still fight, spank again.'"

With great glee at her cleverness, Fran proudly proclaims a work-
ethic approach as her final discipline tactic: "The beaver says, 'Make
them chomp on a tree.'" After the parent ducks compare scripts, they
discover that no two punishments are the same; they then conclude
that the advice "must not be right. . . . So the parents decide to come
up with their own solution." When Fran thinks about a moral to her
story, she replies in a flash, "Take someone's advice, but don't leave
out yours!" I compliment Fran's thinking and creativity.

DEVELOPMENT DIRECTIONS

> If a child is to keep alive his inborn sense of wonder without any such
> gift from the fairies, he needs the companionship of at least one adult
> who can share it.
>
> —Rachel Carson, marine biologist and ecologist

As parents, we need to come up with our own creative solutions, and we
need to expect our children to do the same. We cannot make a child
"live up to her potential" with stern discipline. Besides, there are always
important reasons why children lag behind their potential. When we
have a partnership with a child, we are on a road to discovering creative
destinations at which we can inspire a child to express their talents.

Eleven-year-olds exercise a critical role with alarming frequency,
and they may cast a critical eye toward their parents. As one parent
laments, her daughter's relating seems "harsh—and toward the littlest
things." When caretakers retaliate in the "blame game," the whole preteen crisis escalates. The wise parent in training understands that this
nitpicking role has more to do with being a preteen than anything else.
It takes increased deep breaths on the part of the adult to travel into
self-territory and not let a preteen drag the whole family into aching
just like he is.

Tip for Raising Eleven-Year-Olds

A preteen may begin pushing you away, but know that you are a valued
partner in creating opportunities for your child to thrive in meeting
developmental needs. "One of the things that will shock you deeply
when your child hits the preteen years is how much her personality
suddenly differs from yours." [12]

Tip for Raising Thirty-Eight-Year-Olds

Foster creativity in yourself and your child; use whimsical language,
make up little stories to get your point across on many topics, and polish
your sense of humor daily. "The skills of creative thinking are part of the
skills of thinking but have to be learned directly in their own right." [13]

SOLVING PROBLEMS CREATIVELY

Thinking creatively can happen when parents in training reach for alternatives to their usual ways of handling difficult situations with a child. However, as creativity consultant Michael Michalko describes our usual adult thinking, we usually rely on thinking reproductively. We copy actions we know about already—or conform to past practice—on the basis of similar problems we experienced at other times. This behavior explains why we may repeat the same mistakes that our parents made in raising us. It also helps to explain why we may blame another adult's parenting moves. One father admonishes his wife in front of their two young sons at the beach: "You are supposed to be the adult . . . you are yelling at them!" I watch the exasperated mother glare at her children and deliver a message she surely does not mean: "Your father wants to leave. I'm leaving, and you can just stay here!"

A creative parent in training does not think reproductively. Instead of relying on tried-but-untrue solutions from past problems, creative people think productively; they seek as many different solutions as possible. They look for novel ways to think about and resolve the problem.[14] All childrearing problem solving receives a boost when parents consider options or think of alternatives. Confused children and tired caretakers can respond well to creative choices.

Children need to sort their own laundry; they also need to sort through their own solutions to many of their own problems. Both tasks require adult modeling, and both tasks occur frequently. Being creative when it comes to our own laundry may be tough, but innovative solutions for many problems exist in our children's imaginations. Make use of your child's creativity when you begin to teach your child, at the age of three or four, to resolve simple issues. For example, learning opposite concepts fosters a young child's thinking of alternative behaviors.[15] Psychologist Myrna Shure tells caretakers of young children: "There are DIFFERENT ways to solve the SAME problem . . . [to] evaluate whether their idea IS or IS NOT a good one, help children learn to wait. . . . 'You can NOT go outside NOW. You can go outside LATER,' and 'Can you think of something DIFFERENT to do NOW while you wait?'"[16] Such simple language boosts creative choice making.

Adults reap their own benefits from learning how to teach children creative problem solving, as many discipline scenarios can be averted by teaching your child how to problem solve. Parents in training learn to play with opposite words in conversations with their youngsters before conflicts arise, and this practice actually can prevent certain problems: "Is this a GOOD PLACE or NOT A GOOD PLACE to draw? . . . How do you think I feel when you draw on the wall and NOT on paper? HAPPY OR ANGRY? How do you feel about the way the wall looks? Do you and I feel the SAME way or a DIFFERENT way about this?"[17]

Most parents rely on three common strategies to get a child to do something different behaviorally: they manage by power, suggestions, or explanations.[18] Parenting through power maneuvers has an authoritarian approach, where caretakers will a child to behave in a certain manner. Picture the caretaker pose of placing your hands on your hips and staring down with a glare at your youngster. Much current parenting practice still holds on to this "because I said so" pose, although it is almost certain to fail in the long run. Suggesting solutions, and explaining, prove useful at times. The downfall occurs when a child later becomes dependent upon parent suggestions or explanations and cannot function without another's opinions of what's "right." Using your power, suggesting, and explaining techniques can place a child in a passive role. Eventually, preteens and teens tune out such parental preaching.

As one middle school youth notes, "I don't even listen to my mom anymore. She says the same things over and over." Adults often overtalk an issue, while children underlisten. The adult pursues. The child distances. When caretakers model a creative problem-solving approach, the child has the opportunity to learn decision-making skills before their challenging teen years. Seeking more than one solution to a problem teaches a child to find creative solutions. Shure's modeling of alternatives teaches consequential thinking, or how to determine which solution would best solve the problem. "That's one thing that MIGHT happen next. . . . Think of lots of DIFFERENT things that MIGHT happen next."[19] By age eight, children generally can understand that the first idea that comes to them may not be their best idea: "Can you think of a time when you did something to solve a problem and later thought of a better way?"[20] When caretakers exhibit patience and prompt for alternatives, a child can gain a perspective on conflicts. Realistically, no child's problem has only one or two solutions.

SCAN FOR ALTERNATIVES

Parents and teachers can coach preteen and teenage children to "scan" for alternatives when conflicts arise.[21] Building upon both Myrna Shure's research in children's problem solving[22] and Richard Schwartz's therapeutic model of Internal Family Systems,[23] my SCANNER Problem SOLVING (SPS) model uses computer terms to aid in child understanding. SPS dialogues address the multilayering of everyone's personality roles, needs, and values in the issue at hand.

Just as computer scanners look for patterns, problem-solver partners examine patterns of behavior before they "network" (share information) and "reboot" (restart) their relating with one another. Your child learns which roles or parts in his or her personality "print out" in a given conflict. Your internal "scanner" examines several layers of the problem. (As a side note, notice how infrequently the word "problem" comes up in this approach with children. Many people seem to have problems with the word "problem." They get stuck, seeing some things as so "problematic" that they feel like giving up. Whenever you say the word "problem," add the word "solve." When you talk about problem solving, you lend hope to your family struggles.)

When your child is in a crisis and you want to yell SOS, take deep breaths and think, "SPS: scan this problem and solve it." Sample questions follow each step of the SPS dialogue. Use the sample questions as a model for your own problem solving, but realize that every problem-solving dialogue may elicit different questions. When you model how to resolve conflicts between children, alter the wording appropriately for the ages of the children. A younger sibling needs help in identifying feelings. Once you use this approach successfully with your child, you will find your own phrases for dialogues.

SCANNER PROBLEM SOLVING (SPS)

State the problem; tell what happened in your own words.

- Now tell what parts of your personality "print out" when you remember what happened. For example, are angry or hurt feel-

ings behind your words or actions? Does a lonely or jealous part show up?
- Which values are "deleted" by these actions? What happens to sharing, cooperation, and respect in this situation?
- Do you remember this kind of situation ever happening before?

Clarify or tell the part you played and the part(s) the other person(s) played; begin to understand each other's needs.

- Do you have other parts that have different ideas about the situation?
- What do you notice about the parts and behaviors of the other person(s)?
- What did you need in this situation? What did the other person(s) need?

Ask for alternatives to the problem behavior; name the behavior change(s) you want to see in the other person(s).

- What changes are you willing to "insert" in this issue?
- What changes can others "insert"?

Negotiate a plan of action. Think of negotiation as "reaching an agreement" instead of "having an argument." Changing *your* approach often facilitates a swift resolution.

- What personality parts of each person do you want to see "downloaded" for the present moment?
- Does fairness seem possible now?

Network with the various parts in your personality.

- What parts can you "start up" now?
- What part can you "insert" the next time you have a problem like this?

E-mail a friend or write in your journal; put what you learned about yourself in writing or in a drawing.

- Just as you let your friends know by e-mail when something important happens to you, think of a message to yourself. Use your computer or a piece of paper. What is the most important thing you learned about yourself today?

Reboot your personality for a new "start" with everyone in this situation.

- Update your internal "screen saver" for a new outlook.
- Today offers choices for change.

This idea, that we can problem solve in creative ways, has many proponents. Some refer to the whimsical adage of Austrian philosopher Ludwig Wittgenstein. He asserted that creativity occurs most often during the calm, resting phases in the three Bs: bed, bus, and bath. Writer Julia Cameron suggests that we first grapple with the skeptic role in our personality—then we can unearth the creativity that resides inside of us all.[24] Others refer to creativity in magical ways, as in having a "writer's muse" on one's shoulder. **If we access it, creativity has applications in all aspects of life's problem solving.**

NIGHTMARE PROBLEM SOLVING

Fostering creativity in our children's problem solving requires our daily attention. Not only can children learn to resolve conflicts creatively in their daily lives, but inventive children are also the hope for our collective future.

Bert (6), Wendy (32), and Larry (34)

> Bert's pediatrician refers him for therapy. Bert has trouble sleeping. He warily approaches ordinary daily events. He picks at his food, forking it from one side of his plate to another. Commercials on television scare him. He finds most child videos unsettling. Joy eludes him. In the first therapy session Bert draws a tiny boy swaddled in fear, with his arms raised over his head and a frown on his face: "Me and the nighttime . . . in my bed being scared. . . . I hear noises that I remember from TV."

Bert quickly begins drawing a second scary image, "Cavity Goo," from a TV commercial. "He sings a scary song. It really scares me." Bert points to Cavity Goo's head and makes a ferocious face. I briefly mimic the face, and Bert nods that I can sense the danger. "He's really bad." I ask for a version of Cavity *Boo's* scary song. A garbled, head-swinging rendition emanates from Bert's contorted body. I suggest that Cavity needs voice lessons. We then create karaoke-like Cavity songs, each one slightly different from the previous arrangement. I follow Bert's lyrics for a bit and then add some of my own; my whimsical "bibbidity bobbity boo," paired with goofy arm motions, sends Bert rolling off his chair in laughter. "It is Goo, not Boo!" I agree with Bert that I really *goo*fed up. (Therapists need a humor role.) When I ask what kind of goo ever has feet or fingers, Bert begins to laugh with blaring, belly-shaking howls.

Then Bert turns serious. He asks, "What does drawing do? How can it help me sleep? Are you a magic doctor?" Taken with Bert's astute intellect, I respond in a heartfelt tone: No, there are no "magic" answers. However, we can put our frightening noises and scary pictures down on paper. We can sing about them and look at them in lots of ways. We can "scan" them in a *different* way. When we see them in a new way, we think about them in a new way. Bert accepts this response. I add that Bert can teach me about drawing and I can teach him to find his strong self.

A week later, Bert returns to therapy, a little more rested. Wendy and Lawrence no longer sit with Bert for an hour, waiting for him to fall asleep. Now they read a bedtime story, lead Bert through a progressive relaxation exercise as instructed, and leave him. Bert announces that he now pulls the covers over his head to fall asleep. When asked how that helps him, Bert matter-of-factly reports that, when the covers are over him, "the pictures in my head are not coming out into my room." He eagerly takes paper to document more "pictures."

Bert makes a larger self-portrait this time. He plops a smiling person on a bed under a protective canopy of covers. Then he adds a black Godzilla (again, from a TV commercial) in the top right corner. "He was going like this—" Bert raises menacing arms over his head and delivers his scariest face. I imitate his moves, and we bond as Godzilla act-alikes, lumbering across the therapy room. I ask Bert if he ever goes to the zoo and sees gorillas. He replies that he knows what a real gorilla looks like. I offer Bert a gorilla mask from my zoo-mask collection, and we chatter about gorillas in general. Gorillas become much less frightening as we act like gorillas looking for food. We hunt and share imaginary grub. I compliment Bert on his excellent creativity, and he continues his train of trauma reduction: "If he was shrunken, he wouldn't be so big."

I support Bert's desire to shrink Godzilla's scary part "to any size you want, since we know Godzilla is just a pretend TV drawing made to look scary." Bert then creatively manufactures "shrinking soap"; he mimes holding a huge spray container and aims it at Godzilla. "This is some pretty good soap that will make them go away. I better bring this shrinking stuff home, so I'll put it in my pocket." Bert loads both pants pockets with scoops of invisible soap. "Pretend this is my bed—now I'm going to make all the faces I'm afraid of disappear."

DEVELOPMENT DIRECTIONS

When your head's full of pictures, they have to come out.

—Bill Maynard, *Incredible Ned*

Unlike adults, young children often admit to some of their fears readily, making it easier for caretakers to deal with their sources of discomfort. Older children get embarrassed by night fears or scary-movie fears and often hide them from adults. Parents in training can model how to deal openly with fearful or scary roles. When a car cuts in front of you when you are driving your child someplace, tell your child after the fact, "I got scared when I saw that car swerve. I was afraid it might hit our car. I took several deep breaths so I could calm myself after I stepped on the brakes." Children often have the mistaken notion that adults never experience fear; adults often lead children to believe this fallacy. It is helpful to admit judiciously to some fear.

Tip for Raising Six-Year-Olds

Night fears are fairly common at this age; parents need to monitor the effects of scary movies and electronic "monsters." "Strange men and women are beginning to appear in . . . [six-year-old] dreams, and the dream animals . . . are becoming active."[25]

Tip for Raising Thirty-Two-Year-Olds

Moms have an ongoing task of helping children learn that their fears have important lessons in them. "We have the difficult task of helping our sons learn how to use feelings as guides to solutions, instead of seeing them as emotions to be denied and ignored."[26]

Tip for Raising Thirty-Four-Year-Olds

Fathers lose contact with their sons if they do not embrace both their own and their young child's fears. "In becoming fathers we confront our own boyhoods and our own fathers. Rather than sorting out this internal struggle many fathers retreat to a distant, remote posture of authority or preoccupation with 'manly' affairs."[27]

CREATIVE PLAY

Setting aside time for creative play needs to be a priority in every family and for every person in the family. Almost anything can be used as a toy to invoke creativity; developmental educators suggest common toys rather than flashy toys to promote children's creative processes.[28] Blocks, building sets, dolls, stuffed animals, clay, art materials, riding toys, costumes, and playground equipment all foster fantasy play. Often using objects creatively provides more fun than playing with single-purpose toys. My children loved cutting up refrigerator boxes with Grandma and then duct-taping their new designs together.

Children love being creative in play. Toys like guns are not a caretaker's best choice, as they can undermine play, turning it into the imitation of violence.[29] **When shopping for your child's toy gifts, ask yourself a number of questions before purchasing: What will my child do with it? What else can be done with it? Will it break easily? Can it hurt someone?** If your child receives a toy from someone else and there is some problem with it, you can use the disappointing experience as a problem solving time to dialogue about the toy's weakness.[30]

Preferably, some of a child's creative playfulness occurs *with* parents. Children lead us into wonderful expressions of our own creativity.

We overlook our creative birthright need too much of the time. When is the last time you felt as though you experienced creative play? When is the last time you played with a child? Perhaps these two questions are related to each other. As psychologist Lawrence J. Cohen suggests, family playing skills are much easier to learn than a number of other personality changes.[31] Each family member can remodel their personality story-houses creatively with family playtime.

CREATIVE LONER

Noreen (10) and Keith (45)

Noreen comes to therapy because Keith wants her to improve organizational and friendship-making skills. Keith also seems puzzled that Noreen occasionally gets "very angry." Noreen has a short improvement list for her father: "Stop yelling." Keith admits he "loses it" when he yells. A shy child, Noreen prefers reading to socializing. Her room has layers of "stuff," and she never can find what she needs for school every morning. The weekday-morning ritual consists of her parents asking Noreen repetitively to find her shoes and prepare her school backpack. Noreen's habitual response shows up in her anger role; she bristles, fumes, and sometimes explodes.

Noreen has many creative ideas and spends her free time happily designing inventions on her sketchpad. However, her artistic ability in drawing people lies dormant. When she tries to draw a person in her first therapy session, she produces a simple stick figure. The sketch belies both her age and her intelligence. Only her accompanying story unearths a creative spark: "Once there was a woman. She came home from the grocery store and saw that there were a bunch of birds flying around inside her house. She began to get angry at the birds and to try to get them out the window. They wouldn't go out the window. So then she thought maybe she could bring them outside by giving them something to eat. She went into the kitchen. She got a milk bottle. She cut several holes in the milk bottle. Then she filled it with seeds. She took it outside and hung it on a branch. Then the birds flew out of the windows to the bird feeder she had made. Now she didn't have the birds in the house and she could do whatever she wanted without being disturbed, and she could listen to their wonderful songs."

When I ask what she does during recess, a time when she can do whatever she wants, Noreen tells how she circles the perimeter of the playground by herself. Noreen suggests how boring the other children's games appear to her. She spends her recess energy walking and re-creating stories in her imagination. She thinks of what she has read in a book, and she retells the story to herself in a different time frame or changes details to make up different, creative endings.

DEVELOPMENT DIRECTIONS

A child, lonely and gifted, will employ a marvelous story or poem to create a companion for himself. . . . Such an invisible friend is not unhealthy . . . but the mind learning to exercise itself in all its powers. Perhaps it is also the mysterious moment in which a new poet or storyteller comes to birth.

—Harold Bloom, *Stories and Poems for Extremely Intelligent Children of All Ages*

Parents may not be aware of how much creative problem solving their child engages in daily. Many children become adept in their adaptations to problem solve difficult school and peer situations. Even though they often figure out on their own how to generate some uses of their time, children benefit from adult recognition of their struggles, such as Noreen's attempts to problem solve difficult times like isolation on the playground.

Tip for Raising Ten-Year-Olds

Ten seems so tender an age, yet the thinking ability of many ten-year-old children shows astuteness about their future. "Individual differences in children . . . become even more manifest at ten. The ten-year-old gives a fair indication of the person to be. . . . He may show . . . a wide range of personality traits which have great predictive value."[32]

Tip for Raising Forty-Five-Year-Olds

Fathers can learn about their child's world through creative playtime. "Successful fathering . . . is about slowing down, taking time to be with our children one on one. . . . Children open their hearts to adults in play situations, willingly discussing topics they might never broach while simply being questioned."[33]

ELECTRONIC "SUBSTITUTE PARENTING" INTERFERES WITH CREATIVITY

Many of our children are weaned on television. Parents use electronic appliances as babysitters for their young. Psychologist Mary Pipher observes how many families spend their home hours separated from one another by various electronics: "They may be in the same room, but instead of making their own story, they are watching another family's story unfold."[34] In addition to the glued-to-the-tube effect of too much TV time, youngsters are subject to mass merchandising. At the age of eight, most children can comprehend television commercials. The average number of TV ads a child watches a year can reach forty thousand ads.[35]

Cut down on commercialism in your living room by limiting the amount of TV time allowed in your home. **Also, you can include in your family discipline a simple creative rule: as soon as a commercial shows up, everyone in the room has to get up, dance, stretch, or do jumping jacks until the program resurfaces.** Groomed on electronics, many preteens ask for their own televisions for their bedrooms; surprisingly, they often receive them. Unfortunately, numerous programs on evening airwaves contain sexually explicit material; so while parents may monitor their children's movie attendance, family televisions can end up showing children bits or all of the movies their parents originally banned at the box office. Through watching television and movies and going on the Internet, children can end up receiving adult sex education in the privacy of their bedrooms without any parental guidance. In past generations, families managed "what 'secrets' of adult life would be allowed entry and what 'secrets' would not" be allowed into a young child's consciousness.[36]

Some families opt to remove TV from their homes. One creative family covers their living room walls with bookshelves and books in lieu of a television. The parents check out books on tape from the local library to augment their children's reading exposure. The children draw, practice musical instruments, read, and play outside with neighborhood friends. When play dates are invited to the family's home, none of the children ask for TV because there are too many other exciting choices. Most television watching stifles creativity, making conformity clones out of our children. And yet TV reigned as the most frequent after-school pastime of children in low-income communities in the Out-of-School Time study. Parents of these children said they would prefer to have their children enroll in classes and lessons, but cost, a lack of transportation, concern over neighborhood safety, and a shortage of available options prevented such stimulating activities.[37] American children spend an average of forty hours per week engaged in their electronic education of TV watching and video game playing. Thus, TV functions as the after-school caretaker for many youth. Much of the programming, as well as the gaming options available, keeps children out of their parents' hair, providing substitute-parenting.

How many parents scrutinize the content and cultural values "taught" by such electronic tutors? Children's minds are malleable. They take bits and pieces of TV trivia and store them in their personality story-houses. Not only should there be concern over the values they are digesting through these mediums, but the worrisome fact is that too much sedentary activity negatively impacts children's health and energy levels. Children who watch more TV than the average are likely to weigh more and engage in less play time than their peers.

Energy, discipline, creativity, belonging, and ability issues all get sidestepped when children sit around the TV campfire too long, devouring junk-food values. The most frightening data about children who are fed too much TV suggest that a child's personal aggression and insensitivity to many forms of violence have a linkage to the high level of violence he or she watches on television; an average of twenty-five acts of violence per hour characterizes some programs.[38] Parents seem unaware of the massive daily dose of violence vitamins our children consume. Additionally, not as much relating occurs in families today when electronics eat up elective time for both children and their parents. Youth form their perceptions about life from excessive media exposure rather than from firsthand involvement.[39] The new millennium family cannot afford to lose opportunities to oversee information overload, to take charge of a child's *values inheritance*. When we do so, we fail to provide our children with more child-friendly and creative outlets for their potential.

WAR ON TV AND WAR AT HOME

Savanna (8)

Children play out their concerns in everyday play and in child therapy sessions. Savanna struggles with homeland wars as her parents face an impending divorce; meanwhile, Savanna is also exposed to TV news clips of faraway wars. In therapy she plays "soldiers"; she has two tiny dolls fight inside a plastic slinky. They make shrill noises as they tumble out of control in one direction and then in another. The accordion-like moves of the slinky toss them back and forth in repetitive maneuvers. Within minutes, Savanna's action shifts. A different doll is run over by a careening toy car. The girl doll dies.

The intense look on Savanna's face shows how seriously she plays out each role in her personality. Sadness engulfs her body as she hunches over the pretend accident scene and carefully lifts the limp doll from the wreckage. Suddenly, Savanna shifts gears again. A broad grin erases the strained lines of grief from her face. She now builds bedrooms out of blocks. Savanna's rapid-fire third play scene features another girl doll safe in her block bedroom; the doll lavishes love in taking care of a pretend family's pet frogs, fish, and cats. Symbolically, the Mom and Dad dolls remain together the way Savanna wishes they would instead of separating in a divorce. She wistfully announces that the parent dolls are "sound asleep" in their bedroom.

DEVELOPMENT DIRECTIONS

Creative minds have always been known to survive any kind of bad training.

—Anna Freud, psychologist

Divorce unsettles children. Typically, children do not understand family wars, in spite of parents' best efforts to deliver the divorce news to their children together and to keep blame out of the picture. Children have strong wishes for peaceful endings to family conflict. Sometimes they perceive themselves as being the cause of their parents' breakup. As angry, confused, and scared roles come out of the child's personality theater in therapy, the child feels relief, both from the acting out of emotional intensity and from experiencing the caring witness of another person.

Most children of divorce need extra assurances that *both* parents love them (and consider that the children now belong in two family units, or have a family with *each* parent). The transition into two families takes a lot of time to assimilate; what will the child's place in each new family look like? Under ideal circumstances, children transition from one parent's home to the next on some consistent and agreed-upon schedule. However, many of these shared schedules fall apart, leaving children to question whether they have a "true" family. One teen tells me of having "six families," because he now experiences six family Christmases. Both parents have remarried, so he has collected two step-parents and four new sets of grandparents. Time to be alone is limited.

Tip for Raising Eight-Year-Olds

Children need lots of time for questions about new relationships in the family. "Regardless of their outward reaction, most children this age have an intense desire for their parents to get back together and can come up with elaborate reconciliation fantasies."[40]

RESILIENCE THROUGH PLAY

Children routinely work out issues in their lives through their play. As psychologists Dorothy Singer and Jerome Singer point out, imaginary play with threatening themes helps a child gain a sense of control or mastery over the real dangers they fear.[41] One child handles his parents' separation by focusing his play in the therapy office on being a baby horse. Although the baby horse faces all kinds of dilemmas, he faces and solves each problem. At the end of the imaginary story, the wise baby horse offers this moral or lesson: "Don't waste your time. Think before you do it, and stick with a friend 'cause it gets things done faster."

Parents can participate in such creative child stories at home. Most young children want their parents to sit on the floor with them and make block cities, Lego neighborhoods, or My Little Pony families. When adults mistakenly believe that play time lacks meaning, they shortchange themselves an opportunity to learn something important about their child, and they overlook their child's truth.[42] The dramatic stories made up by children often reenact bits and pieces of important issues in their lives.

Many children want caretakers to engage in the fantasy alongside their story-making efforts; others prefer a reflective caretaker who makes a few comments but mainly observes the process of play. You do not need to read up on play therapy to be capable of following your child's lead in creative play scenes. Your child will let you know which type of participation seems most supportive. Moreover, parents in training do not need to make interpretations about their child's play. Simply witnessing the play and treating it as creative means so much to a child. You find a creative role when you follow your child's lead into imagination.

YOUTHFUL FEARS OF WAR

Daren (13)

> Daren rebels against his parents' gentle rule, but mostly he rebels because he is scared that he does not measure up to peer standards. He plays violent video games and watches TV more often than hanging out with his peers. War breaks out in his family room when he watches the TV evening news and sees soldiers dying. In an uncharacteristic move, both for his age and for his personality, he comes to a therapy session saying he wants to tell a puppet story for his therapy session. Daren lines up "good guys" and "bad guys" before noticing that the "good" soldiers consist of troops of the smallest puppets, while "bad" soldiers have the largest puppets in their ranks. "Wait a minute—the bad guys are bigger!" He decides not to change his course.

Soon enough, the largest puppet, a red ball of fur with huge, puffy eyeballs, sweeps through the smaller "good" guys and crushes them to death. Daren adds a narrator line: "It is like dodge ball. You know how you 'die' and then you come back in the game again?" The bad warriors prevail, killing their enemies over and over again, although the bumblebee general manages to sting just about every bad soldier at least once. When asked for a moral to the puppet carnage covering the therapy-room rug, Daren looks blankly at me and shrugs his shoulders. Spent, he sighs and slowly begins to pick up the puppets. We discuss Daren's fears about violence and war.

DEVELOPMENT DIRECTIONS

The research results are clear: in spite of the protestations of media executives, exposure to violence in films, on TV, and in video games can and does have an important impact upon the behavior and feelings of children and adolescents.

—Elliot Aronson, psychologist, *Nobody Left to Hate: Teaching Compassion after Columbine*

Fears present opportunities for creative mastery at any age. We need to encourage sons to express grief and talk about what they find scary in their lives. Too often our culture presents the silent-strong manhood image for boys and men. When we do not encourage boys to express their complete personality story-house of experiences, we foster only limited development for them. This restricted version of becoming a man quite possibly leads to domineering roles within their personalities. Children of all ages deserve chances to express grieving and fearful stories. They require a caring adult, in one interaction at a time, to understand and accept their personality roles as legitimate.

Tip for Raising Thirteen-Year-Olds

War scares everyone, but it particularly scares young males who may be asked to serve their country in the future. "For the majority of boys, adolescence is a period of emotional ups and down as they struggle for control—or the appearance of control—over their lives."[43]

CREATIVITY AND THE LOSS OF A PARENT

Death is a topic that unsettles children and adults alike. One of the more difficult grieving issues occurs when a child loses a parent.

Haley (27)

> As a young woman, Haley grieves for her lost childhood. She was twelve years old when her mother died of a sudden heart attack. Roles of her personality trip over each other; sad scenes crammed with guilt, regret, remorse, and anguish swirl around in rapid succession, while fear and anger further tangle up her thoughts. She recalls through dreams a catch-up childhood, made up of her unmet needs. One early dream that Haley recalls paints a relationship picture between her parents that works out well, when in reality her storyhouse of parent memories contains multiple physical confrontations and affairs.
>
> In therapy, Haley relives childhood fantasies from the age of nine, when she orchestrated families of stuffed animals into mostly happy compositions. One fantasy she recalls is of a large stuffed bear living "in the basement with all her bear children. . . . The father bear is 'invisible.'" Once, her mother tape-recorded Haley in her fantasy play. As a grown-up, Haley remembers this early tape and now listens to it. She feels embarrassment at hearing her little girl voice, but she also feels incredulous amazement and joy at hearing her loving mother's voice again. The early stages of her story-house memories contain fragments of her caring mother in one-interaction-at-a-time relating.

DEVELOPMENT DIRECTIONS

> That is what learning is. You suddenly understand something you've understood all your life, but in a new way.
>
> —Doris Lessing

Experiencing the death of a parent in one's childhood can cause one's needs to cascade many times through the down escalator of apathy, blues, conformity, disorder, and ennui. The incredible loss of stamina that occurs in meeting energy, discipline, creativity, belonging, and ability needs affects each grieving person in unique ways. Some experience arrested development; others skip certain key developmental stages. The grieving for a beloved family member does not follow one particular route. Rather, it has a spiraling effect that catapults the bereaved through some memories at particular times and other memories on other occasions. When the death is sudden, as in Haley's mother's death, no one can prepare for the loss. A child often manages the grief of significant losses through creative fantasy, just like they manage the rest of their issues. Merely *telling* a story does not compel as much interest as *relating* a story, because there are many kinds of nonverbal poses involved in our relating; we actually embody some of our stories. So do not exclude your stories of loss and grieving. As writer Judith Viorst wisely counsels, every person struggles with issues of loss. In fact, she terms lifelong losses that need expression in the family as "necessary losses."[44]

Tip for Raising Twenty-Seven-Year-Olds

Open the pages of your story-house of memories; recapture some meaning from the losses you experienced. "By taking in the dead—by making them part of what we think, feel, love, want, do—we can both keep them with us and let them go."[45]

CREATIVITY CROSSROADS

Psychologist Howard Gardner suggests that at as early as age five, children already have a sense of themselves and of other people as participants in their life stories. **Children dearly appreciate stories and become adept at creating their own.** They put together "scripts" in their play scenes. Furthermore, five-year-olds begin to take on poses of leadership versus followership.[46] Gardner maintains that adult leaders reach their effectiveness primarily through the stories they *relate* to others. The most innovative adult leaders are adept at storytelling. Many leaders take an ordinary story and highlight a particular aspect of the story, but the visionary leader creates "a new story, one not known to most individuals before, and . . . conveys this story effectively to others."[47] All of us have untapped ability reservoirs.

Psychologist and chemist Teresa Amabile suggests that adults seek the "creativity intersection" of children, the arena where their ability, skills, and interests overlap.[48] One mother recognizes her teen son's budding interest in directing movies. Instead of telling him how difficult it would be to enter the film industry, she takes his interest seriously. The two of them watch movies together and discuss how they are directed. One movie leads them to the next. Whatever this creative young man eventually decides about a career, he will have precious memories of one-interaction-at-a-time relating when his parent *listened* to him and his interests.

Each person in the family has a "tree" of innovativeness. **If we conceive of creativity as a tree's innermost energy and the tree branches as our inventive ideas or thoughts, each one of us branches our originality into different shapes and directions.** Some creative geniuses are like the redwood tree—giants like Einstein, with ideas that reach to the sky and beyond. Others are like slender shrubs that grow a few clever limbs. Whatever our growth cycle, and wherever we are on our developmental raising road, branching out our own ability potential and our children's ability potential leaves families with hope.

CREATIVITY MAPPING

We all yearn for something. "Something" is not the same as "some things," in spite of our cultural values that propel us to keep buying things. One of the yearned-for aspects in life is creativity. Since everyone's definitions of innovativeness are quite unique, there is no particular set of directions to lead you to find your brand. Many "aha" discoveries by inventors happen when they are on the way to look for "something" else.

- Set aside time in your week to focus on just "being." You may have to get someone to watch young children so that you can take a walk or be alone. Take turns with other caretakers so that each of you gets opportunities for solitude.
- **Learning to cherish time alone can feel like a gift in itself. When we can step out of the cultural values that would**

shape us into conformity clones, we can begin to set sail on our own creative voyage.

- Take some deep breaths, whether you are walking, driving, or just sitting. Make time for self-territory exploration. Use your one-interaction-at-a-time focusing upon yourself. You can find *one* thing you yearn for.

- Some people use journaling. Writer Julia Cameron's wonderfully worded permission for the creative wave in each of us can help provide discipline for this practice. She proposes we write "morning pages," three pages of longhand writing from our here-and-now thoughts.[49] I began this book in this manner.

6

BELONGING NEEDS: ARE YOU A BUDDY OR ARE YOU BELITTLED BY "BELONGING BLUES"?

The greatest thing in the world is to know how to belong to ourselves.

—Michel de Montaigne, French philosopher

People seem to need a marriage between autonomy and attachment, a way to belong to themselves in some respects and a way to belong to significant others. In the past, psychology overemphasized the autonomy end of the continuum, calling for individuals to differentiate themselves from family members. As psychiatrist Jean Baker Miller points out, much of our American theory of psychological development stems from the notion that people need to *separate* themselves from others at nearly every developmental stage. After the first stage of psychiatrist Erik Erikson's eight stages of man (basic trust versus basic mistrust), the agenda of every other stage until the young-adulthood stage (intimacy versus isolation) relies upon increased *separation*.[1] Freudian thought emphasized such independence themes. Psychoanalyst Peter Blos interpreted adolescent independence as relying on conflict in order to *separate* from others and become an adult.[2]

An alternate viewpoint by psychologist Alexandra Kaplan and psychiatrist Rona Klein casts conflict as only *one* of the important roads along the adolescent girl's journey of *connection* with significant others. **Conflict does not have to *separate* people; sometimes people**

move closer together in facing their differences.[3] Adolescents want autonomy, but they also crave belongingness, needing to be recognized and valued. Actually, all of us want both autonomy and a variety of acknowledgments from others whom we perceive as significant. Finding a balance between autonomy and attachment proves difficult.

Has our culture taught us to value autonomy to the exclusion of valuing belonging attachments? Psychologist Dana Crowley Jack suggests that the dominant ideologies in the United States are individualism and capitalism; she argues that capitalism fosters independent individuals making economic decisions in their own self-interest. "The intermeshing of ideas from political theory, philosophy, and cultural legends—of the lone cowboy, the hero, the warrior—has supported the psychological theory of the separate self. . . . These ideas add up to an individual for whom relationships are primarily functional, who should not 'need' relationships, but merely have them."[4] A rugged individualist stance takes us down roads that often bypass belongingness.

"BLUES" IN MOMS

Latisha (43)

Latisha brings her recalcitrant teenage daughter to therapy, but she soon engages in therapy herself, as her child's issues of feeling "lost" begin to trigger her own unmet needs. Latisha realizes that she has lost a sense of belonging in her life. She keeps a journal and sings her blues in writing: "I'm lost . . . I came into this forest to find something, and I've lost my way. Every path leads to nowhere, as I frantically try one or another. I had my red hood on and my basket of food, but I felt cold and hungry and alone. I met the wolf and although he looked ferocious, his words were kind, and he offered me shelter and warmth and friendship. I went with him, but he took my basket of food. He told me if I wanted to feel safe I would need to sleep with him, so I did. When I got up in the morning, he was gone, and when I looked in the mirror, I had no face.

"I met several other wolves. Some of them needed my strength and I gave it freely, asking only for acceptance in return. But I forgot my name and lost my red hood. I looked in the mirror and had a face, but it was not mine. . . . I wandered the forest for a long time surviving on whatever I could find. I forgot there was life outside the forest. One day I came upon the cottage of my grandmother. I ran in and she was lying in bed. 'Oh Grandmother,' I said, 'I'm so glad to see you! I'm so scared and so lonely.' 'My dear, come lie down with me. I will keep you safe and warm.' And I lay down with my grandmother. But when I woke up in the morning, I was lying with a wolf. 'Didn't you read the story when you were a little girl?' he asked."

When I asked for the moral or lesson to Latisha's journal entry, she produced it in further writing: "I don't have a strong sense of self, so I look to others to give it to me. It works for a while and I feel good, but then I find it's not really the person I want to be. . . . My identity is tied in to other people; when they go, I not only lose the good feelings, but I lose part of myself. . . . How do I develop a self of my own?"

DEVELOPMENT DIRECTIONS

"How can you love a liar?" "I don't know, but you can. Otherwise there wouldn't be much love."

—George Bernard Shaw, playwright, *Heartbreak House*

Many parents in training share Latisha's sense of feeling "lost." They experience the deceptions of other adults, who appear as "wolves in sheep's clothing." Not many of us have received training in recognizing deceptive body language. Psychologist Paul Ekman studied lying and found that the emotions a person wants to hide can ooze out in "micro-expressions" consisting of less than one-fifth of a second. Without special instruction, who knows that lying can accompany such characteristics as increased pupil size, voices pitched higher, or lips pressed together?[5] All of us wish to experience meaningful belonging with significant others, and all of us make mistakes in detecting the lying of others. When others lie to us, we end up not being close to them at all, but distant.

Tip for Raising Forty-Three-Year-Olds

When we feel as though we belong to ourselves, we accept responsibility for our own actions, instead of blaming others for our suffering. "[Initially] each [person] believes the problems lie somewhere 'out there' . . . rooted in external circumstances. They also believe that the solutions to their problems are 'out there' too—the right man, the perfect woman, a more appreciative boss, a more interesting job, the right diet."[6]

Ways of conveying unconditional belonging with our children take place in: power-sharing communications, intuitive perceptions, coping with our own childhood memories, and friendship coaching.

Parenting-Trip Tips

- Create a partnership with your child through power sharing (which is "power with" communication) rather than dominance (which is "power over" communication).
- Practice using your intuition to *sense* your child's feelings about belonging actions in everyday situations.
- Keep uncovering your own childhood story-house of memories so you do not push off your own belonging baggage onto your child.
- Coach your child in forging friendships with peers.

"POWER WITH" BELONGING

Our first *connections*, both to others and ourselves, occur in our families. With luck, we get basic training in belonging from loving parents. If children cannot find love at home, sometimes a loving relative or kindly teacher provides a meaningful attachment. However, even though a child might establish a strong foundation in their belonging skills, the larger world can present hostile forces that translate into belonging heartbreak.

One caring mother anguishes over her thirteen-year-old daughter's exclusion from a friendship after she comes home from school one day sobbing. The daughter's best friend had blithely announced, "I had a dream last night. I was climbing the social ladder. You were behind me, hanging onto my ankles, and pulling me down. I can't be your friend anymore." Devastated, the daughter traveled into "blues" land, feeling utterly powerless to belong in this friendship. Belonging-blues experiences are common occurrences in childhood and adulthood. Psychiatrist Jean Baker Miller and psychologist Irene Pierce Stiver focus on such poignant moments when a person experiences the pain of not belonging. They believe this can result either from not being understood or not understanding the other person, and they term this stressful time a "disconnection."[7]

When parents in training constantly argue with their children, a disconnection or a sense of belonging blues can ensue. One mother admits that in the heat of an argument with her teen, "I never considered what my daughter was feeling; I had to take care of my own feelings." Another mother confides that she becomes preoccupied with her own "childhood wounds" whenever parent-child conflicts arise. Such detachments, and the resulting "blues," are especially distressing when differences in power exist between the people in the relationship: parent-child, teacher-student, and employer-employee pairs are some common examples where dominance, or "power over" relating, often occurs. In these couplings, the person without power often fears the more powerful person, and mutual problem solving does not seem possible. Belongingness cannot exist for a child when that child feels at the mercy of someone else. Meaningful relating calls for people to be *present*, able to listen and communicate to each other in a respectful manner.

Our challenge in belongingness requires that we view people with what theologian Martin Buber calls, in his book *I and Thou*, 'I and Thou relating.' In this view, acceptance abounds. When people can *dialogue* with one another with their "whole being," they erase arbitrary boundaries between them.[8] The focus of a dialogue is on caring about understanding another person and caring about being understood. In the words of historian Theodore Zeldin, true communication hands feelings "back and forth until an intimacy develops, and the other person's concerns become one's own."[9] Some believe that such dialogues have a "religious" connotation, but others refer to such caring in a relationship as "spiritual," important with or without any reference to organized religion.[10] Sometimes our descriptions become the focal point instead of the actual *present* dialogue.

Miller and Stiver's work on childhood development reveals that girls and women often approach life situations from an inner sense of belongingness; *connections* with others are the centerpiece, or foundation, of many women's lives. This type of belongingness does not convey a "power over" others but rather a "power with" others, or a power that increases as it empowers others.[11] "Power with" relationships can foster creative problem solving. Psychological development from this perspective focuses on mutuality within relationships.

Sons often are groomed to embrace autonomy more than belongingness. However, research shows how supportive male mentors can enable adolescent males to be more open emotionally. Psychologist Renée Spencer studied male mentoring in a Big Brothers Big Sisters group. Male teens without a father figure in their homes received continuous, supportive relationships for one year with a male mentor. As a result, the teens increased their self-confidence and perceived a greater ability to manage their emotions through having surrogate "big brother" relationships.[12] Whenever we can relate one interaction at a time, we slow down our agenda, and we begin to see that another person has similar needs. We find common ground for belongingness. All ages have incredible belongingness needs along the raising road. Fathers and mothers, as well as sons and daughters, want their viewpoints heard and mutually considered.

CONNECT OR DETACH?

While many of us highly prize our verbal skills, much of the way we relate and belong to each other arises from our nonverbal communications. Psychiatrist Dan Siegel and preschool educator Mary Hartzell focus on the topic of *resonance*, another way of looking at "power with" relating between two people. When parent and child align their emotions through their nonverbal communication, they form a resonance, or *memory of the other*[13] that *connects* with the intentions of each other. **Through our sensing of another's particular intentions, we either connect or detach.** We perceive ourselves as either belonging or as experiencing the "blues" of alienation.

However, we may not be free to experience belongingness with others when we are not aware of our own emotional states. Additionally, when caretakers and children focus primarily on their own loneliness, or "blues" detachment,[14] they put up emotional shields that block any connections. When parents cry the "blues," they are locked into anger, worry, and sadness poses, and they are not available to extend appropriate belongingness to a child one interaction at a time. Nor can they listen to their child's story. They quickly lose sight of the meaning behind a child's requests when they are invested in their perceptions of their own emotional distress. This investment is something of which they may not be consciously aware. Many times we are only conscious of having a nagging sense of negativity, and we do not understand the origins of this worrisome attitude. Our personality story-house likely holds the reasons for our behavior, but we are not always aware of the memories that could explain our actions. We commonly disconnect ourselves from our stressful early stories.

Children can sense disconnections, or belonging blues, in their caretakers. For example, children report to me very often that a particular teacher does "not like" them. After meeting a lot of such children's teachers, I could see exactly what the child saw: the teacher appeared embroiled in personal issues and, being preoccupied, was not very *present* around the child. This state is what the child sensed. When we focus on caring for too many of our own feelings, children will try a variety of behaviors to get our attention. When a child reacts to our inattention with their own blues, they may exhibit isolating moves or raw aggressiveness. Caretakers and teachers then often make the mistake of getting caught up in these secondary behaviors instead of perceiving the child's initial desire to belong. Our challenge in relationships with children comes back to self-territory. We need to feel grounded in self-territory in order to sense what our children are feeling. We need to be *present* in order to respond to a child's needs.

EVERYDAY BELONGING TIES THAT BIND

Remember the courage and extraordinary sense of belongingness shown by the New York fire fighters and police officers as they rushed into the World Trade Center towers to save people on September 11, 2001. Their tragic and heroic legacy reminds us of our deep connections to other people and even to sisters and brothers who are strangers to us. Interesting enough, much of our newfound computer connectedness is used to link absolute strangers. This practice occurs despite the fact that we do not find enough time to talk to the people who live next door to us. While we are interconnected with one another, we also have isolating roles in our personalities that frequently keep us apart from others. Our shielding roles hold us from closeness or proximity with other individuals, who also have their own protective sheathing. As caretakers, we cannot afford to raise such shields between our personalities and those of our children.

All of us search for a sense of belonging or *connectedness*, both to ourselves and to others. Cultural historian Riane Eisler reinforces the idea that you first need to address the issue of having an inner relationship with yourself.[15] Eisler proposes that we work on six kinds of relationships: intimate relationships, workplace and community relations, national community relations, international and multicultural relationships, our connection with nature, and our spiritual relations.[16] Psychiatrist Edward Hallowell believes that we are both happier and healthier when we develop and increase our connectedness in six domains of belonging: familial connectedness, historical connectedness to our past, social connectedness to friends and colleagues, information connectedness to knowledge, institutional connectedness to our schools and jobs, and "beyond knowledge" connectedness to a religion or a transcendent connection to nature.[17]

There are many reasons why we seek religion and bond with nature, but one of the most basic reasons relates to the very meaning of the word "religion":

- "Religion" comes from the Latin words *re* ("backward" or "again") and *ligare* ("bind," "fasten," or "tie").[18]
- One definition describes "religion" as "a vivid awareness of kinship and affinity with a life larger and more lasting than our own."[19]

We *bind* or *fasten* onto belongingness in our religious practices. **When we make an effort to fasten or bind to something again and again, we feel we *belong*.** People of all religious backgrounds want their children to have a perspective on life that affirms belongingness on multiple levels. Initially we exercise our sense of kinship in wishing to spare our children pain. When we realize the impossibility of this hope, we then wish for our children to have a life of meaning. For many parents in training, "meaning" in life includes their family's religion. Children sometimes recognize needs for connections and belongingness that adults overlook.[20] Children can have rich spiritual lives, as psychologist Tobin Hart writes about so poignantly. Hart suggests that caretakers view parenting as a practice of their own spiritual growth.[21]

What changes in your personality perceptions if you view parenting as one of the most growth-producing and spiritually fulfilling endeavors of your lifetime? What differences in your relationship might occur if you embraced your child as a present "miracle," and you felt honored to have a connection to such a miracle? How might your life be different if you threw yourself into present moments, finding more belongingness with your child and relating one interaction at a time? When parents discover present moments with a child, they also uncover self-territory inside their own personalities. Self-territory holds both a caretaker's most important values along with a consideration of a child's needs. Trust, fairness, respect, and responsibility are key values in this caretaker-child belongingness. Our connections with our children run along many values tracks simultaneously, covering all of our basic needs.

Belonging mutuality surfaces when parents can detect a child's needs. The confirming parent looks at the *whole* child, not just some troubling surface role or pose. When true belonging takes place in a family, there exists an awareness of mutual self-territory. Psychologist Daniel Stern takes this interplay between two individuals a step further. He suggests that when we jointly share our experiences in a mutual and intuitive manner, we can address past traumas and even "rewrite the past."[22] We can remodel our personality story-house memories so that they do not hurt us anymore.

INTERGENERATIONAL BELONGING

Many grandparents experience and share utter joy as they spend time with their grandchildren. Their faces beam with the all-out smile of the gentle Dalai Lama, who appears to radiate a purity of happiness that many seek. One adoring grandfather glowed as he spoke of his seven-year-old granddaughter: "She's one in a million. Probably every grandfather says that, but she really is!" Many grandparents grasp the importance of belongingness. As one grandparent describes her new grandmother role, she explains that she feels the freedom now to enjoy an intimate belonging relationship: "When I was a mother, I'd be thinking of forty things I had to do. . . . Now as a grandmother, I'm happy to just sit still and play in the water with Lucy as long as she wants!" The glow on this grandma's face shows how deeply this connection with her granddaughter resonates within her. One-interaction-at-a-time relating connects a caretaker and a child in the present moment.

Another grandparent also admits that he feels "freer" with his grandchildren than he ever felt with his own children "now that I don't have the responsibility for them." When I ask him what he means by this statement, he offers somewhat apologetically, "I am trying to do a better job of relating the second time around." Another grandfather explains his new role in these terms: "I love to love 'em, because I know I can leave 'em at the end of the evening." Having a break in the responsibility realm helps these retired fellows throw themselves into creative play and experience energetic belonging when their grandchildren visit. In the precious miracle moments, when adults connect with offspring or grandchildren, the belonging appears as smiles mirroring one another, as if a mutual "aha" realization reaches both parties simultaneously. In such belonging moments, people realize that separations between them are mere illusions.

RITUAL IMPACT

Psychologist Alan Loy McGinnis sees rituals as one of the necessities in quality family relationships.[23] **Most children love holiday and birthday rituals, but other simple daily customs like bedtime are also wonderful chances for child-parent bonding.** Children grow up quickly, but certain rituals stay with them. I helped my daughter make sense of her school days by making up stories at bedtime when she was in elementary school. Then I would start a story about "Annabelle," who happened to have a strong physical resemblance to my daughter. I would pause at dramatic moments and have my daughter fill in "Annabelle's" next steps. In this manner, I found out about my daughter's stress points at school and helped her problem solve what to do about them. Rituals within the family build partnerships.

Leah (5), Lane (7), Joyce (38), and Noreen (65)

For twenty years, Noreen keeps company with a special flower, Virginia bluebells, in the springtime. For the past several years, she has extended her spring ritual to include three generations. Leah and Lane look forward to sharing one interaction at a time with their grandmother. They know the routine. They travel to a nature preserve where bluebells proliferate. Lying down in the bluebell sanctuary, they ground themselves and their belongingness to nature. This year, the sojourners turned solemn when they found their path to the bluebells blocked by a gate. Disappointment swarmed the family carload, and Joyce slowly turned the car around. Abandoning their family ritual for the day brought on the "blues."

Five-year-old eyes brought problem solving to the forefront: "I see blue," yelled Leah. Along the side of the roadway, an open area of bluebells fluttered. The children tumbled out of the car, with the adults not far behind. Everyone lay in the blue bed. Leah enthused, "Every other year we can come here . . ." as she adopted the new bluebell patch into the family's tradition. Noreen then took Lane on a brief walk. In eloquent first-grade thinking, Lane shared empathy with Noreen: "Nana, I was so disappointed when we found the gate closed. I was going to go home tonight and cry in my room." Noreen responded to her grandson's words in the present moment. "I was really sad, too," she confided. Lane continued, "Leah saved the day because she saw blue out the window." Noreen breathed in the honesty of her grandson's admission, recognizing that in a few short years he might not admit such tenderness to any adult.

DEVELOPMENT DIRECTIONS

The grandparents and the children . . . [have] lives . . . closest on the circle.

—Joseph Bruchac, Abenaki storyteller, *The Circle of Thanks*

Family rituals create meaningful connections between an adult's story-house and a child's story-house. Belonging times spent with a loving caretaker fuel us for decades. Grandparents were elevated figures in ancient cultures. In earlier generations, family rituals were held sacred. One Native American symbol represents "grandmother growth"; the female elder had the role of praying for the health of children.[24] When caretakers offer rituals and prayers to their children's lives, an ancestral legacy of belongingness permeates those lives. In turn, children learn to honor their elders through simple acts.

Tip for Raising Five-Year-Olds

Nature exploration delights most five-year-olds; they are much closer to "grounding" themselves in nature than adults. "Children [from five to seven] are especially nourished by contact with the world of living things because their own life forces are so strong."[25]

Tip for Raising Seven-Year-Olds

Young school-age children often are sensitive to adult emotions and adult needs. Five- to seven-year-old children "can 'hold on' to a concept in their heads."[26]

Tip for Raising Thirty-Eight-Year-Olds

Parents do not have to despair when their children experience some disappointment; some of our most powerful life lessons surface when "things go wrong." "Negative experiences can serve as superb opportunities to empathize, to build intimacy with our children, and to teach them ways to handle their feelings."[27]

Tip for Raising Sixty-Five-Year-Olds

Vital experiences with grandchildren keep grandparents young at heart. "[In] my quest for the fountain of age . . . [I looked for] people who seemed to be 'vitally aging' as compared to the image of deterioration and decline. . . . I found that they were everywhere."[28]

ANIMAL BELONGINGNESS

The animal kingdom, it seems, always has something to teach. What can

families learn about the importance of belongingness from animal behavior? Hurricane Katrina swept into New Orleans and broke belonging ties not only among family members but between individuals and
their treasured pets. When one blind evacuee was rescued, he had to
leave his seeing-eye dog behind. Fourteen days after the storm, the
forlorn dog was still watching over their abandoned home. When man
and dog were reunited, television cameras captured the emotional re-
union of the overjoyed dog and his overwhelmed best friend. Animals,
like people, need and want to belong. Primatologist Frans de Waal
researched the behavior of chimpanzees. Immediately after a chimpanzee conflict, the opposing chimps appear in need of a physical sense of
belongingness; fighting chimps embrace, kiss, and groom each other
within a minute of their fight.[29] Apparently chimps do not tolerate
disconnection or the loss of belongingness for long.

The following chimpanzee parenting story demonstrates how connected these animals are to one another and how they follow a sophisti-
cated set of group norms. Two chimp mothers watch their two children
play together. But when the youngsters' playful wrestling turns into
throwing sand at one another, one mother chimp intervenes with a
threatening grunt. The second mother goes to the sleeping dominant
female nearby and pokes her in the ribs to awaken her. This grandparent female then takes one threatening step forward and quells the peer
uprising with a wave of her arm and a loud bark.[30] **These primate
members have grown into certain roles within the family system;
how they belong and fit into the colony has meaning for the
entire group.**

Other animals also exhibit the power of belonging. Whales have
strong belonging ties. In fact, blue whales call to one another across two
thousand miles of ocean. Sea otters in captivity share their food with
one another. When fish are tossed into the aquarium tank, each otter
swims gracefully to the bottom and scoops up many fish. Instead of
eating the fish immediately, the otters stash their catch into their ab-
dominal pouches and then come to the surface to share. Even vampire
bats share their meals with those less adept in hunting and gathering.
Elephants are known to have very strong attachments to their young.
This elephant story re-creates the force of belongingness and caring
within a herd: when a baby elephant falls into a drinking water hole and
the mud appears to swallow the young elephant, the entire herd mobi-

lizes. At the risk of their own safety, the elephants work cooperatively with one another to free their herd "brother."[31] Apparently elephants, bats, otters and whales all comprehend "power with" relating.

BELONGING BAGGAGE

As parents in training, we may start with virtuous intentions, but sometimes we collapse under the weight of a confusing variety of personality roles. When we angrily complain about our baby (or, later on, about our teenager), our frustration wells up if we do not recognize our own unmet belonging needs: "The relationship with the baby offers a new venue for the drama played out in the parent's childhood."[32] **Unmet needs travel across generations.** Parents in training have to gather up their own personality story-houses of memories, sorting and accepting the whole lot of them so that they do not push their belonging baggage onto their children's shoulders. Otherwise, our childhood frustrations can transfer to the next generation.

FIRST ATTACHMENTS

British physician John Bowlby originated many of his theories on attachment from his careful studies of homeless children when he worked for the World Health Organization. His keen observations led to changes in hospital and orphanage rules for children. Specifically, previous policy had ensured that caregivers were rotated frequently so that youngsters could avoid further separation issues upon leaving a facility. However, many of these orphans became listless and died. Bowlby observed that when the children received care from the same caregivers regularly, belonging attachments formed, and the orphans thrived. The importance of tender, close relationships applies to people of all ages. However, who we belong to—and belong with—changes as we travel through the lifespan. By old age, we may seek to belong to younger people, as our peers and age-mates may no longer be living.[33]

Some of us are blessed to receive incredibly devoted caretaking; others of us miss out on secure attachments in parent-child bonding. A belonging balancing act exists between every caretaker and child, and a child can become tangled in a caretaker's stress. For example, if a caretaker overcontrols, an infant adapts and "downregulates," or behaves submissively. For some young children, the task of switching belonging gears in accordance with their parents' functioning proves too difficult. One youngster adapts to parental overcontrol by gazing into space before doing what she was told. Later, when playing alone, the child remained aloof from any real engagement with things.[34] In the case of a depressed caregiver, the youngster "upregulates" energy levels and tries to act perky. **Whether a parent's unmet needs reflect one's own childhood or simply a bad day at the office, spillover blues can carry over to the dinner table right along with the knives, forks, and spoons.**

UNMET BELONGING NEEDS AND TEEN PREGNANCY

Noelle (23)

> Noelle grew up in a home where she always felt blamed for "everything wrong." The oldest of seven children, she had only one brother. Her mother married after finding out she was pregnant with Noelle, and Noelle believed her father would not have been her mother's choice of a mate without this pregnancy. Nothing in Noelle's childhood seemed "easy." Mealtimes were noisy, with bickering as the main course most evenings. Noelle grew up with little sense of belonging to her family, and at fifteen she latched onto the first boyfriend who declared he cared for her. "He was the first person to ever tell me that he loved me," Noelle says in a quiet voice.
>
> Noelle's boyfriend's mother showed Noelle warmth, and she allowed the pubescent couple to "have their privacy" in her home when she worked. With little guidance or belonging attachments in her own family, Noelle became infatuated with her feelings of belonging to her teenage boyfriend. Within a short time, Noelle was pregnant and starting her own family. Noelle describes her early mothering days as filled with "having the blues" detachment. Noelle would prop up her daughter's baby bottle instead of holding her for feedings. Noelle ignored all but the most pressing of her baby's needs. Cuddling did not exist; rocking never happened. With little attachment to her own mother, Noelle initially did not form a secure attachment to her own infant.

When Noelle became pregnant with her second child two years later, she reacted in an entirely "different" manner. She felt a sense of belonging to this child; she wanted this baby. Warm feelings flooded her throughout pregnancy. With this newfound budding belongingness, Noelle now could look with maternal eyes upon her firstborn. Today, she cannot believe her maternal instincts could have been "as different as night and day" in such a short time span. She has made every effort to repair her relationship with her firstborn child.

DEVELOPMENT DIRECTIONS

I had a beautiful daughter, and we've been growing up together for twenty-seven years!
—Chris Vitale, "A Journey to Self," *You Look Too Young to Be a Mom*

Most adolescent pregnancies are unintentional. Many teenage girls are looking for belongingness rather than babies when they become sexually active. Teens are not good at planning ahead, and often they do not use birth control. Sexual spontaneity often takes priority, and birth control planning seems unromantic to teens. Additionally, naive adolescent assumptions about pregnancy produce further deterrents to safe sex: "I didn't think I could get pregnant the first time. . . . I heard that you won't get pregnant if you have sex standing up. . . . I thought I would not get pregnant during my period." With the reality of their actions hitting home after missing a period and having early pregnancy symptoms, many teens panic, feeling unprepared for parenthood. Pregnant teens are equally challenged by an abrupt transition into adulthood. Carrying a baby creates all kinds of issues for what previously was simple day-to-day functioning. In the best-case scenario, the teenager's parents offer support; however, parents who are about to become grandparents have to confront their own unmet needs.

Tip for Raising Twenty-Three-Year-Olds

Review your values for yourself and the new family you are forming; what do you want most to teach your child? "The twenties represent a period marked by audacity and grandiosity, self-doubt and emotional instability, playfulness and risk taking, intense learning and mental rigidity. For most, it is a scary wonderful time."[35]

BELONGING TO PEERS

Initially parents have a hand in choosing appropriate friends for their children, as caretakers are the ones who set up play dates for their youngsters. Later, children make their own play dates and join group activities that foster belongingness. Often turmoil accompanies these early bids for connection. One mother reported to me that her fourth-grade daughter and many of her friends left their Brownie group in tears one day after a confrontation with some peers. The Brownie troop moms discussed the malicious behavior shown by the girls in the troop with the school social worker. Many cliques start by fifth grade, and children can spend their middle school years trying to break in or out of various groups.[36] Research finds that reciprocated friendships positively influence middle school students' overall adjustment, with this positive influence staying strong even up to two years later in eighth grade.

Sixth graders without strong peer friendships have higher levels of sadness and less self-worth. Their grades slip, too. While many social needs get fulfilled through trusted peer relationships, some middle school youth are not ready for this step. Some preteens prefer more adult-oriented friendships, and they form ties with their teachers rather than their peers.[37] **This practice of making either peer or teacher buddies pays off when the middle schooler later adapts to the widening social scene.**

PEER ISOLATION AND CUTTING

Katrina (12), Theresa (36), and Darryl (38)

Twelve-year-old Katrina hated the thought of having to change school buildings for middle school. One initiation step for entering middle school included a group visit to the new building. While her classmates were bubbly with enthusiasm, Katrina kept to the middle of the packed hallways, fearful of getting lost and not wanting to lose face with her boisterous classmates. When she finished her tour, she felt only nausea, not relief. Whereas fifth graders had one basic class-room, the sixth graders' routine of moving from classroom to class-room unhinged Katrina. She worried about forgetting her schedule, although she rarely forgot things.

Once the school year started, Katrina felt isolated in her new school building, separated from her closest friends. She moved tenta-tively about in tiny steps, as if she was walking an acrobatic tight wire, and she feared she could tumble off course at any moment. Katrina recalled fifth grade at her elementary school with much fondness, and she lamented over how secure she felt in her old school building. As one of the youngest students in the school for sixth through eighth grades, Katrina imagined that the older students would look down upon her.

Katrina did not join the noisy, hormone-driven throng at recess. She preferred staying inside the school building during the break. A previously close girlfriend ditched her friendship with Katrina when she captured her first boyfriend. Other girls urged Katrina to hate the ex-friend's boyfriend "because he stole her friend." When Katri-na objected to such snide behavior, the other girls glared at her, said "whatever," and walked away from her. Katrina's world quaked with an unsteadiness she could not calm. One day, Katrina cut her arm, drawing blood, in order to "get out of class."

Theresa anguished over her daughter's disconnections. Katrina's struggle paralleled long-buried memories from Theresa's own child-hood. Theresa worried for Katrina's future. Darryl took the long view; he surmised that both his daughter and his wife could weather the preteen storms. He promised to have ongoing, supportive chats with Katrina about her daily grind. Both parents stayed connected to Katrina, lending their power to help her problem solve her peer pressure dilemmas and reminding her of her love for academics. The sense of belongingness her family provided gave Katrina a welcome nest for her fledging flights into preadolescent territory.

DEVELOPMENT DIRECTIONS

All the lonely people, where do they all belong?

—Paul McCartney, "Eleanor Rigby"

The "tween" years of middle school are difficult for many children. Not quite a teen but definitely not a mere child, this youngster experiences awkward body changes and awkward feelings. For many, transition to a new school building looms as a clumsy step. Lost security in terms of knowing the way around a new school increases the uncertainty in a normal twelve-year-old's general sense of insecurity. There is a tendency for this age group to believe that they are the "only ones" who ever felt "lost." Overly anxious roles in the preteen personality can take over, leaving the student to feel they cannot possibly solve the problems of the day. When parents share memories from their own story-house of schoolhouse transitions, it helps the preteen realize that such transitions are universal. Creativity in the approach to belonging and ability needs also helps most preteen children meet the challenges of middle school.

Tip for Raising Twelve-Year-Olds

Encourage your preteen to bring home their friends so you can get to know the cast of characters in their social life and have empathy for the up-and-down nature of tween relationships. "The more problems that children have in interacting with their peer group, the more time they need doing just that."[38]

Tip for Raising Thirty-Six-Year-Olds

Raw emotion expressed by preteens rattles the windows of a parent's story-house of past memories. Acknowledge your own emotions from your preteen years. "Often our children are more open about their needs and their feelings than we allow ourselves to be. . . . We can learn from them that it's possible to feel something intensely one moment, act on our feelings, and then feel better and move on to something else. Our kids are experts at that."[39]

Tip for Raising Thirty-Eight-Year-Olds

Parents need to model friendship with one another at times of high stress in a child's life; sharing emotions and sharing chores are two forms of support. "Egalitarian fathers always feel that their experience of being involved in caregiving has made them better fathers than they would otherwise have been. . . . Women in more egalitarian relationships appear to be more satisfied in their motherhood role in this society."[40]

PRESSURING PEERS

In high school, teens must navigate even more complicated issues that relate to belongingness than those in middle school. Most teens seek independence from their families, and as a consequence, their range of social opportunities expands. Not only do teens feel tempted to experiment with drugs and sex, but adolescents frequently find themselves in situations where they feel forced to join "the crowd." Many teens participate in the gossip mill, too, grinding out daily news reports of who did what with whom. "He said, she said" chitchat pervades teen conversation. With the prevalence of computers and cell phones, teen social wars extend far beyond school hours; instant messaging, cyber-bullying, and gossipy text messaging elongate the hours that teens experience peer pressure.

Briana (15) and Andrea (44)

> Troubled belongingness issues echo throughout several generations in Briana's and Andrea's stormy relationship. Andrea worries that Briana makes the wrong choices, especially in terms of boyfriends. The personality story-house behind Andrea's worry, however, began with blueprints from a previous generation. Andrea related how her own mother "failed" in love relationships. Andrea then sighed as she told how she put herself into the same love-challenged category as her mother. Andrea married a man whom she claimed was so violent that he eventually was disowned by his relatives. She suffered much abuse at the hands of her bullying husband, and although she has left him, she now worries that Briana "will be the third generation unlucky in love."
>
> Briana's mother and grandmother chose the distancing of divorce to deal with their "blues." Grappling with a history of belongingness going awry and the raw responsibilities of single parenthood, Andrea feels drained and ill equipped to create closeness with Briana. In a

similar vein, Briana has distanced herself from her mother, mirroring what Andrea does when relationships challenge her. Arguments abound in their household. Silence intervenes. Pain pervades the parent-child home atmosphere.

In therapy, Andrea focuses on Briana's ability; she wants her daughter to excel in academics in order to obtain a high-paying career to support herself. However, Briana's attention is on belongingness. Typical of many adolescents her age, Briana has no interest in schoolwork. Her homework seems like busy work, and she only pretends to do any of it while she sits at her computer instant messaging anyone who pops onto her screen. Since she spends most of her free time at school with her boyfriend, she goes to the computer for girlfriend company.

Andrea yelled when she received teacher notification that Briana is failing. When Andrea forbids Briana to spend any time on the weekend with her boyfriend, Briana dissolves into tears. She says she has cut herself off from her old girlfriends because they socialized predominantly through alcohol, and Briana does not want to become an alcoholic like her absent father. Briana described her old peer group as living for weekend drinking parties: "All they do is take off their clothes with boys they don't really know." She elaborated on the topic of teen sexuality for the new millennium—her girlfriends engage in casual sex with different boys under the guise "friends with benefits." Briana is opposed to teens that "hook up" sexually and do not relate emotionally as a couple in any other way. Briana rejects her friends' manner of relating as "shallow."

Briana confides in therapy that she never intends to smoke pot "because it messes with your brain," and she feels proud of being able to say "no" to her drug-using friends, even though they tease her for being a "wimp." Then Briana turns wistful. She understands that her mother worries about the impact of her sexual intimacy with her boyfriend. She also misses having girlfriends. Her need for belongingness is strong, yet every pathway to meeting these needs appears to have roadblocks.

DEVELOPMENT DIRECTIONS

By keeping her distance, Miriam realizes too late that she has made her daughter more like her than she ever intended.

—Myla Goldberg, *Bee Season*

Adolescents have a difficult time keeping their personal behavior private. Rumors among peers add to an adolescent's general confusion about their social choices. While parents and other caring adults still play an important part in a teen's life, the high school peer group can influence a teen to veer sharply away from family and community values. The wise parent uses their teenager's belonging struggles to reminisce about their own value-laden crises when they were in high school. Parents in training need to review their own personal struggles without judgment and with an eye for the lessons that can be learned. When judgments do not take over a caretaker's lingo, many important values dialogues can take place among parents and teens. Sometimes an older brother or sister can take on a caretaking role for a teen who craves a skilled listener. School counselors and teachers often provide a sounding board for teens to explore belonging needs.

Tip for Raising Fifteen-Year-Olds

Encourage discussions about what your teen values most; ask whether these values are the same or different from what the peer group values most. "Our best hedge against the risks of adolescence is to fortify our girls with a sense of their own value, their own power, and their own capacity to . . . make wise choices for themselves. They need to know the difference between a stupid risk . . . engaging in unprotected sex of any kind . . . and a good risk that challenges them to learn, stretch, and grow stronger."[41]

Tip for Raising Forty-Four-Year-Olds

Cultivate your own friendships; you need a source of support for yourself when you are raising a teen. "At midlife, when we aren't sure ourselves of who we really are, the love and containment of friends offers strength, support and an opportunity to know how much we are loved."[42]

FROM BELONGING TO DRUG "BLUES"

The "herding" belongingness that is forged among some teenagers can result in risky behaviors without any benefit of "power with" relating. **Most teens believe that they are immune from truly dangerous consequences.** For example, if one teen is hospitalized for a drug overdose, peers often make up reasons why that same result could *never* happen to them. Many teen bids for belongingness end up in "blues" land.

Todd (16) and Ruth (46)

Todd came to therapy after enduring a psychiatric hospitalization for drug abuse. His mother, Ruth, explained, "This is no simple kid. . . . He's in a serious relapse. . . . He is very resistant to talking about it, or to even admitting that he's using drugs." Todd's marijuana pattern included smoking at school lunchtime, missing a class or two, and showing up sleepy and "out of it" by the final class period. When Todd attended concerts, he extended his drug usage to include LSD and Ecstasy. He stole money to buy drugs. School woes followed Todd's regular drug use: one more absence in English, biology, and math class would mean failure. His art teacher reported that Todd "goes into a trance" in her class. Todd worked in spurts, but very slowly, so that he fell behind in turning in the required four sketches each week.

Todd named the part of his personality that uses drugs as "boredom": "I am bored fifty to seventy-five percent of the time." To understand how his roles belong to one another, we mapped them on paper. Todd's first map was a jumbled cacophony of words—some written sideways, some written in neat print, and others were merely scratched onto the page. His depiction of his self-sphere in the center of the page appeared small, almost lost in the crowd.

One role, Todd's artistic role, seemed to rise off the page; it appeared in giant puff letters. Todd rated his creative leanings as the number-one functioning part of his personality. Todd found solace in writing poetry. Then he linked the parts of himself that he saw as belonging together: artistic, compassionate, happy, smart, enthused, self-reliant, and creative parts made up an "I'm together" persona that Todd wished to project to the world. However, a more familiar stance that Todd played out daily among his peers and family was signified by these roles: scheming, spontaneous, sneaky, bored, and angry. A third role grouping revealed Todd's fears and insecurities: stressed-out, regretful, sad, lonely, tired, manipulative, scared, empty, irritable, and pessimistic. Three roles in Todd's personality did not receive any grouping; optimistic, courageous, and brave parts simply floated on the map like tiny islands waiting to be discovered at a later time.

DEVELOPMENT DIRECTIONS

I am a completely isolated man and though everybody knows me, there are very few people who really know me.

—Albert Einstein

Teenage angst often relates to emotional distance, or a lack of belongingness. Drugs are one way that teens try to "fix" their isolation, and they temporarily can put aside the personality roles that normally clamor for company. Drugs become the medication of choice for their "blues." Sometimes, adolescents medicate their various personality roles to such an extent that they perceive a drugged state as more of a reality than a sober one.

Tip for Raising Sixteen-Year-Olds

Outings are good times to have discussions with teens; the privacy of a long car ride gives an adult and a teen a chance for an uninterrupted values dialogue. "The loneliness of men has to be addressed in the lives of boys. Boys need to be encouraged to initiate friendships, maintain them, and experience the conflicts that arise in male friendship from different levels of athletic skill, from teasing, and from competition for the attention of girls."[43]

Tip for Raising Forty-Six-Year-Olds

Just as important as working on belonging needs with your teen are your own belonging needs and how you "fit" into this world. "At midlife, regardless of the relative health of our family of origin, there is a need to look back, to understand where we came from and how we are contained by our family. . . . What did I learn about myself and the world as I grew up?"[44]

BULLYING "BLUES"

Peer harassment often takes place on school playgrounds or during sports competitions. Playground bullies hold incredible power over their victims, because most of these interactions occur out of earshot of teachers or playground supervisors. As a result of their harassment, some bullies increase their social standing; some even qualify as "cool" when rated by peers.[45] Many youth face peer harassment. **The effects of bullying can range from poorer grades in school to homicide or suicide.**

Bullying starts up in kindergarten and continues throughout children's schooling. Psychologist James Snyder and colleagues report that some kindergarten children are targets of verbal or physical harassment about once every five minutes. When Snyder and his research team observed boys on playgrounds, they observed youngsters valuing physical prowess, such as who can run the fastest, and preying upon those who were perceived as "weaker." Name-calling, poking, pushing, and shoving were the customary bully tactics for this kindergarten group. The young victims showed a range of insecure behaviors, with parents of the teased targets telling of their children being more aggressive or more withdrawn at home. These victims were likely to bring home poorer grades than nonvictims.[46] Children often do not understand why someone "picks on" them. They end up feeling "lost."

Psychologists Amie Grills and Thomas Ollendick found that middle school children who report being victims of bullying experience more anxiety than nonvictims; they also have more negative self-views.[47] Those who receive the bullying feel humiliation. Researcher Jaana Juvonen found that peer harassment does not make victims tougher. Consequently, many victims suffer in silence and blame themselves, believing they somehow are responsible for being targeted. Often these students perceive they are being rejected by all their peers, whether true or not. The bystanders of school teasing also reap negative consequences. There is a high level of anxiety for both the teens who receive harassment and any bystanders who watch someone else being victimized.

Researcher Nan Stern begins classroom discussions on bullying by raising student awareness of the differences among joking, teasing, and bullying.[48] Bullying behaviors are hostile and focus on "power over" intimidation; teasing tends to carry a mixture of hostility, humor, and ambiguity.[49] Often comments begin with joking and teasing before sometimes crossing a nasty border into bullying. The reasons we bully are various, but one underlying reason is our inability to cope with our own faults. Sociologist Richard Sennett calls for "fidelity to oneself" in order to be honest about looking at our own mistakes.[50] Making fun of others' weaknesses overlooks one's own flaws.

ATTENTION-DEFICIT HYPERACTIVITY, BULLYING, AND BELONGING

Scott (9), Melinda (34), and Wayne (39)

> Nine-year-old Scott dresses well and has a snappy haircut. His boy-next-door appearance belies his use of foul language. His physician has given Scott a diagnosis of attention-deficit hyperactivity disorder, and impulsivity may as well be Scott's middle name; every situation described by Scott's parents exhibits rash behaviors on Scott's part. School troubles abound for Scott, especially when it comes to completing assignments. Nightly homework hell takes the form of much family screaming and crying. Fights on the playground appear to rotate between Scott initiating name-calling to his classmate throwing the first verbal punch. The change both Melinda and Wayne seek in their son seems reasonable: "We want to teach him to control himself."
>
> Before the end of the first session, the desired change already needs revision: Melinda and Wayne both confess to their own "crabby" behavior. "Yelling" happens regularly in their family. Wayne shows impulsive, rash behavior just like Scott, and he likely shares Scott's attention-deficit challenge. Melinda alternates between crying when family disorder ensues and raging at her husband because he rails so frequently at Scott. Swearing is par for the course for every member of the family. All three family members need a few house rules. The first rule everyone agrees on is to "talk in a normal tone of voice without swearing."
>
> With only a short time left in our first session, I spend time alone with Scott. We draw. Scott produces a square, boxlike boy with no hands, and he shares a telling story from his frustrating school day: "This kid was in school, and he is in recess. The kid got his jump rope

out and started jumping rope. His friends said, 'Do one hundred,' and the kid said, 'I can't do one hundred.' He wanted to go tell the teacher that the kids were bothering him, telling him stuff he didn't like. And then the teacher said, 'Could you please bring the kids here who are aggravating you and tell them that the teacher wants to talk to them?' And then he went to go get the kids. And the teacher said, 'Why?' They said, 'Because we just felt like it. Then the teacher said, 'Are you sorry for what you did? Why would you want to hurt him in any way? He is your friend.' They said, 'We were just bored.' And the kids had to go stand on the sidewalk. That was their punishment."

DEVELOPMENT DIRECTIONS

Question: "How do you help give children the sense that they'll be OK?"

Answer: "The key factor for children is having relationships they can count on . . . a place to turn, that they're not alone in the world.

—Stanley I. Greenspan, psychiatrist

The challenges in Scott's family span all five basic needs. Scott's agitated actions result in a difficulty getting to sleep at night, so his sagging energy often sputters as overtired behavior. Everyone in Scott's family suffers from a lack of a few simple rules or discipline. Swearing peppers many arguments. The marital relationship suffers along with parent-child connections. Melinda knows that her husband's "power over" relating with Scott does not work. No one here can muster much creativity to solve family problems, as each person yells louder than the next to ensure being heard. Bullying and belonging struggles abound in both the family and the schoolyard for Scott. Like Melinda and Wayne, Scott speeds through each day; the family swerves from one conflict to the next. Ability needs are "lost" in the shuffle.

Tip for Raising Nine-Year-Olds

Children with an attention-deficit challenge require a few rules to help them chunk their homework into smaller segments; timed breaks in between the chunks offer the chance for them to renew their energy.

"Once you get a handle on . . . [the procrastination, the disorganization], you can start benefiting from the positive—the high energy, the creativity, the open-heartedness, the resilience, the willingness to work hard, and the ingenuity."[51]

Tip for Raising Thirty-Four-Year-Olds

Arguments over childrearing mask expressions of love and belonging-ness between the marital couple, as well as among family members. "Mate relationships are unique in being the only social tie that encompasses all three forms of love . . . [a child's love for a parent, a parent's love for a child, and the romantic love of the couple where sexual, physical, and emotional closeness occur]."[52]

Tip for Raising Thirty-Nine-Year-Olds

Start with one interaction at a time to change your own behavior. "All strengths can be worked on. . . . However, the temperance strengths, like patience . . . are hard to work on. . . . Something like kindness is easier."[53]

ANTIBULLYING INTERVENTIONS

Most children need help preparing for the rough-and-tumble world of playground politics. Caretakers need to reinforce with their child that they are *not* to blame for being bullied. They also can role-play both verbal and nonverbal ways to handle teasing, such as walking away from bullies.[54] Psychiatrist Stanley Greenspan suggests that caretakers can help their youngsters look for various roles in bullying peer and adult personalities: "I like Mr. Guthrie most of the time, except when he slams the eraser against the chalkboard."[55]

Some proactive schools have programs that foster acceptance of the differences among children, and teach tolerance. After the senseless violence at Columbine High School in Colorado in 1999, a nonprofit organization, Community Matters, proposed a student-led antibullying intervention, the Safe School Ambassadors program. Since 2001, more than five thousand student ambassadors have worked diligently in hundreds of middle and high schools to stop bullying among peers. Students who are "opinion leaders" from diverse cliques receive training in nonviolent interventions and communication skills.[56]

Another program, Operation Respect, builds upon the acceptance themes in Steve Seskin and Allen Shamblin's song, "Don't Laugh at Me,"[57] which was popularized by folksinger Peter Yarrow of Peter, Paul, and Mary fame. Yarrow built an educational curriculum teaching second through eighth graders to create a "ridicule-free zone" in their classroom and on the playground. Operation Respect also delivers a summer-camp experience and after-school programming.[58] A Chicago group, Hey U.G.L.Y. ("Unique Gifted Lovable You"), helps children create positive acronyms for disrespectful labels. Innovative students developed their own definitions to transform derogatory epithets:

- "Geek" means "gifted, enchanted, educated kid."
- "Loser" stands for "living outside society's everyday rituals."[59]

Creative responses are needed in both homes and schools for children to feel accepted in a bullying culture. Parents in training should help children scrutinize occurrences of teasing and bullying on an ongoing basis and recognize that there are more roles within a child rather than just being a bully. **Wise parents also teach children that they are not just a label, like "nerd" or "wimp."** However, some parents instruct their teased children to use physical force on the playground. The teasing of a son, for example, can raise all kinds of past injustices in a father's memories. Nonetheless, all of us have to take a few deep breaths first whenever we feel the stirrings of such anguish. There are alternatives to every piece of child or adult behavior.

Teaching your child to identify alternative behaviors should underscore all problem-solving dialogues. Some children do best to ignore a bully and walk away from their cruelty, as the shy child finds it excruciating to say something to a bully. Parents can coach more assertive behavior in response to future taunts by suggesting verbal responses such as, "I don't call you names; don't call me any." This strong statement only has punch if it represents the truth. Part of the difficulty of the teasing culture exists in the whirlwind effect that it generates. Many children begin with a one-word name-calling step. They do not anticipate how winded they will become in a moment with back-and-forth name-calling steps.

More key coaching from a parent on the topic of teasing needs to address angry roles. The shame of being a victim stirs up retaliation plans in many children. Painful memories can bubble up to a boiling point in some students. Too many school shootings have occurred as a result of teasing. These students did not know where to turn to meet their needs to belong. Both teachers and students report that a victim getting angry in a teasing situation does not effectively stop the teasing.[60] When a bullied child makes a retort, their fiery rage usually elicits an even more vicious degree of bullying. Such "power over" relating fuels the relationship inequity. Teaching children strong values and how to connect in "power with" friendships takes repeated coaching. The first lesson needs to instill a child's belief both in self-territory and an assertive personality role. Impart the knowledge to your child of how to make a true friend, one who knows how to relate one interaction a time.

IMAGINARY FRIENDS AND INTROSPECTION

When adults believe they need company, they may look for it in a variety of places other than marriage. Husbands and wives sometimes look for belonging companionship in affairs. Adults and children alike watch television or go to movies for company. Online chat rooms offer solace to some lonesome adults and teens. Daydreaming suits others, because they address their belonging needs through imagination. Many forget to look for belonging in self-territory. **Children have many ways of meeting belonging needs other than interacting with their peers. They play, read books about others' relationships, or even create an imaginary companion.**

Psychologist Marjorie Taylor studied children's imaginary playmates and found the practice to be both relatively common and healthy.[61] Children with imaginary buddies might have advanced social understanding, but they are not very different from other children their age. The average ages of children who engage in imaginary companionship are three to six. Most of these masterful fantasy makers control the content of their imagination, understanding that the pretending does not equal reality.[62] Imaginary playmates may be another child or an animal, and the fantasy friend sometimes serves as a scapegoat:[63] "I did not dump out all the toys; [imaginary] George did it," claims one solemn four-year-old. This child wishes that "George" could materialize so that he is not alone in picking up the mess.

BEING "ALONE" VERSUS BEING "LONELY"

Aloneness is different from loneliness. Many creative children are content to spend hours by themselves, as they revel in their imagination and their spontaneous resourcefulness. Parents in training often can tell whether their child enjoys such "alone" time through observing nonverbal signals. The "lonely" child does not look content. Rather than viewing aloneness as something only another person can fix, sociologist Martha Beck sees loneliness as stemming from a lack of fulfillment when a person is alone. Beck asks her adult coaching clients if they ever had an imaginary friend or have anything they do on a regular basis that erases a sense of time.[64] In that way, loneliness simply consists of a frame of mind for both children and adults. Again, while both adults and children have a lonely role in their personalities, many children are better at pretending and filling their day with interesting activities than adults are. During "alone" time, they are creative, filled with passion about their play, and appear very capable of reaching self-territory. **We seem to forget that we belong to our very selves.**

What happens to our strong sense of self-fulfillment as we grow into adulthood? We all feel "lost" as caretakers at times, and we all sing the belonging "blues." We do not know where to search for a map out of our loneliness. We assume that we are the only ones who lack a buddy; however, loneliness touches every person, young and old, at particular transition times throughout life. We assume that famous people have marvelous connections with the rest of the world. We view movie stars and professional athletes as lucky because of their glamorous lives. However, many so-called stars turn to the same drugs that adolescents stumble onto in a desperate attempt to numb their loneliness. Friendship appears to elude them, and the belonging blues prevail.

Every person has the same basic needs for energy, discipline, creativity, belonging, and ability. Some famous people turn their affections to their easier-to-meet ability needs. For example, British historian

Theodore Zeldin discussed the life of the famous psychiatrist Erik Erikson. Zeldin found that Erikson, as a child, never knew his father, so he espoused "a philosophy . . . inspired by a longing for a normality he never experienced."[65] Belongingness eludes far too many. Throughout history, people have grappled with belongingness issues. In the United States, 26 percent of adults rate themselves as chronically lonely; almost as many married people rate themselves among the lonely as the unmarried population.[66] Zeldin has proposed four strategies to combat loneliness: (1) become a noble or professional hermit with a cause, (2) look to introspection to define your own uniqueness, (3) take on an eccentric pose using huge doses of humor, and (4) have faith in a greater power, believing in a divine spark inside you (for those without such faith, create a life of being useful to others).

Indeed, perhaps the most powerful argument for finding belongingness in self-territory is the idea that most human progress comes from individuals who can act solely on their own, even defying persecution, because they perceive an inner truth.[67] In the words of Irish philosopher and poet John O'Donohue, when we stop fearing our solitude, we can find creativity: "Your forgotten or neglected inner wealth begins to reveal itself. You come home to yourself."[68] One of our most important needs in all of our personal growth revolves around our belonging needs. Yet, like so many other issues in life, aloneness and belongingness are in the eye of the beholder. We and our children need to feel as though we belong, both to ourselves and to others. When we enjoy belongingness, we can use more of our ability.

BELONGING MAPPING

There are many synonyms for the verb "like": "Fancy, enjoy, care for, delight in, get a kick out of, be partial to, dig, love, adore, take pleasure in, be fond of, appreciate, relish, have a soft spot for, esteem . . . want, choose, prefer, care, feel inclined."[69] These are some of the words we feel when we have a sense of belonging with another person.

- Write down the names of the adults in your family of origin and your immediate family. Beside each adult family member's name, write down some of the characteristics or personality parts that you "enjoy" or "relish" in that person. Example: "Marie: Funny, loyal, caring, smart, honest, creative."

- From the list of people's roles that you "like," circle all of the roles that describe you as well as the other person(s).
- Now list these same individuals again. This time, think of any characteristics or personality roles that you do not like about them. Example: "Marie: Jealous, manipulative, critical, impulsive, and overly talkative."
- Again, circle all of these roles that describe you as well as the other person(s).
- Make a separate list of all of your circled roles. **Which of your roles draw you closer to others, and which ones may get in the way of your belongingness with others?**
- Now make a list of your child's roles, both those that you like and those you do not. Circle any roles you have in common with your child. What do you notice about the circled roles?

7

ABILITY NEEDS: ARE YOU AN ARCHER, OR ARE YOU ALIENATED WITH APATHY?

You were born with the potential for genius. We all were; just ask any mother.

—Michael J. Gelb, *Discover Your Genius*

How many of our children walk into school classrooms every day with the belief that they are "stupid" and that only the other students qualify as "smart" kids? How many of our children compare themselves to siblings, cousins, or neighbors and imagine that someone else qualifies as "bright" but they do not? In what ways do teachers and parents in training play into such belonging and ability misperceptions? Smartness comes in many flavors. When we expect our children only to flourish in the three Rs of reading, 'riting and 'rithmetic, we are limiting the possibilities of child genius.

Many achieving adults have near failures in their early school histories. The great Indian leader Mahatma Gandhi struggled in school as a child.[1] Stories of Albert Einstein's early development include the fact that he was slow in learning how to talk; one teacher stated that young Albert would never amount to much![2] **Ability does not show up at the same age or in the same manner for everyone, as there are many intervening factors in each person's story-house.**

Grades are only one marker for achievement. I meet many children who do not think they have any ability. Children cannot conceive of doing their best in any area because they have no reference for their personal best. They lock on to worst-case scenarios, as if they have some date with failure. We need schools and homes to value *each* child's potential and expect *each* child to meet this potential. Adults need to expand their expectations regarding childhood abilities and their own abilities. Our society needs each and every child's and adult's unique talents.

Master teachers groom students to realize their potential by having powerful expectations of their students' potential. Through one interaction at a time, one mentor or caretaker who expects excellence can reach generation after generation of potential learners. Through her experience with one teacher, one learner slowly unbuttons her doubts and comes to realize her incredible inner worth. As she studies, she tries on new poses and roles. She uncovers self-territory and finds belongingness with other knowledge-searching scholars. She no longer wears her old personality wardrobe, which had a "loser" label stitched into nearly every role.

Unconditional love for our child relates to all of the basic needs, but parents in training often link such love to certain abilities the child displays. Enlarge your perspective to embrace your child's true interests and multiple talents and your own creative potential.

Parenting-Trip Tips

- Expect children to achieve through encouraging the discovery of what really interests them.
- Acknowledge your child's feelings about their abilities in schooling, sports, and extracurricular activities.
- Foster learning connections between your child's homework and everyday life.
- Display a love of learning by working on meeting your *own* potential.

EXPECTATIONS AND ACHIEVEMENT

Adult expectations prove to be critical predictors in children's achievements. Expectations carry both power and energy. For example, parental expectations have a bearing on teenage daughters' career aspirations. Adolescent girls desiring careers that require at least a three-year training program beyond high school report higher parental expectations of their career level than similar-age daughters planning a career involving two or less years of training.[3] The "I think you can" messages from adults to children have far more effects than you might imagine.

A classic study in teacher expectations, the Pygmalion effect, found that adult expectations about a child led the child to behave and achieve in ways that met those expectations. Psychologist Robert Rosenthal and elementary school principal, Lenore Jacobson, found that elementary school children made measurable strides in school achievement when their teachers expected excellence. Their research model selected 20 percent of a classroom's students randomly; they then told the teacher that these targeted students possessed "unusual potential for intellectual growth." Hearing this, the teachers expected more of an outpouring of ability from these students than from the rest of the class. Sure enough, eight months later, the targeted students had performed according to the teachers' heightened expectations; through more teacher encouragement and attention, the random 20 percent continued to excel through the end of the year.[4]

Teacher expectations, like parent expectations, can become a self-fulfilling prophesy. And the reality is that teacher evaluations of students—on such characteristics as body build, gender, race, ethnicity, name, attractiveness, dialect, and socioeconomic class—occur daily. Teachers often size up students on the first day of school and make internal predictions regarding certain students' academic achievement. These potent predictions show up in the teachers' classroom climate, feedback, and relating. Often teachers convey these expectations nonverbally; a disapproving look sent in the direction of a student speaks loudly and with authority. Teachers' feedback follows both *affective* (praise versus criticism) statements and *cognitive* (intellectual) information.

Teachers, like parents, operate from their own personality storyhouses. Therefore, teachers can enhance student-achievement "diets," as in the Pygmalion effect, or they can starve a student's confidence. When a teacher pegs a student as a troublemaker and not a scholar, the learning environment for that student becomes compromised by the teacher's ongoing negative expectations. Negative expectations impact children just as powerfully as positive ones, and these "archers" become unable to hit the bull's-eye of education and A grades.

EXPECT EXCELLENCE THROUGH DISCOVERY

Many adults believe that control is what works best in terms of children's achievement. When children are told to study "because I said so," the caretaker is assuming control, relegating the student to a passive role. However, children need an active role, rather than a passive role, in order to achieve well. Besides, parents in training cannot make a child achieve. Erroneous expectations about the role of control when it comes to schooling follow the "mimetic" school of thought, where adults are presenting themselves as the unquestioned keepers of knowledge for the young.[5] The child's job simply rests upon memorizing the information presented by an adult. Having to mimic the parent or teacher does not have much probability of instilling a love of learning in a child. And where is the inspiration for the adult's continued learning when the rote memorization route becomes tiresome?

Real learning comes from the process of discovery and an emphasis placed upon creativity, values, and discipline. Research among middle school and high school students found that students who received teaching that fosters their creativity and practicality, in addition to their analytical skills, achieved at higher levels than students who received lessons filled with rote memorization. The creative learners also achieved at higher levels than students who were taught critical thinking or analytical lessons. Another interesting finding was that the creatively focused students even outscored the other students on standard multiple-choice tests, which rely largely upon memory.[6] Children are by nature keen explorers and action seekers.

Caretakers who understand children's exploratory ability use more of a "transformative" teaching style, where the adult functions more like a coach in engaging the child actively in the learning process.[7] This caretaker style utilizes what psychologist Ellen Langer terms "mindfulness"; the children receive adult encouragement to notice new things and to try on creative or artistic roles.[8] The classic example of mindful or transformative teaching is when nineteen-year-old Annie Sullivan overcame her blindness and then reached a breakthrough with deaf, blind, and mute Helen Keller in getting her to grasp language skills.[9] Sullivan's careful training of a previously unreachable Helen demonstrates one-interaction-at-a-time relating.

Sometimes too, the more playful the interaction, the more a child engages in learning. As child-development researchers point out, the many discoveries of children often do not take place in specific lessons or on computer programs but in more play-like settings: "Play equals learning."[10] Parents in training do not have to set specific goals for playtime in order for a child to learn something important in the activity. Children are born learners. Parents who make time for action play with their children will discover that a wealth of ability in problem solving and creativity underlies children's play. For example, many children work out their ability and belonging issues within their play.

SIBLING RIVALRY AND ABILITY

Dylan (4) and Shea (7)

> Sibling rivalry describes Shea's and Dylan's relating poses. Following his older brother around like a second skin, Dylan impedes on Shea's freedom. Shea devotes much effort to planning ways of losing or avoiding Dylan. Sometimes he locks himself alone in his room until the heaving cries of his brother waft under the door and tug on his heart. After hearing about the latest infraction of Shea's privacy, when Dylan interrupted Shea's reading, I ask Shea to choose some puppets for a story.
>
> Shea gleefully gathers a chicken and a Native American talking stick with flowing feathers. The brother props, the chicken and feathered stick, have feathers in common. "Hi! My name is Shea Special. I am now a chicken. I would like you to meet my brother and his name is Stick. That's not true—his real name is Dylan." Shea shoots an evil eye in the direction of Dylan the Stick and takes on a foreboding chicken voice: "Stop it, Dylan. Stop it, Dylan. Now I'll have to use my beak on you." Dylan the Stick tries to run away from Shea the Chicken, but he does not get very far because Shea's two hands direct the chase scene. Dylan the Stick screams, "Mommy! Save me from Peck Man! Stop him! Help me! Protect me! I'm too little."

Shea sobers after uttering these words and has his chicken representative apologize: "Come on Dylan, I'm sorry." Dylan the Stick replies a little too easily, "It's OK, Shea. I forgive you." The two puppets share in playing with a slinky next. Here they take turns and genuinely appear to enjoy each other's company. After witnessing this quick turnaround, I ask Shea for a lesson to his story. Shea grins as he says, "The lesson to this story is happiness and sadness." I inquire how Shea can make the move from being sad with his brother to being happy. Shea smiles broadly; he has the ability to answer because he has played out this scenario in real life before. "It's easy. You have to calm yourself. You have to take three deep breaths and think about it."

DEVELOPMENT DIRECTIONS

Man is but a reed, the feeblest thing in nature, but he is a thinking reed. . . . All our dignity lies in thought. . . . Let us endeavor then to think well; therein lies the principle of morality.

—Blaise Pascal, French mathematician

Children often pick up skills quickly. But a caretaker's engagement in a child's skill development is what helps to keep the learning fresh. Through caretaker comments about noticing the various roles in a child's personality, a youngster learns to accept that both sad feelings and happier ones are part of the same personality system. Similarly, children learn that feeling both insecure and smart about their abilities is normal. Parents in training can teach a child how to shift from one opposite role to another by sharing some of their own story-house of childhood memories that illustrate the opposite roles in parent personalities.

Tip for Raising Four-Year-Olds

Copycat actions are common among four-year-old children, so help preschoolers discover their own special areas of ability. "Older preschoolers are only beginning to suspect that they are not the center of the universe—and the idea is not entirely welcome."[11]

Tip for Raising Seven-Year-Olds

Seven-year-old children are so eager to master first grade and their newfound school skills; provide ample opportunities for your first grader to read, spell, and create stories for family members. "Children don't need to be treated equally. They need to be treated uniquely."[12]

ACKNOWLEDGE A VARIETY OF ABILITIES

Many parents make the mistake of pushing their children to achieve at a particular skill area "as if they were the [sole] sculptors of their children's character and self-concept."[13] Parents' expectations for their children need to support the child's discovery that they have a variety of abilities, instead of demanding compliance and progress in one arena alone. Not only does the former put incredible pressure upon parents to make their child achieve some particular level of proficiency, but it narrowly defines a child's options. **Children need exposure to a range of skill areas in order to determine what interests them most.**

When they are teetering on the edge of an educational abyss, I often ask children what they wish they could do instead of going to school. I often hear, "Watch TV." I then say, "No, that's not doing anything. . . . What have you ever really wanted to do?" Many appear clueless in response. How can we raise children to meet their potential when they are not aware that they have alternative abilities?

Another common kind of expectation oversight occurs when caretakers are at cross-purposes in expectations of their children. Caretakers commonly have different ideas about a child's ability levels. When this happens, a child sometimes learns to turn to the parent with the least expectations for their achievement, because it gives them "the easy way out" of homework.[14] Such divisions between parents often reflect the unresolved ability needs within one or both of them.

ABILITY NEEDS *CONNECT* TO OTHER BASIC NEEDS

Many parents in training sadly reflect upon their own difficulties in learning to read when they tell me about their child's reading challenges. They cannot process the anxiety reactions of their child over learning struggles because they feel fearful themselves. Some parents also confess that they get nervous whenever they have to go to their child's parent-teacher conferences. These parents tell me that going into an elementary or middle school "just brings up too many memories of my own learning problems." Instead of focusing solely on regret about the past, parents can use their own anxious memories of past unmet abilities to better understand what their child faces today. This perspective not only supports the child but also leads the adult to consider new learning opportunities.

Caretakers need to adjust their expectations for their own achievement as much as they need to alter their expectations for a given child. They can do this through pursuing new avenues. For example, there are many adult education classes. There are no prescribed times in a person's life to study a foreign language, audit a college class, or even enroll in a particular course of study for credit. Parents can use the *present* to engage in new opportunities for themselves.

Another parental snafu occurs when adults expect and demand achievement from a child who has not been effectively meeting his or her needs along the energy, discipline, creativity, belonging, and ability escalator. Specifically, when parents value "top dog" status above all else, this compels them to demand that a child achieve at all costs. However, A grades are not as important as a child's ability levels. Ability is what counts. Yet teachers too frequently make a similar error in regarding As as the most meaningful result for a child.

Adults cannot expect a child's ability levels to soar and increase exponentially when basic nutrition, sleeping, and exercise energy needs are unmet. While sleeping needs are not as frequently addressed in public education, nutrition and some exercise needs now are increasingly viewed as critical factors to a child's learning capabilities. Fuel, or healthy food, for the school day needs to be the first stop on the achievement route. Related to a child's need report card is a parent's need report card. How can we expect a child to meet their daily needs if we are not meeting our own daily needs?

The way in which homework rules are developed also makes all the difference in peaceful evenings and achieving students. Maintaining some discipline in the house in order that children can focus on homework makes an enormous contribution to a child's excellence. A truly motivated child shows energy and discipline levels that can surprise us. Next on the escalator is creativity. Our imagination sparks enthusiasm and discovery, which can make learning fun. Belonging needs often intertwine with learning potential. We sometimes assume that our children are using their learning potential, when learning rates as the last thing on their minds. Think of how often we go to our jobs and our own thoughts wander. Children also keep their minds busy with myriad thoughts. Many of them have yet to discover ability highs, or the value of learning.

School learning theories often do not encompass the value of learning from children's internal worlds—from their imaginings, thoughts, and feelings. Thus, students often complain of unending and boring assignments. Those children who exude any excitement about a piece of school homework often have multisensory projects in which they can employ their individuality in producing some unique piece of work.

UNHAPPY AT SCHOOL

Nita (11)

> Nita rates herself harshly among the learners in her classroom. She outlines her thinking for me: she perceives herself as hopelessly deficient in math and grammar assignments. When I ask about her best subjects, Nita brightens and gives herself a top rank in reading, science, and social studies. Still, Nita does not average her rankings— she rates her overall scholastic abilities at the lowest rating of her perceived weaknesses. She considers what she does *not* know as more important than what she knows.
>
> We map Nita's concept of her personality. Her various personality roles are faces with smiles—fun, cheerful, friendly, and thoughtful—and faces with frowns—afraid, nervous, angry, bored, and tired. Slowly, we add smart and curious roles. By her choice, all of these drawings are made with a black marker. Her one exception, her self-sphere, stands out as a huge brightly colored pencil. We then work on the idea that she can be her own creative artist who keeps drawing or discovering who she becomes.

Meanwhile, a new assignment at school takes on a special place in the family's busy calendar. Nita has a project assignment, her favorite kind of homework. She decides to illustrate a Native American cookbook. Nita works diligently in researching her topic. The energy in her voice is melodious as she eagerly tells about her plans for the menu selections. I tell Nita that she rates as "out of this world" in creativity, because there is no way to contain anyone's creativity in any kind of grading system. Nita smiles broadly.

DEVELOPMENT DIRECTIONS

Until we possess our own version of ourselves, we are prone to all manner of mishaps.
—Julia Cameron, *The Vein of Gold: A Journey to Your Creative Heart*

Every child deserves an education that enhances their particular abilities. While this notion seems obvious, there are many children who slip through the cracks and never feel that they have *any* worthwhile abilities. Parents in training must be the major advocates for children who do not learn at an average pace. Alerting your child's teacher(s) as soon as you become aware of a child's distress over schoolwork gives them the best chance of forging new learning opportunities. Some teachers are advocates for students when they detect faltering patterns within the classroom. However, students often hide their concerns, making it difficult for teachers to pick up the troubled learner's clues.

Tip for Raising Eleven-Year-Olds

When you see your child struggling in school, find their pockets of strength within your community to round out their learning program. "The school of the future might have the 'student-curriculum broker' . . . to help match students' profiles, goals, and interests to particular curricula. . . . There should also be . . . a 'school-community broker' . . . for children who exhibit unusual cognitive profiles."[15]

EMOTIONAL BLOCKS

How many children are like Nita in seeing the glass half empty instead of half full? They catapult themselves into an ability abyss when they focus predominantly on their weakest subjects. Learning struggles can lead a child to apathy if their deficits are not understood by caring adults or given the proper attention. Sometimes parents also focus on half-empty glasses. Apathy can bury ability or achievement potential. Psychiatrist Stanley I. Greenspan points out that children's intellect, achievement, sense of self, and morality all have their roots in their earliest and continuing emotional experiences.[16] When we understand intellect and ability as standing on the shoulders of meeting our emotional needs, we value parenting/teaching relationships in a new light.

Parents often ask me about particular wording to use with children to motivate them in productive ways. Parents may borrow another's words, but there are no magic words; a parent's self-territory meets a child's self-territory without any special wording. Besides, each child in the family responds to the same words differently. **What works with one child may backfire with another.** In this manner, each child in the family raises our parenting growth.

While children have many different reasons for experiencing learning difficulties at school, sometimes our notions about why Johnny or Susie "cannot learn" are wrong. As many teachers point out, often children who fail in math do not necessarily need *more* math practice: they simply do not concentrate on math while they are in class. Caretakers can identify their child's possible emotional blocks to learning by these telltale warning signs: a lack of any identifiable interests, an inability to experience fun with *any* school assignments, an unwillingness to take any risks due to fears of failure, a lack of ambition, a tendency toward giving up easily, an insufficient ability to "think on one's feet," or an inclination to clam up with few questions asked of anyone.[17]

Researchers have found that the learner's emotions are central to the learning process. Emotional roles in a child's personality are not an outcome of learning; instead, emotion interlaces classroom and homework scenarios every day.[18] Neuroscientist Candace Pert discusses how important emotions are in the role of memory as well as actual performance.[19] While this may be news in some circles, anyone who observes a child in a classroom setting can explain how important that child's emotions are to the learning process. Young children seldom mask their feelings well; the look on a child's face gives many clues as to whether a particular learning situation is a thumbs-up or thumbs-down experience for him or her. When it is a thumbs-down, some learners act as if they are an animal in a laboratory cage; they appear restricted or apathetic. When a child does not capitalize on his or her ability, negativity wells up over time and spills over into many other facets of life. Self-territory appears only in fleeting moments, because the child usually appears *lost*, afloat in a sea of self-doubting and fearful roles.

Fear and apathy do not make good learning buddies. In his research, psychologist Donald Hebb let lab rats have the run of his household, where they doubled as pets. Later, when the rats were tested, he discovered that the free-spirit rats ran a better maze than caged laboratory rats. Furthermore, Hebb found that rats raised in "enriched" cages with toys also ran better mazes than those kept in sterile cages with no stimulation available.[20] Discovery and exploration are key to learning success.

"LOST" ABILITY

The cost to society of restricting a child's potential can never be measured, but often the cost to the individual child shows up dramatically. Frustration precedes anger or apathy in many children with learning differences. Depression follows, with a fearful role of not being "good enough." Our competitive cultural values exacerbate such fears with a "first place" mentality; too often winning gets emphasized more than the value placed on learning. Our culture's preoccupation with competition extends to some parents in training who compete with each other to be the "better parent."[21]

Partially, this competitive dilemma exists because our families and our schools are not working on the angle of finding and promoting *each* learner's unique potential. "Education in the United States has long given lip service to the development of individual potential and a concern for equity, but attention has focused primarily on the preparation of future workers."[22] The focus on winning workers takes a higher priority than that of cooperative teams of workers in our society. Children who are not at the top of their class notice a competitive pecking order even in elementary school. This causes them to lose confidence in themselves.

Many studies document that significant declines in girls' self-confidence occur as the girls move into puberty. On average, 69 percent of elementary-age boys and 60 percent of elementary-age girls report being "happy the way I am." The figures of self-acceptance in high school are alarming for both sexes, but especially for girls: 46 percent of adolescent boys are "happy the way I am," while only 29 percent of girls register this basic acceptance of themselves.[23] How many mothers still have such a lack of self-acceptance?

Many girls carry embarrassment, often a signal of their low self-esteem, through years of their lives. Journalist Peggy Orenstein documents how such *lost* girls attempt to navigate childhood and adolescence. When these girls cannot command a strong sense of self-territory, they sometimes resort to hopelessness and acts of self-destruction. Sexual harassment nips at the heels of many of these girls and further creates a hostile learning environment.[24] Early motherhood can delay ability pursuits for some. Others jolt themselves into pursuing their own advanced education only once they become mothers and can sense the power they can have in their own lives.[25] One young mother attests to the difficulty of her adolescence in this manner: "I'm so glad I'm on the other side of seventeen!"

Boys also have ability challenges. They often have few male models in elementary school, where the teachers are predominantly female. Family counselors Don and Jeanne Elium tell how frequently boys are criticized for behaviors that seem aggressive, inattentive, and/or unruly.[26] Psychologists Dan Kindlon and Michael Thompson suggest that many parents and teachers do not understand that boys' anger has its roots in fears. Early schooling focuses on reading, writing, and verbal ability—all skills that frequently develop more slowly in boys than in girls.[27] Many boys also struggle for self-respect, and their impulsive acts largely reflect emotions they cannot name.

Some boys simply get *lost* in educational cages. More than two-thirds of all students in special-education programs are male, in spite of research on learning disabilities showing more equal numbers of both boys and girls. Girls who sit quietly in their classrooms frequently get ignored, but active boys who are disruptive sometimes get placed in special programs that do not truly meet their needs.[28] Wielding incredible energy that does not find positive outlets, such boys career from one sort of trouble to the next in school. Recess provides some welcome time for movement, but the rest of the school day registers as tedious and slow. Too many students become known by their disability cage, as in, "She's developmentally delayed," or "He's behavior disordered," rather than known for their abilities. Why do we pay more attention to youth weaknesses than strengths?

SCHOOL LABELS FOR LEARNING CHALLENGES

Our current educational labeling system helps to identify some troubled learners and provide them with needed support. However, the labeling and identification processes in our schools are different state to state, and sometimes even the labeling differs across school districts within the same state, which makes "learning disabilities" a subjective label.[29] Labels do not cure.

Lumping children together under the "learning disabilities" umbrella rarely defines any particular teaching strategy, because individual learners are a diverse lot. In general, the term "learning disabilities" (LD) refers to difficulties in acquiring and using listening, speaking, writing, reasoning, or mathematical abilities that are assumed to relate to central nervous system differences within a child. "LD is a broad term that covers a pool of possible causes, symptoms, treatments, and outcomes. Partly because learning disabilities can show up in so many forms, it is difficult to diagnose or to pinpoint the causes. And no one knows of a . . . remedy that will cure them."[30] Social or self-regulatory concerns in a child are not a specific learning disability but can accompany children labeled as learning disabled.[31]

Many LD-labeled youth have no understanding about the "hidden curriculum" cues of school—how certain clothes can draw negative attention, how the lunchtime culture has rules, and how the classroom has unstated norms. For students with nonverbal learning disabilities, social interactions around these topics "are tested . . . hundreds of times each day."[32] When deficits exist in attending, prioritizing, sequencing, goal-setting, and overall problem solving, the challenged learner faces an agenda that makes learning any particular subject much more demanding than it would appear to the casual observer. These same deficits affect belonging interactions, so it is little wonder that school for some students takes inordinate energy. Children with a combination of learning differences and social differences face many challenges in competitive schools.

Many children do not understand the amount of work needed in order to be successful in school. All students learn best when *connections* exist between their studies and their interests. The best efforts caring parents and teachers can make for *each* unique, individual learner in school are as follows: understand a child's learning *strengths*, provide a combination of class and individualized instruction (from a specialist, teacher's assistant, tutor, coach, music teacher, or caretaker), and offer a scheduled evaluation system for some. However, knowing what helps a child's academic progress does not equal the task of making it happen. Even the parent who understands the complicated ability and belonging picture for a child with learning differences may have a difficult time implementing a supportive school/extracurricular program.

ATTENTION-DEFICIT HYPERACTIVITY AND READING CHALLENGES

Owen (13) and Evelyn (45)

Evelyn's concerns about her son's academic status are justified. Diagnosed as ADHD or attention-deficit hyperactivity disordered, Owen already has a medicine chest of medications to help counter the effects of his short attention span. One medication produces elevated liver enzymes, another generates severe depression and confusion, and a third causes insomnia and loss of appetite. A reading challenge further impacts Owen's schoolwork success.

Evelyn calls her son's school frequently in the beginning of the school year to make sure Owen is off to a good start. She requests teacher reports of Owen's progress. But by the third week, Evelyn finds out that Owen already has failing grades in English and science classes. She inquires about the school providing books on tape, as requested in his educational plan, but none of his teachers appear aware that Owen was supposed to receive them. Meanwhile, Owen is suspended from school for punching another boy who called him "gay." In-school suspensions become a frequent occurrence for Owen due to his repeated tardiness and missing homework assignments.

We discuss a typical school day while Owen draws his personality roles and self-symbol. He reports that all classes are boring, but he likes football. He enjoys being able to "hit people" and "get away with it." He reminisces about fifth grade; when he started "not to follow any rules." He describes how he "blows off" his homework and how his mother then "takes things away from him." He initially shrugs when I ask if this discipline system works, and then he looks up briefly from his drawing: "Nah." Owen finishes an intricate sketch. Fear and anger punctuate his depiction of his self-symbol, which is cloaked in armor, rather than being any particular recognition of a wise self that can transcend everyday scrimmages. He has yet to make the acquaintance with self-territory. With his foreboding identity of power and fear, I imagine Owen setting off to school each day, like a knight in heavy head-to-toe armor, who needs to slay a few dragons before first period begins.

DEVELOPMENT DIRECTIONS

Boys are driven by psychological self-protection. . . . Much of their energy is devoted to sustaining their defensive perimeter, seeing threats where they don't exist and staging preemptive strikes against any feared incursions into their fortress of solitude.

—Dan Kindlon and Michael Thompson, psychologists, *Raising Cain*

Schools are busy places. Following up on educational plans falls into a caretaker's lap. Parents in training are the most invested people in a child's learning struggles. Having an ongoing way of communicating with school staff ensures that all involved are focused on a child's potential. Some youth benefit from individual or small group help with their homework. Many caring teachers extend their workday to meet with challenged learners. However, early teens have so many belonging needs on their minds that they frequently do not tune in to their ability needs. The caretaker's job relies upon helping their adolescent discover *something* of interest that they can energetically pursue with their seemingly boundless energy levels. For many, athletic, musical, and artistic endeavors are vital to the talent search.

Tip for Raising Thirteen-Year-Olds

Early teens often enjoy teaching something to younger children; find opportunities for your teen to be a coach's helper or other helper at community events. "I was in a session with [child psychologist] Dr. Ginott and heard him say something about treating our children, not as they are, by as we hoped they would become. That thought revolutionized my thinking. It freed me to look at my boys with new eyes. What did I hope them to become?"[33]

Tip for Raising Forty-Five-Year-Olds

When your child has ability pain, it seems to radiate to other limbs of the family tree; focus on how you handle your own ability challenges. "Do your family members bottle up their feelings and pretend everything is fine even when they're seething inside? Or do they have ways of communicating and resolving conflicts that are not abusive to themselves or others? Which do you find yourself doing?"[34]

LEARNING DIFFERENCES

For the parent in training who shares the same learning challenges as his or her child due to genetic influences or a lack of academic opportunities, backlogged memories in his or her personality story-house may interfere with effectively processing any of the child's academic difficulties. All this parent sees relates to weaknesses—his or her own, the child's deficits, and perhaps the school's lack of responsiveness to particular learning differences. Other parents simply cannot grasp how confusing the school day appears to their child who is a challenged learner. Caretakers may wonder about their child's complaints of frequent stomachaches or other bodily symptoms, but they do not necessarily *connect* these signals with experiencing learning differences.

Danny (9)

"Dear Therepest [therapist], I swich [switch] for math." Danny hands me this note shortly after I come to observe him in his classroom. With a hooded sweatshirt over his head, he resembles a tiny medieval monk as he bends over his seatwork. Minutes later, Danny abruptly exits the classroom. His teacher does not notice him coming or going because she has a group of students surrounding her desk. Upon returning to class five minutes later, Danny begins cleaning out his desk, which is stuffed with so many papers that it seems as if he kept last year's assignments there, along with those from the current year. As soon as Danny peruses one paper, he shoves it back into the desk. He continues shuffling the contents of his desk until his teacher catches his actions with a sideways glance: "Whatever it is that you are doing, put your papers in your desk."

Danny complies with this request immediately, adding the contents from his desktop, including a paper for the current class assignment. He sits and awaits further direction. In a twenty-five-minute class segment, Danny "works" approximately five minutes. Later, I ask the teacher if this day represented a typical language-arts class in terms of Danny's meager academic efforts; the teacher sighs. Danny seldom finishes *any* task he begins. I follow Danny to his math class, hoping for a more productive class experience.

As the children file into math class, the teacher announces, "Mix it up! Don't sit where you sat yesterday!" Danny appears to hang back, not choosing a seat until nearly everyone else slides into place. "Homework up!" fires the teacher in a commanding voice. Everyone except Danny waves a math paper high overhead. His teacher glances in his direction but does not say anything. Danny fumbles with a whole fistful of papers he produces from his math book, and he finally flies one of them triumphantly in the air. "Hold up your red pen!" More hands wave their red pens like flags at a Fourth of July parade. Danny launches his pen aloft nearly as fast as the rest, while one girl crawls on the floor looking for her lost pen. Many eyes drop to floor level, carrying with them some fluttering papers and pens. "Everything should still be in the air!" With all arms flying again, the whole room looks like it might lift off into space.

The math teacher begins by reviewing the first math question on the day's homework assignment: "One-fourth and two-eighths . . . are they equivalent? And do you know why it would be a travesty if you didn't spell 'equivalent' right?" There are no responses except for the rustling of papers. Every desktop now sports only two items, a math-homework page and a red pen. The unspoken rule about a tidy desktop seems clear to every student. Danny bites his lip. He no longer has his sweatshirt hood covering his head. He squirms in his seat. The teacher continues: "Is 'equal' a wrong response? . . . I am going to accept it, but I would prefer 'equivalent.'" Silently, I wonder what will happen if Danny's spelling issues prevent him from putting down the correct word, "equivalent," in this math class. Fortunately, Danny figures out a clever solution to this possible snafu. He saves himself from spelling embarrassment in math class, avoiding the "equal"-versus-"equivalent" spelling travesty altogether by listing his answers as "=" or "not =." Ability winks its eye.

DEVELOPMENT DIRECTIONS

Virtually everyone has a learning disability in something, but society chooses to recognize only some individuals with the learning disability label.

—Robert J. Sternberg and Elena Grigorenko,
psychologists, *Our Labeled Children*

All teachers need to have discipline, or a few rules, to structure a class. Some students require additional caretaking to get their assignments rolling during a class period. If you perceive that your child needs help at school, speak to the teacher(s) about what "works" at home. Some children respond better to class directions that have been written on the blackboard; they are not always attentive to spoken or auditory directions. If you do not have a workable homework process, create homework discipline. Simple structures can help a child begin a task. The most important learning structure involves having your child know what *to do*. Many students focus on homework by keeping assignment notebooks, where they write down daily homework directions. However, the challenged student may forget to take the assignment notebook to or from school each day. E-mails between teachers and parents are another way for dispensing homework directions, although sending these messages to parents removes responsibility from the student.

Tip for Raising Nine-Year-Olds

As school assignments become more difficult, many children can benefit from a partnership in learning. "Within every family unit, a boy should feel there is at least one mentor upon whom he can count. At school, ideally every boy should know that he has at least one such person upon whom he can regularly rely."[35]

TRAUMA BLOCKS LEARNING

Children react and respond in unique ways to their learning differences. Many children suffer silently in their classrooms. Other students are noisy, perhaps in attempts to distract teachers from their learning challenges. One rebellious teen assumed that apathy was the only path to take; he thought that every teacher was "against" him: "My mom quit school, and my dad was a troublemaker. So when my teachers would ask about my name, I knew what they were getting at." Other students fail to achieve at school because some trauma provides another obstacle to the learning process.

Many unforeseen events can cause trauma in children; for example, accidents and falls, medical or surgical procedures, violent acts and attacks, grief and loss, and environmental disasters such as hurricanes or fires all have the possibility of eliciting trauma in a child.[36] Traumatized youngsters often restrict their ability potential because they replay trauma lessons over and over in their minds.[37]

Steven (5)

> Steven announces to me that in his school "you have so many learning goals! It's like infinity—it never ends!" When I inquire about what learning goal this eager scholar is pursuing currently, he gushes, "Frogs! I love frogs!" He dazzles me with his frog data. However, within minutes, the brightness dims on his tiny face, and he takes on a different, somber pose, one of intense sadness. I mirror the look on his face and marvel at the rapidity of his chameleonlike change in his personality. Steven brings up the tragedy of the Columbia space shuttle dissolving into thin air: "It is bad for the astronauts—they died. I can't figure out what happened. I usually figure things out,

but you need a science dictionary for this one." I validate Steven's sadness over the shuttle crash. We share a few silent moments and a few deep breaths. Then I ask this perceptive boy if he would like to have a job someday figuring out space questions. He beams. "Yes! I could be a scientist!" I tell him that he already can call himself a "frog scientist." He shakes his head affirmatively and returns to his tadpole ability tales.

DEVELOPMENT DIRECTIONS

> Optimism is the faith that leads to achievement.
>
> —Helen Keller, advocate for the deaf, blind, and mute

Children often show an amazing amount of empathy for events in the world. We mistakenly assume that their youth prevents them from seeing or hearing about so-called adult problems. All children (and adults) need permission for the expression of grief. Our culture tends to blanket grieving with pillows of denial; taking pills, keeping busy, and ignoring losses are commonplace. However, children are not as adept as adults at denial. If someone can *listen* to them one interaction at a time, they will frequently bring up the losses in their experience. Some of their impressions of death and loss show both their creativity and ability levels. Having someone hear their pain, acknowledge the truth of the loss, and show compassion for their grieving sends a message to children that life's transitions are meaningful.

Tip for Raising Five-Year-Olds

Children's ability levels are sidetracked by all kinds of issues, but various losses can consume a great deal of thinking time. "Early on, children pick up whether it is okay to express their feelings, or whether some feelings are fine while other feelings are not acceptable. . . . It is common for children to fear that all of their close relationships are in jeopardy when . . . a person or pet dies."[38]

UNRESOLVED TRAUMA

Trauma often leads to another type of apathy abyss. **When stressful situations are not acknowledged in childhood, the trauma can fester and erupt at some later date.** For example, unresolved crises in childhood may lead some youngsters to drop out of school. Many students drop out of school as a way to cover up the fact that their academic progress does not measure up to parental standards. These children drop out before considering how ill prepared they are to meet the demands of the job world. Furthermore, teens leaving high school precipitously are at risk for using alcohol and drugs, carrying weapons, thinking suicidal thoughts, and engaging in sexual activity.[39]

Some students drop out of school for an entirely different reason: because they have been put in jail. Taking a closer look at jailed youth, we find that as many as eight out of ten jailed juveniles have the additional trauma of learning disabilities.[40] Some of these students drop out too because they have experienced the trauma of school retention. An eight-year study on retention in the Chicago Public Schools shows that 78 percent of eighth graders who repeat the grade ultimately drop out of school. Records of students retained in third grade show no greater academic gain than those third graders who have been allowed to pass without meeting school standards. In spite of such research, the decision about promoting a child to the next grade rests solely upon standardized test scores in nineteen states.[41]

What are the adult expectations that land upon the youth who have been held back? Do the adults *expect* excellence from them during their second year in the same grade? Or is it as researcher Susan Stone found: students simply disengage from academics because they go over the same material time and time again.[42] Likely, the student considered for retention needs someone to pay attention *one interaction at a time*, both at home and school.

As shareholders in the process of education, children need involvement in their learning. Psychologist Howard Gardner terms the routine, repetitive teaching that occurs in many schools as a "drill-and-kill" curriculum that tends to "dull [the] perceptions" of the learner.[43] When students cannot *connect* with the learning process, they often do not feel that their teachers care. Many students do not feel positive about school because they do not feel "liked" by their teachers or school community.[44] Yet the emotional well-being of students frequently gets taken for granted. Often, the adult assumption is that learning is simple: "Just do your homework," expresses one tired parent, "and then you will be done." Hopefully, our children are never "done" with meeting their ability needs.

EDUCATION IN LAST PLACE

When nearly one out of three public high school students fails to graduate,[45] we are experiencing an educational crisis in America. Where do we place the value of education among our culture's values? We pay attention to strengths in sports. Students often are labeled in terms of athletic prowess rather than academic ability: "She's a runner," or "He's a basketball player." For some students, sports motivate them to learn, as they must maintain a certain grade point average to stay on a team. Many athletes report on liking "to be busy" and say they use their time better when they are involved with their sport.

For other youth, their athletic participation brings out their parents' childhood issues. Some struggle under critical and explosive parent personality roles, when parents forget that their best way to support a child athlete is from the sidelines with praise for good effort. Yet other students believe that their sport equals schooling. They only enjoy the athletic portion of their day and the camaraderie it brings; they find nothing else redeeming during the school day. Why does athletic success and a winning school team rate higher than academic achievement? Many pages and pictures in our local newspapers are devoted to student athletic success; minimal pages and only the occasional picture appear about academically and artistically talented students. After all, we pay athletes higher salaries than most others at the top of their professional game.

Judy (14), Loretta (41), and Kenny (44)

> Judy's freshman year of high school begins with intoxication. After Judy comes home drunk several times, Loretta and Kenny come to family therapy. Judy begins her first session by stating she wants to be "independent." She also wants her parents to refrain from grabbing and physically shaking her in their discipline efforts. However,

Judy admits that she lied to her parents "because it is the only way I can go out to do things with my friends."

Loretta and Kenny demand to know who these friends are, but Judy does not want to tell her parents about her friends' situations—she fears they would tell her she cannot hang out with them. For example, one friend has four siblings, and each child has a different father. She also cannot tell them that she has a kissing roster on which she lists sixty-two boys. When she proclaims that she is "everybody's psychologist" in her peer group, I wonder if kissing is her preferred treatment approach.

Judy begins a fragile adolescent alliance with her parents by promising to be truthful for one week in exchange for Loretta's and Kenny's agreement to "listen to what I have to say" without grabbing onto her. Yet her progress stumbles as the weeks go by. Because Judy swims on a team, she declares that she has no time for homework. Smart enough to "get by," Judy maintains high-enough grades to continue swimming—until she is suspended for smoking at school. She rails at her mother for chiding her, because Loretta smokes also. Meanwhile, Judy tells of arguments with her father where he calls her "a bitch," and we uncover where her own "bitch" name-calling originates.

Judy drifts into a long saga of boyfriend woes. She finds "bad boys." On a map of her personality, Judy identifies a tomboy/bitch role as the part of her that is attracted to these boys. Judy believes "everybody at high school is doing drugs" and admits that her "crazy" role enjoys a "buzz." In terms of her girlfriends, one friend who has intercourse with a new boyfriend believes she is pregnant. Judy and her friendship gang pledge that they will help care for the baby. Another friend runs away from home. Then Judy attends a weekend antidrug program at school and meets a whole new set of friends. The very next weekend, though, she sees the student leaders of this antidrug program get drunk at a party. She confesses that she is thinking of trying "acid," or LSD.

Judy choses Darnell as her new boyfriend. He is an eighteen-year-old school dropout. Judy identifies with Darnell because she has been kicked off the swim team and Darnell was suspended for fighting. She likes Darnell "because he listens to me." However, Darnell does not always listen, and he has a quick temper like Judy. The contentious young couple finds more fights than fun in their relationship. Judy breaks curfew to spend time with Darnell. After Loretta and Kenny tell her that she will be grounded for the rest of the year,

Judy sneaks out of the house to be with Darnell. When Judy comes home after fighting with Darnell one evening, a time in which she barely escaped a physical altercation, she almost gets into a physical battle with her father. She calls a friend, who in turn calls the police. No homework happens this night.

DEVELOPMENT DIRECTIONS

The consequences of the sexualization of girls in media today are very real and likely to be a negative influence on girls' healthy development. . . . We need to replace these sexualized images with ones showing . . . the uniqueness and competence of girls.

—Eileen L. Zurbriggen, psychologist, APA Task Force on the Sexualization of Girls

Parents in training cannot "shake" sense into a teen or screen a child's friendships through verbal warnings. Like the infamous Romeo and Juliet, youth somehow can find the "forbidden" lover. Belonging needs cannot be ignored in adolescence. Handle them, though, through focusing on *values dialogues* about what makes a person a candidate for a close friendship. This approach has the most likely chance of making an impact. Every child deserves a chance to meet their basic needs. School staff cannot afford to place a student's ability potential in "last place" by kicking them off teams, giving them extended suspensions, or expelling them.

Tip for Raising Fourteen-Year-Olds

Discussing moral dilemmas that surface in movies, TV, and news helps provide teens with a forum to consider which values they should live by. "The early teen years are truly as gray as it gets. Barely out of that pollywog stage, girls are very fuzzy about what they think and feel and want and need, and so are their parents. . . . Friends are still as important as oxygen . . . but somehow, the thought is emerging for the early teen that it is time to grow up—somewhat, some days."[46]

Tip for Raising Forty-One-Year-Olds

As your child grows *up*, you also grow *up*. Consider your own values and how you really want to live the rest of your life. "It is no simple task to live your own life. It is far easier to pack your schedule so tight with busy, productive activities that you do not have to confront the feeling of emptiness you hold inside."[47]

Tip for Raising Forty-Four-Year-Olds

Children, especially teenagers, often challenge the ideas and ideals of their caretakers. It takes many deep breaths to hold onto your temper when your child rebels. "Men are used to loving from a position of strength, yet children lead us into a new kind of vulnerability: how to be emotionally close and responsive. . . . Fatherhood is a confusing swirl of feelings, of love and hate . . . wanting to spend private time at home and wanting to . . . be a public success."[48]

CONNECT HOME AND SCHOOL

When parenting advocates Charlene Giannetti and Margaret Sagarese asked teachers in a survey to list the problem situations their students faced, the response "in with bad crowd" headed up the teachers' concerns. Two-thirds of the teachers rated a negative peer group as more of a problem than drugs, major depression, or violent behavior.[49] I am concerned about the label "bad crowd," though, as the adolescents who qualify as "bad" are just as much entitled to discover their energy, discipline, creativity, belonging, and ability needs as those who might qualify as "good." **Caretakers and educators need to mentor fragile youth, not label them negatively or ban them from public schooling. What values do we follow when we prohibit our youth from attending school?**

Project Spectrum, a ten-year research collaboration, focuses on alternative curriculum methods that respect the diverse interests and abilities of youngsters in preschool and elementary school. Key findings of the project maintain that a child learns best through repeated contact with engaging or creative materials and that persistence pays off in learning.[50] Project Spectrum embraces psychologist Howard Gardner's concept of "multiple intelligences." Gardner defines intelligence as the ability to "solve problems or fashion products that are valued in one or more cultural settings."[51] He suggested that all normal individuals are capable of at least eight forms of intellectual accomplishment: linguistic (verbal) and logical-mathematical abilities; musical abilities; spatial abilities; bodily-kinesthetic talents (using one's whole body, as in dance and sports); intrapersonal and interpersonal skills (understanding oneself and others); and naturalistic abilities (keen interest in the natural world). A ninth intelligence, existential intelligence, relates to one's ability to grapple with meaning in life and death.

Gardner asserted that while everyone has *all* of these intelligences, no two people (not even identical twins) show exactly the same combination of strengths.[52] What is similar across children though, is the finding that when youngsters recognize they are good at something and their skill receives validation from others, they can reach their ability levels and experience achievement success.[53] Such talented teens connect with teachers who are supportive, and they model their enjoyment in a particular academic subject. These excellent students tend to spend more time with their families and have more one-to-one contact with their parents than average teenagers.[54] What is sad but true, though, is that some people go through a significant portion of their lives before they feel like they have *any* recognized strong area of intellectual prowess.

Psychologist Deborah Stipek advocates making real-life connections in learning to increase a child's academic motivation.[55] Caretakers can make these valuable connections between a child's homework and everyday life when they link learning assignments and life experiences. For example, when one sixth grader had a project to study some aspect of Great Britain's economy, her caring parents steered her to look at the fashion economy, because they knew that fashion held her interest at that time. Mom, Dad, and daughter all discussed the economic history of trench coats and miniskirts. When another student studied a foreign language, his supportive mom looked for real-world opportunities to make use of that language, such as through reading books, watching movies, visiting museums, and even traveling to vacation destinations.

IN THE ABILITY "FLOW"

Creativity researcher Mihaly Csikszentmihalyi and educators Kevin Ra-thunde and Samuel Whalen studied talented youth to determine what made it possible for them to use their ability to achieve well. They gathered more than seven thousand self-reports of achieving adolescents' everyday experiences. The reports came in the form of journal entries, which students were triggered to write by random signals from electronic beepers they wore. They found that high school students' motivation for excellence blossomed when they *enjoyed* learning tasks. When students could immerse themselves in learning, they lost track of time and ignored other distractions, focusing on the activity at hand.[56] This "flow"[57] expression of talent occurs when students receive clearly stated goals followed by "immediate and unambiguous feedback" regarding their actions. Since specific goal setting and feedback happen fairly frequently in sports, music, and other artistic endeavors, these activities feed into "flow" experiences quite easily.

A secondary feature of "flow" of talent relates to the depth of involvement of the student. Motivated students seek greater challenges.[58] Underlying these students' desires for reaching their ability potential are supportive family members and teachers. Supportive families and schools furnish "information . . . encouragement . . . and discipline, or the set of habits that allows a person to study and concentrate."[59] **When parents experience their own sense of "flow," or passion for a certain topic, they model this zest for living to their young, assigning learning as a prominent value in the home.**

HOMEWORK HELPER

One of parents' most frequently mentioned problems regarding children's schooling revolves around the issue of homework procrastination. But the term "procrastination" does not describe just one kind of behavior. Some perfectionist students procrastinate because they worry that they cannot produce good-enough work, although there are other reasons for dawdling. Consider psychologist Linda Sapadin's six styles of procrastination: perfectionist, dreamer, worrier, defier, crisis maker, and overdoer.[60] Some children who put off homework assignments do so because they have a very large worried role in their personality. Usually, these worries are about legitimate problems, such as being worried about teasing.

Some youth cannot tackle their homework due to agitated thinking, as if they perceive themselves in a crisis. They place so many roadblocks in their ability path that they increase the initial crisis by geometric proportions. **Missing two assignments soon doubles to missing four; as the procrastination continues, the child becomes more overwhelmed.** Yet others constantly overwork themselves; they do twice as much work on assignments as called for by their teacher, until at some point they cannot keep up.

One nine-year-old girl procrastinated because she valued her after-school time for carrying out her many creative ideas. In her case, traditional "drill-and-kill" worksheets seemed counterproductive; her imagination stimulated her to use her free time in a different way. Caretakers can provide appropriate help for such a child when they engage in a values dialogue with their child about their school day and homework. Working as partners with a child's teachers also sets action plans. Parents can work with teachers to ensure homework assignments have a creative flair, although this approach takes time and energy on the part of the homework helper.

Still, many teachers on their own, now give pupils choices about book reports. Instead of traditional reports that cover a book's plot, characters, and themes, innovative options are offered. The student can dress up as a character from a book and pose the story as that character sees it. Students with good verbal skills might create an advertisement for a book and then "sell" the book to the class. Other students can make a diorama or present a brief one-person play of the book's highlights. Many children engage in hours of work when they are the proud "stage manager" of their own production. One father reported his amazement when his twelve-year-old daughter put sixteen hours of concentrated time into a school project; he claimed that the lawyers in his office did not work as diligently as his daughter did while working on her chosen project.

PROCRASTINATION HABIT

Kiara (10) and Nan (35)

Kiara often feels overwhelmed by homework. Nan admits that she too feels overwhelmed by the amount of homework her daughter brings to the kitchen table on school nights. While Kiara appears motivated to go to school on a daily basis, she wilts when she comes in the door after school. All she wants to do on school days is flop onto the sofa in front of the TV. She then claims that she never can finish all of her homework. Kiara's lack of energy, which is connected to a loss of sleep and late nights, exacerbates her homework complaining. Nan confesses that she is also a procrastinator at her job. Both mother and daughter alternate between procrastinator roles and guilty roles.

Kiara portrays a tiny figure drawing in the upper left corner of a piece of paper when I ask her to draw a person. The figure has an oversized head with large, frightened-looking eyes and a tiny open mouth. The too-small body shows short stick arms with no hands. The figure's legs are spread out in a wide-open stance; the top-heavy figure looks as if it will topple over because it is drawn on a slant. Jagged grass appears as a slippery base. A large question mark hovers over the figure's right ear. After some reflection, Kiara erases the question mark.

She begins her accompanying story tentatively: "I'm not sure . . . kind of reminds me of, well, I don't know . . . a younger person . . . I don't know . . . maybe eight years old. She's . . . I don't know . . . a new kid . . . um . . . she likes to . . . I don't know . . . sometimes she gets lost in the school because it is so big. Well, she looks in every room to see if any of her classmates are in it, and she passes her room. And she was late for this class with a really strict teacher about being late. She was forty-five minutes late and now there were only five minutes left in the class. . . . She sneaked to her desk. Her teacher paused from her teaching and noticed her. When asked for a lesson to the story, Kiara just shrugged her shoulders. Her face seemed to hold onto the erased question mark from her drawing.

DEVELOPMENT DIRECTIONS

> The events of childhood do not pass, but repeat themselves like
> seasons of the year.
>
> —Eleanor Farjeon

The procrastination abyss that can develop around homework describes
many households. We address energy and discipline needs first, but
Kiara has unmet ability needs that weigh upon her small shoulders.
Children can worry just as much as adults about a myriad of needs.
Many of their insecure roles relate to unmet belonging needs. Fitting in
socially often occupies more *space* in a child's mind in the upper elementary grades than fitting in academically. Kiara's procrastination
pose stems from worry; her creativity seems missing. She stores up fear,
is an indecisive thinker, and requires help in finding *self-territory* in
order for her to use her academic abilities.

Tip for Raising Ten-Year-Olds

Hobbies and chores actually help with establishing solid homework
rules. Getting used to spending time in chores can set the stage for
good homework habits. "Chores develop a sense of responsibility. Start
in preschool years . . . [putting dirty clothes in the laundry basket] . . .
Chores foster skill development . . . a sense of accomplishment . . . [a]
feeling of pride."[61]

Tip for Raising Thirty-Five-Year-Olds

Take some deep breaths and find the space to have presence for one
interaction at a time with your child. "The next time you go into overdrive, just stop . . . think about it, there are two hundred eighty-eight
five-minute segments in a day, two thousand sixteen in a week, and if
you are thirty-five years old, over three and a half million have passed
by already . . . taking an infinitesimal fraction of your life to try something different is not going to be the thing that finally does you in. And
it could open up a whole new world of possibilities."[62]

VALUING HOMEWORK

Parents help enforce a learning value by helping children to have good homework habits. Setting up a student "home office" space makes a student's work seem important to family life. Children, however, do not need a special room for their home office, although if they are in high school they may need private space for their several hours of homework each day. Many children do their homework at the kitchen or dining-room table. If this practice works well for your child, have a pencil cup of sharpened pencils and any other supplies needed for daily assignments handy at the table. This signals the importance of homework.

Some children need parental help with assignments, but sometimes parents feel energy strapped about spending *any* time doing homework with their child. Other parents in training do too much for their child (one parent routinely writes the book reports for her middle school child). Whose needs are met by parents taking on a child's school assignments? Psychologist Sylvia Rimm suggests that parents should not sit with a child nightly to pore over homework, but they should have children try working on their own initially. She counsels that the average child needs to review a problem three times before asking for help.[63]

America is a country of individuals, and as such, how we handle homework as a family varies from household to household and person to person. Some families set times aside each evening for homework. Other families have so many evening activities, both for children and parents, that adhering to a specific homework schedule cannot work. Some students need a short break after school before beginning homework; others like getting their homework out of the way so that the rest of their evening is free. Some early elementary-age youth require caretaker help on a consistent basis; they wait to start assignments until their parents come home from work. Many older children can handle homework on their own, and they work out their own nightly schedules.

However, the Brookings Institution, a Washington, D.C., nonprofit organization, found that the number of students spending more than one hour per evening doing homework has dwindled over the last two decades. Only about one-third of seventeen-year-olds in the United States spend an hour or more a day on homework. Another study found that U.S. high school students have one of the lightest homework loads in the world! Of twenty countries studied, the U.S. students tied for next-to-last place.[64] What values do American families place upon homework? What meaning does homework have in encouraging us to *connect* with our ability?

INSTILLING A LOVE OF LEARNING

The best learning happens in schools and families because of (1) an underlying love of learning, (2) the value placed on the search for underlying meanings, and (3) the value of sharing that learning with others. Many parents erroneously center most of their motivational efforts upon a system of rewards and/or punishments to obtain a child's compliance in schoolwork. But it is through praising a child's efforts and the use of new, innovative strategies and ideas that a child tends to work harder and try more problem solving techniques.

Children whose mothers encourage them to problem solve independently have been shown to be academically more successful than children receiving either rewards or punishment for doing homework and getting good grades.[65] There are several key ingredients in the love of learning "recipe." Children need to feel capable and confident that their abilities can increase as they develop competence, they need a sense of some autonomy or choice in what they are learning, and they need to feel loved and respected by their parent(s).[66] One-interaction-at-a-time relating shows such love and respect. Because a caretaker's role in advancing a child's learning rests upon helping the youngster connect new situations to more familiar ones, every situation holds learning possibilities.[67]

ABILITY TRAINERS

In general, my advice is that caretakers take on a trainer pose. Do not assume your child cannot measure up to the task at hand. However, if your child needs so much help that you feel overwhelmed, it is time for a conference with the teacher. How many school conferences are needed each school year depends entirely on the individual student, but many parents wait too long before contacting their child's teacher. It is helpful to check in with your child's teachers at the beginning of each semester to get the best measure of their ability expectations.

Caring parents are constantly training, helping a child create a personality story-house of adaptive and efficient learning. **Much learning for children takes place outside of the school classroom.** Ideally parents in training provide the time and space for their offspring to enjoy many valuable nonacademic experiences, such as music lessons, athletic opportunities, and community volunteer activities. Furthermore, researchers suggest that positive out-of-school experiences have a beneficial effect upon a student's ability in school.[68] Children's upbeat feelings about their achievement in extracurricular sports, music, art, or other endeavors spurs on their own expectations for success in academics. Again, some of these valuable, teachable moments are nonverbal; a child discovers much learning by watching adults *do* something. Yet parents often are unaware of the power of their training until some poignant moment occurs and they see their child's eyes focused squarely on them.

ABILITY MAPPING

The Chinese word for "learning" means "to study and practice constantly." Within this ancient wisdom, the Chinese must assume that everyone knows how to *begin* this process of ongoing training. However, the beginnings of any project can daunt us, especially if we have no experience in the subject area. We cannot assume that our children know how to begin a new task when we have difficulty with our own adult beginnings.

- **What do you wish to learn at this stage of your life? Choose one topic for a beginning learning focus.** Think of all the ways you might approach this topic; jot down salient ideas as they come to you.
- Gather information on three or four of the most important ideas.
- *Gulp!* I would say *breathe* some deep breaths, but sometimes it feels more like an initial "gulp" to me. Remember taking it *one interaction at a time?* Now's the chance for you to practice a *beginning* to something *you* want to learn about or do in your life.

Move out of your comfort zone of doing what you always do, and take your first step toward mastering new learning. Now, take long, deep breaths. Breathe into any parts of your body where you feel nervous or anxious. Everyone has poses of the jitters when beginning something new. Remember how Einstein perceived his own learning process: "I grope."

- Consider something your child needs to learn that requires a *beginning* move. Do you have more empathy for your child now that you are in the same position of trying out your learning wings in a new flight pattern?

- Share your winning techniques of starting something new with your child. Ask what helps your child in taking the first steps for new learning. Be start-up partners by supporting each other's efforts. Children have the mistaken idea that everything "comes easy" to adults. They do not understand that adults struggle just as much as children when they encounter something new.

Too often both adults and children wrestle with transitions in silence, thinking they must have some defect or crisis in their personality. There are two Chinese characters for the word "crisis." One character means "danger," which we often feel when we experience change in our lives. The second character means "opportunity." We can model our new beginnings for our children as **creative** opportunities.

Part III

Modeling How to Relate One Interaction at a Time

8

YOU CAN MAP YOUR PERSONALITY

The visions that we present to our children shape the future. They become self-fulfilling prophecies. Dreams are maps.

— Carl Sagan, astronomer and biologist

Native Americans considered life as a journey with the goal of discovering wisdom and a *connection* to all of life; for example, every Zuni has a life road, or "breathway." The Navajo call life's road trip the Pollen Path; the Sioux travel the Good Red Road.[1] Yet discovering the *territory* of *self* may seem to you like taking a distant journey, like what faced army captains Meriwether Lewis and William Clark as they set off to map the unknown West. To make sense of their journey, Clark took a crude map drawn by Blackfeet chief Ac ko mok ki; it was the only written guide available for their odyssey. Along the way, however, he meticulously recorded their routes, combining his observations with the Blackfeet map to create a composite guide to the region. Clark's notes led to eventual maps of the entire territory.[2]

Maps help orient us when we feel lost. Road maps point us in a particular direction for our car journeys. Similarly, we can orient our parenting routes with a map of our personality for both ourselves and our children (if we discover self-territory for ourselves, then we can help each of our children find self-territory). Sometimes, though, children are the ones in the family to lead caretakers in the direction of self-territory. While children may flit from subject to subject, from one activity to the next, often they are very involved in both their actions and words in the present moment; they frequently help raise our capability to be in the present moment with them.

In the words of psychologist Daniel Stern, "Present moments are unbelievably rich. Much happens, even though they last only a short time. . . . The feeling of presentness seems . . . to require a sense of self."[3] Stern elaborates on a time frame for present moments; he notes the constantly changing world of our daily existence and views our here-and-now moments as occurring from several seconds to ten seconds in duration.[4] Philosopher Alfred North Whitehead discusses such micromoments in even smaller segments than Stern. He considers one "specious present" as consisting, on average, of one-twentieth of a second, although there may exist even shorter time estimates for the atomic level![5] All of us have experienced these poignant moments either when we grasped something in the present or held another person's gaze and felt that there was a special connection.

PRESENT INTERACTIONS

Whatever the clock says about present micromoments, we experience our present *family* moments in movie fashion, with scene after scene flashing by us. While we often consider the separateness of such bits of time, all family life is made up of *one interaction* leading to the next. **There are meaningful bits of "being here now" moments in all our life stories, although we may not notice them as we attempt to meet both our children's and our own daily needs.**

Meanwhile, we keep assembling memories in our personality storyhouse, story by story. We chunk together[6] a beginning, middle, and ending as well as some meaning for ourselves from the fast-paced transitions in our busy lives. Yet, on a daily basis, it is often a struggle to find *any* particular direction for our present actions in the countless transitions of our lives. Conflicting roles swirl in our own personalities, and we do not seem to know if we are coming or going. Like Dorothy's searching for Oz, we can feel *lost*.

Psychologist Carl Jung referred to our struggle to find ourselves as "individuation,"[7] the lifelong process by which we chip away at our unique personality sculptures. Jung considered the development of our personalities as our lifetime's task.[8] Psychologist Carl Rogers outlined this basic notion of finding our unique identity as "becoming" a person. Rogers also believed that we spend our entire life learning to identify and accept our personality roles, looking for directions that take us *home* to ourselves. Hopefully, throughout our lives we keep learning to access any previously denied roles within our personalities and begin to take ownership of even our most negative thoughts. When we no longer think that all evaluations come from outside of us but recognize how much we evaluate from the inside of our personalities, we grasp a basic acceptance of who we are.[9] Through learning about our personality roles and self-territory, we learn the meaning of our storied memories. We even learn how to remodel our personality story-house.

Thus we can learn how to connect with significant others in meeting everyone's basic needs. All of us have a better chance of meeting our basic needs and reaching our own potential if we access self-territory; then we can base our actions upon unconditional love for our child. We see how parents and children learn from each other, how our personality roles connect, how connected we are to others, and how we have choices.

Parenting-Trip Tips

- Consider that raising *up* a child means that you raise *up* yourself into your parenting identity, as you integrate many of your previous life encounters throughout the course of your parenting trip.
- Draw a *map* of your personality roles. Visualize how various personality roles form the basis for your interactions with your child and others.
- Recognize that in locating self-territory, or becoming conscious of your self and others' selves with here-and-now awareness, you find meaning in connections with other people.
- Review your own life needs. What else can you do with your time that *really* matters?

FINDING SELF-TERRITORY IN ONE INTERACTION AT A TIME

Marriage and family therapist Richard Schwartz describes one's "self" as the seat of consciousness with an ability to provide leadership within one's personality.[10] He views a person experiencing such self-leadership as having "a pervasive sense of physiological and mental calm."[11] Body and mind make space for a peaceful sense when self-territory is accessed. Spiritual consultant Eckhart Tolle refers to the spaciousness concept of self-territory in this way: "Whenever you can, make some room, create some space, so that you find the life underneath your life situation."[12] **Whether we realize it or not, an intuitive self remains "there," even though we may not be consciously aware of our ability to have inner roots.**

A pioneer of mind-body health, Joan Borysenko suggests that tuning in to oneself intuitively happens quite naturally: "Too often portrayed as the stuff of seers, [or] fortune-tellers . . . [intuition] is less about divining the future than it is about entering more authentically into the present. Intuition is always operative, so common that it often evades conscious recognition."[13] Whether you consider yourself a user of intuitive reflection or not, you can learn to make space between the bossy, critical roles in your personality and the overwhelmed ones that chronically have too much to do, too many worries, and too much stress.

You have choices in your approach to every situation. If you want to practice being in self-territory, becoming conscious in here-and-now awareness, find spaces between your personality roles each day. Realize present moments. In one interaction at a time, you slow down the rapid-fire pace of action-reaction that characterizes much of your days.

SELF-SPHERE

To acknowledge self-territory, remember that your *listening body* has sensory awareness. So take a deep breath to enter your self-sphere; then slowly read aloud each of the following phrases, taking a new breath when you read each new phrase. Self-territory includes:

- The origin of possibility and potentiality
- The sense of being *awake* in and *aware* of the moment
- Listening to every one of your thoughts you ever think
- A fount or source of wisdom
- A place of solidarity
- A vital essence
- An anchor
- A peaceful harbor
- Unmistakable energy
- Solace in *this* moment
- The experience of spaciousness
- A lighthouse for the mind/body
- One interaction at a time

For the next few minutes, just consider that there is a uniting self underlying your personality roles that knows and remembers how to focus on the *present* moment.

A connection to exquisite sensory experiences is important for every person and does not require a mind-altering drug to get there. Many people find they are capable of experiencing one interaction at a time, or being in self-territory, when they are in nature, such as when they are hiking, walking along a lake, or spending time in a garden. Self-territory has an interior feeling of openness and spaciousness, much like the feelings one experiences in open-air arenas or while looking at the boundless stars in the night sky. Irish poet and philosopher John O'Donohue speaks of the senses as being guides to one's self.[14] Our ties with nature can calm "frenetic streams of thought. . . . The elemental nature of the self takes over . . . rather than taking us out of ourselves, nature coaxes us deeper inwards."[15]

Perhaps we are less distracted from self-territory when we are surrounded by beauty or nature, but there is no certain "there" that one needs to travel to in order to find self-territory. Similar to creativity researcher Mihaly Csikszentmihalyi's concept of "flow,"[16] in which no one activity results in a person's intense awareness of being in the present moment, self-territory can be accessed anywhere and anytime.

ANCIENT WISDOM

The idea that self-territory lies underneath one's day-to-day functioning reverberates throughout ancient philosophies and modern poetry. **People have sought the wisdom of self-territory in every age.** Greek scholars focused on the concept of the mind's inner workings. Socrates, born in 470 b.c., provided contemporary advice for all millenniums: "The unexamined life is not worth living." His protégé, Plato, born in 427 b.c., followed with his version of searching for life's meaning: inner reflection, or introspection, rates as a human obligation. Plato believed that morality arises through one's understanding of one's self. Born in 384 b.c., Aristotle continued the internal search for the "essential whatness"[17] of a person.

Ancient people from the central part of Mexico, the Toltecs, explained our existence in 200 a.d. in terms of a mind being capable of talking, listening to itself, and recalling the past. The Toltec people comprehended a self that knows and remembers. French mathematician René Descartes declared a partial definition for self-awareness in the sixteenth century: "I think, therefore I am." For Descartes, the very nature of humanity denoted the existence of the self, a sphere that knows and remembers. He believed that the pineal gland set the boundary where one's mind and body met, and he received credit for his attempt to locate the seat of consciousness in the brain. Although incorrect about the pineal gland being the site of self-awareness,[18] Descartes started a search that opened pathways for exploring our mind's map.

RIGHT-HEMISPHERE TERRITORY

Philosophers, theologians, poets, and artists appeared as the leaders in understanding the *inner space* of consciousness until quite recently. Increasingly, scientists have joined their ranks. Brain researchers provide us with fascinating facts. For example, while the brain's left hemisphere contains the seat of our language and motor activity, the territory of our right hemisphere appears to hold a sense of self and consciousness that exists without the benefit of language. While left-brain language plays an important role in conscious thoughts, nonverbal emotional communication appears to stem from a dominant right hemisphere.

Neurologist Julian Keenan explains the brain's inner complexities: "By casting the right hemisphere in terms of self, we have a revolutionary way of thinking about the brain."[19] People can learn to use their right hemispheres to become "cognitive Goldilocks: instead of having to literally try out each of the beds or sample from each of the bowls of porridge, self-aware individuals are able to cognitively cast themselves into each possible event and plan before acting."[20] Parents in training thus can be the "cognitive Goldilocks" kind of caretaker who translates what it may be like to experience life in their child's "chair," or particular developmental phase.

This ability to model another's mental state begins to develop in children at age four.[21] Many young children in play can be overheard expressing empathy for a pet cat or stuffed animal. Yet many of us as adults seem less attuned to such self-awareness. We become busy and overbooked with life's chores and duties. In our constant pursuit of the best in life, we sometimes miss tasting the daily porridge in front of us.

FINDING THE *PRESENT* MOMENT

Scott (8), Maria (29), and Norman (31)

> Scott comes to therapy due to intense anxiety, which shows up in having trouble falling asleep at night and frequent stomachaches. Simple, consistent rules at home do not exist; Maria grew up in a regimented family and does not want to repeat her family's rigidity. She has the notion that her child "can decide what to do" without anyone having to tell him. However, Norman desires establishing a lot of rules so that his household can run more smoothly than his remembrances of his chaotic childhood home, run by what Norman called "apathetic" parents. Each parent wishes to reverse the parenting gears from their childhoods, but they lose sight of too many *present* moments with Scott. Scott appears lost in the midst of his parents' battles about day-to-day family organization. The anxious look on his face conveys too many cross-fired messages.
>
> When asked to draw a person in his first individual session, Scott sketches a forbidding masked monster with muscles of a bodybuilder

and limbs that have no hands or feet. Without any grounding, the masked figure looms eerily on the page and casts fearful vibes. Scott's accompanying story reveals unease both about his inner resources and his family's uncertainties; he fantasizes that a wizard-like strength, which only comes from a magic crystal, can help the masked, scared monster-man cope. "He was in a car accident and everybody thought he was dead, but it turned him into this guy. His face was all burned, so he got a mask for it, and then he built the rest of his suit. It made him really strong. He found this crystal and it made him really powerful. And then after that he hid the crystal. He threw the crystal far away so no one could find it. If anyone found it, it would take away his powers."

Scott envisions that power only comes externally and that he needs to protect both his hidden source of power and his weaknesses. I ask Scott for the meaning in his ominous figure with a few follow-up questions. When I ask if his masked guy has any friends, Scott looks sad, saying, "No, no one knows his identity." I tell Scott that the guy can make friends when he is ready to take off his mask. Scott's intensity loosens. He smiles.

DEVELOPMENT DIRECTIONS

We don't see things as they are, we see them as we are.

—Anaïs Nin, French-Cuban writer

Maria and Norman do not function in many *present* moments. They are so judgmental about their families of origin that they cannot focus on their own inner resources, their self-territory. Working at cross-purposes, the parents do not realize how their brand of discipline might cancel out the other's discipline. Parents in training need to partner with each other and with their children in the new family they establish. The discussion of how each parent's family of origin handled developmental ages and phases reveals differences in every couple. But the differences are not the most important issue. Each parent has similar needs. Accepting where we come from and acknowledging unmet needs makes a beginning move toward deciding where we want our new family car headed in order to meet every person's current needs.

Tip for Raising Eight-Year-Olds

Parental arguments are painful for most children, but eight-year-olds are just beginning to detect contexts and implications. "The child is becoming enough aware of . . . 'self' to use the term. . . . The child is more conscious . . . in the ways in which he differs from other people."[22]

Tip for Raising Twenty-Nine-Year-Olds

There are no rigid rules for good parenting; each parent in training becomes the "best" he or she can be with acknowledging one's own personality story-house. "There are no perfect mothers. There are no perfect fathers. Fortunately, perfection is not required for the development of a healthy real self. The mother and father who are simply 'good enough' are sufficient."[23]

Tip for Raising Thirty-One-Year-Olds

In our culture, fathers often have less preparation for their parenting roles than mothers. "Becoming a father is not something that many men think about years before the event. Unlike career achievement or working which we rehearse and practice for even as children, fatherhood is not a crucial part of our identities until we actually become fathers."[24]

"SELF-ACTUALIZATION" REVISITED

Marvin Minsky, cofounder of the MIT Computer Science and Artificial Intelligence Laboratory, captured the essence of the self-definition dilemma. He placed the self within a context of an identity underlying everyday experience: "Self is the part of mind that's really me. . . . It's the part that's most important to me because it's that which stays the same through all experience . . . and whether you can treat it scientifically or not, I know it's there, because it's me. Perhaps it's the sort of thing that science can't explain." Minsky further explained that our self-definitions are only clear-cut in logic and mathematics: "When it comes to understanding minds, we still know so little that we can't be sure our ideas about psychology are even aimed in the right direction."[25]

Psychologist Peter Fonagy also addressed "identity" in defining the self: "The essence of the self . . . rests in the process of reflectiveness. . . . Paradoxically, when selfhood is authentic there is little need for the concept. . . . Identity is a consequence or a property of the self."[26] **However we view ideas of our internal identity, most of us can relate to the notion of a self-territory that recognizes the part of mind that's "really me."**

What do self-definitions have to do with raising children? We often do not take the "selves" of others into consideration; we often miss others' true nature, or what Aristotle termed the "essential whatness" of a person. We cannot take our children for granted if we want to be *present* in our relationships. We need to have a framework for understanding their personality roles and self-territory, too.

The generation of the sixties followed psychologist Abraham Maslow's theory of the hierarchy of basic needs as a framework for understanding personalities. Maslow described a hierarchical list of basic needs for one to meet *before* one achieved self-esteem (liking and respecting yourself) and then, finally, "self-actualization."[27] These needs, in the order of Maslow's progression, are the following: physiological needs (for food, water, rest, and sexual expression), safety needs (for security and freedom from fear), and belongingness/love needs (for affiliation). Upon meeting these basic needs, Maslow believed one might next reach an esteem need (a sense of worth and respect). The final pinnacles of personality development in Maslow's hierarchy are "self-actualization," or fulfilling one's potential, and an aesthetic need for beauty and creative expression.[28]

Yet Maslow's concept of self-actualization placed the terrain of self as a distant opportunity, one discovered by only a few special explorers in life. Reading his list of self-actualized people presents a who's who list of the famous few: Albert Einstein, Eleanor Roosevelt, Jane Addams, William James, Albert Schweitzer, Aldous Huxley, Benedict de Spinoza, Abraham Lincoln (in his last years), and Thomas Jefferson. Maslow considered a list of "contemporaries" for "partial cases," although their names did not appear in writing.[29] Describing self-actualizers as a small proportion of the general population, Maslow made it clear that mounting the self-actualizing slopes took a Herculean effort. In fact, Maslow had few women climbing to the "top."

Maslow used childhood as an example of how a self-actualized adult might behave, yet he excluded youth from "self-actualization." He viewed children as "innocent" and less critical than adults. These very qualities were esteemed by Maslow in the self-actualizing adult, who cared not just about individual needs but for others' needs as well:[30] "Self-actualized people have a wonderful capacity to appreciate again and again, freshly and naively, the basic goods of life with awe, pleasure, wonder, and even ecstasy, however stale these experiences may be for other people."[31] Children do have the capacity to view the world with present eyes.

My opinion is that we need psychological models that are inclusive, not exclusive. Research shows that, indeed, self-awareness occurs very early in childhood. Children are the most likely ones to exhibit wonder and a naive understanding to savor the simple pleasures in a day. It often seems that a child has more self-territory presence than a parent who juggles too many household and office tasks with a gut-churning acidity that overpowers any semblance of present moments. Repair the past mistakes! Fix the future! Breathe and remember: our parent-in-training goal calls for us to be present one interaction at a time. **Who has time and energy for present interactions? Your child has time and energy. In this aspect, it is our children who "raise" us to the level of awareness that we need when we are with them, and they do this one interaction at a time.**

Maslow's concept of self-actualization focuses on an end state achieved by those he viewed as people of accomplishment. But what if psychology endorses the expectation that *every* person deserves an ongoing renewal of self-territory? Rather than needing to reach some zenith of life achievement to reach selfhood potential, we can experience self-territory as ever-present. It is the underlying support available daily to every one of us on every step of our journey in life. All of us have a better chance of reaching our potential if we access self-territory along the path to accomplishment. Realize your own potentialities through acknowledging self-territory alongside the steps of day-to-day living. Attune your senses to savor the delicacies of the here and now. And begin encouraging this potential in your children, too. Relate to your child one interaction at a time.

GROWING *UP* AT EVERY AGE

Kathryn (52)

Kathryn raised her children and sent them off to college, but now she wonders whether she has raised herself enough. She turns wistful when she discusses her own mother, as she did not experience affectionate vibes in her childhood home. Patience did not make the roster among her mother's varied personality roles. However, Kathryn's face lights up when she recalls spending time with her patient maternal grandmother. As a young girl, Kathryn sensed that she better not ask her mother any "real" questions, so she saved her important questions for her grandmother. One time she asked her grandmother, "What is eternity?" The answer both surprised and scared her. When Grandma told her that eternal life goes on and on forever, Kathryn felt panicky. At that moment, time sped up for her instead of extending itself. Kathryn recalls how her heart raced, her palms felt clammy, and she had trouble catching her breath all of a sudden. "Eternity" did not make any sense to her. Kathryn did not recall her age at the time of this question.

Another time, Kathryn asked her grandma about God. The two of them were coming home from a funeral, and twelve-year-old Kathryn did not understand the life-death connection. She did not *see* God, and she wondered how everybody kept talking about an entity they did not see. Kathryn recalled that Grandma thought for a moment before answering her sensitive grandchild's penetrating question. Then Grandma pointed to some trees. She asked Kathryn if she could *see* wind. Kathryn studied the treetops. She saw tree limbs swaying in a breeze. She saw leaves rustle. But she did not "see" wind, she said. Grandma agreed with Kathryn's astute analysis, and she then explained divinity with a wind metaphor. Kathryn did not *see* wind, but she saw the actions of wind. She did not *see* God, but she saw the actions of God. Kathryn feels lucky to have had such a wise grandparent. She recalls the wind story whenever she feels lonely in life.

DEVELOPMENT DIRECTIONS

Most important, Grandma's time was my time, and there was plenty of it.

—Demi Moore, actress, from Jennifer Gates Hayes's
Pearls of Wisdom from Grandma

Kathryn looks back on her personality story-house with acceptance and understanding. Too many people spend large chunks of their life wishing that they had a different parent or spouse. While Kathryn acknowledges that her belonging ties with her mother did not measure up in terms of a positive attachment, she feels eternally grateful for the unconditional love she received from her attentive grandparent. For those who cannot depend upon a positive values inheritance from parents, your adult path can challenge you to delve into self-territory and find your own sense of interior wisdom. Perhaps there are loving siblings, grandparents, teachers, or friends who can inspire you to find and utilize your potential if your parents did not meet this need.

Kathryn models a lot of her life on the lessons she received from her grandma. For example, Kathryn attributes her love of color to her grandmother. While Kathryn's creativity stems from childhood memories of spending quality time with Grandma, her most important gift from her caring grandparent was the modeling of how to relate one interaction at a time.

Tip for Raising Fifty-Two-Year-Olds

Finding acceptance for our past aids us in living with awareness for our here-and-now actions. "What was not modeled in the family of origin, what was not made available in the popular culture, becomes a personal task for each of us in the second half of life."[32]

PERSONALITY MAPPING FOR ADULTS

We can continue to grow and develop our personality story-house throughout our life span. While we relate to all kinds of people in our lifetime, we take in our own perceptions of these interactions. We filter our experiences in unique ways, utilizing our personality story-house as a repository for our memories. When we recognize the roles making up our personality story-house, we more clearly see how these roles form our interactions with our child.

We often travel to our personality "edges," or insecurities, while facing daily life. Drawing a personality map helps us acknowledge these insecure edges instead of just feeling lost. In understanding the various personality roles we play in our lives and the roles played out in the lives of our child, we need to consider our personal sense of boundaries. Our personality map provides a kind of personality boundary, a knowing of what roles belong to our personality. Family members also require boundaries when two people in the family try to work out a conflict in their relating and another person keeps distracting or interrupting them.[33] The distracter needs to watch quietly, allowing the twosome space for their dialogue.

All of us can benefit from the ability to detect one personality role from another, to appreciate that a person uses that role for a reason, and then to grasp how our own various roles intersect with others' roles every day. These intersections, though, make one-interaction-at-a-time relating a challenge. Personality maps show us the intersections of our many different roles. Sometimes these role intersections cause personality traffic jams.

We map our personality roles to differentiate one jammed role from another and, perhaps most important, to differentiate our personality roles from self-territory. **By "mapping," or describing an inner compass that is different from our darting, ever-changing, personality roles, it becomes clearer that we can access self-territory whenever we want.** We can use our maps to see the so-called big picture. Drawing a personality map helps enforce the idea that we can push away from busy or overwhelmed roles and locate self-territory. This manner of being present for one interaction at a time in our relationships with other people is what seems lost when we are busy tackling life in our multitasking millennium. We find new eyes for a child's behavior when we can respond from self-territory in one interaction at a time.

We also draw maps to circumnavigate our way through lost byways of our personalities. When we learn to map our own missteps along the raising road of meeting our basic needs, we are in a better position to raise *up* the next generation. Insight into our parenting fears and frustrations grows with the guidance of this homemade map. By telling stories of how our personality roles tried to handle a situation, we uncover some lost opportunities to meet certain basic needs. Our drawing also brings back a few stories we forgot about from our past trek along the raising road of learning how to meet basic needs. We can learn to acknowledge how certain roles help us meet our basic needs.

A world of introspection opens up when we draw. Ideas occur to us in new ways. Our right hemisphere's spatial/intuitive sensing also gives us essential nonverbal feedback, for art therapist Helen B. Landgarter suggests that art provides us with "a different kind of attention."[34] Artist Betty Edwards maintained that drawing allows a person to use their brain in such a way that new perceptions surface.[35] **Both children and adults engage in new learning when they use the nonverbal motion of drawing.** Drawing brings the abstract world to hands-on awareness. By drawing a particular thing, you concentrate on a select perception, leaving out other perceptions that might complicate your understanding.[36] For those of us accustomed to using verbal cues and our left hemispheres most of the day, art encourages exploration, a kind of map-making of Oz, or some internal place of wisdom.

Yet caretakers often overlook creativity as a basic need. Some have a commanding critical role that believes they have no drawing ability, denies any responsibility for unmet ability needs ("It's my father's fault that I never went to college," says one young mother), and thinks they cannot change their personalities. Another personality posture stems from stern discipline needs; a perfectionist role demands a map is made in an exact manner. Some people have a major pleaser role, wanting to please whoever looks at a drawing product; they overfocus on belonging needs. Hopefully, you dismiss any personality parts that are skeptical of what seems like "child's play" and allow unfettered creativity to emerge as you draw your personality roles on paper. (This exercise generally gets a very positive response from most adults once they actually begin.)

DRAWING YOUR PERSONALITY MAP

An introduction to personality mapping for adults begins with acceptance: *You cannot make a mistake.* You draw a map of your personality roles that seems right for today. Maps change; another day your map might be different from the one you draw today. Then select markers, crayons, or colored pencils to draw a symbol representing "self-territory." You may choose a particular color or find you want several colors. Somewhere near the center of the page, draw a design or shape that stands for your internal compass, the "core" you. It is a symbolic self-representation.

Just as a road map may portray a city as a star or a circle—an image that does not capture the essence of a real city—your mapping of a self-symbol is just a representation. Everyone draws something unique and creative for their core. One parent draws a branching tree. Another draws a deep blue triangle with "vibrating sides." Still another parent pictures an abstract design with many different colors floating inside.

After drawing the "core" you, downshift from the rest of your busy day by taking a few long, deep breaths. You can choose to have some quiet time for reflection, some uninterrupted space to be in the present moment. A calm and peaceful feeling comes when you find space for self-territory. If you do not find space for a few peaceful moments, do not despair. You still have inner self-territory, but you just are not accustomed to making the time or space to recognize present moments. Have patience.

Continue your map. Add designs for your personality roles, one at a time, around the centered symbol of your self. Just draw whatever comes to mind. **Visualize your roles without judgment.** Remember, a picture can express a thousand words. Sketch first the role of your personality that seems to describe you during much of your day. How do you present yourself frequently? Choose a role that you experience every day, several times a day. How do you envision the size of this part? How do you imagine its placement on your map in relationship to your self-symbol? What color(s) do you associate with this role? Many different responses are possible. Some familiar parts that are first drawn by adults are caring/loving roles and tired/overwhelmed frames of mind. Label each part of your personality as you draw it.

Draw a second role in your day-to-day personal story. It may be quite different from the first. It represents another aspect in your per-sonality story-house. How do you envision the size of this personality stance in relation to your self-symbol? How do you imagine its place-ment on your map in relationship to what you have drawn already? What color(s) do you associate with this role? Draw a third aspect of your personality. Where does it stand in relation to the first two roles?

By this time, most parents draw three roles of their personality that describe either the ways they *like* to see themselves or, in some in-stances, one or two symbols representing challenging roles in their per-sonality. This is because our brain tracks scary pathways just like a road map rates certain roadways as safe for travel. **However, both brain maps and road maps do need updating from time to time.**

PERSONALITY-MAP READING

There are many different adaptations available for continuing the mapping process. One option is to take time with each drawn role, spending as much time as needed. Your map can evolve over a period of weeks with additional roles added when they occur to you. Another option delineates getting down as many roles as you can think of today; you can draw a map in one sitting. Do not erase or cancel out roles when they seem opposite of other roles. Remember that all of us have a personality comprised of opposite roles. And do not judge yourself; judgment does not help in identifying the roles making up your personality.

After drawing several roles and picturing the usual workaday personality roster, we look for roles that may not have favored status. Can you identify an opposite role to any roles you have drawn? Maybe there are stances in your personality that you do not show others. Maybe there are roles that you do not want to see very often. Where do these roles fit on your map? How do you envision the sizes of these roles? How do you imagine placement on your map in relationship to the self-symbol? What color(s) do you associate with these roles? What relationship do all these parts have with one another? Notice where opposite roles appear on your map. Do you banish them to the edges of your paper? Do you make them a different size from roles you prefer? Do you use colors that represent your least favorite colors?

We can encounter a mazelike system of diverse personality roles. Personalities, like magnets, have two poles: so-called positive and negative poles. Sometimes we see inner roles as negative, but often they are as positive or helpful as the outer roles already drawn. Our least favorite personality roles also protect us; they just have different methods of protection. Your child has layers of protecting roles as well. As you consider the similarities and differences among the different personalities in your family and peer circles, certain patterns in roles may emerge. You "see" others' variety of personality roles, as well as your own different roles, in a more complete manner. Personality poles, or opposites, keep surfacing, but it is in the "eye of the beholder" to perceive their meanings. Sometimes you cannot admit to having some roles that you feel uncomfortable with, and thus you may not represent them initially. One parent in training says, "This is a closed door—it is locked."

Many adults show "locks," or unknown roles, on their personality maps. The locks initially are a mystery. One mother says, "This corner holds a question mark—I don't know what it means." Others respond openly: "This is my intolerance," or "This is my anger." Personality map making often uncovers postures in our daily lives that we initially say we dislike. However, these roles have purpose and await our discovery of their wisdom and for their storytelling. When you find a personality role that is active as you travel through each day, process what that part means in terms of your parenting and in terms of taking care of your own needs.

Some stories from your past may surface if you begin to recall the first time you saw a role show up. Take notes if you find journaling helpful. Each person's map will present a unique pattern in the same manner that each thumbprint has originality. Also, a person making maps in different time frames of life will focus on different personality roles each time. Just like our world maps require updating when countries take on differing boundaries and names, our personality maps shift along the raising road of learning how to meet our basic needs.

The important learning in our mapping efforts is our realization that while some personality roles may switch in their importance from time to time, or take on different forms and meanings throughout our life, our core self-territory remains intact. In the words of mythologist Joseph Campbell and journalist Bill Moyers, there exists "that life within you, [there] all the time." When you become aware of such an inner landscape, "you put yourself on a kind of track that has been there all the while, waiting for you, and the life that you ought to be living is the one you are living."[37]

MAKING CONNECTIONS FOR A NEW DIRECTION

For your final map guideline, look for connections or the lack thereof among your roles and your self-representation. You may choose a marker or crayon to draw roads or bridges among your various roles. If you perceive a strong connection between two roles or between one role and your self-symbol, draw a thick line connecting them just like in an AAA road map, where highway roads are represented by thick, bold lines and country roads by smaller lines. Decide between wide highways or narrow roads when connecting personality roles. You also may find that some roles are reached only through certain other roles; it can seem like a one-way road leads to some parts of our personalities.

Now, are all your roles connected, or are there roles that stand alone as islands? One parent in training has four isolated islands on her map; each appears in one corner of the paper, far away from all other roles and her self-symbol. These areas are her guilt, grief, sad, and depressed roles. Only when she explains her map does she realize, "They aren't connected to anything." Then she suddenly understands that she cannot meet her belonging needs because she has overfocused on rejections from her past. Her present connections with other adults are tenuous at best, and now she needs a new set of personal directions to meet her basic needs.

Connections are what we need in this world. Too often we rush through our day without making any real connections with those around us. Our child's needs simply loom as monumental energy takers. Children often are eager for one-interaction-at-a-time relating. They find it is easy to "lose" themselves in pretend play, and they access their creativity and ability potential without judgment. To parents, though, their every need seems difficult to meet, and every person in the family appears needy.

Remember, as caretakers in training, we have to consider *both* our own and our child's needs. All of us require periodic reviews of our current directions in the map of our personality journey through life. **When parents in training feel confused about some difficult stage of development in either their own life or their child's life, they can use their creativity to map their current personality roles.** All benefit from making space for self-territory, where we engage in one interaction at a time, allowing for creative routes on today's journey.

A CHILD'S EYE INTO SELF-TERRITORY

Follow the creative journey that a child and I take while the drawing of her personality map unfolds:

Child: "My self is a big, big house . . . it has strong wood."

Therapist: "Your self is very strong."

Child: "There is a table on the deck. It's dark. Put some candles."

Therapist: "The self can light up dark spaces."

Child: "What should I draw there now?"

Therapist: "You can draw whatever you can think of. . . . There are many ways to draw one's self."

Child: "A tunnel . . . the tunnel goes up and you can look out."

Therapist: "What do you see?"

Child: "Trees . . . a door."

Therapist: "A door . . . and that's how you find your self?"

Child: "Yes! And there's light!"

Therapist: "What kind of light?"

Child: "Happiness light!"

Therapist: "I think that's a door you want to open lots and lots of times."

SELF-TERRITORY MAPPING

When we are in self-territory, we are capable of being in the present moment. We are not flooded with a rush of preoccupations, a "to do" list that seems endless, or yesterday's glories and stories. Within this open space, this terrain of present being, we are most able to show loving and compassionate actions.

- How could you tell when your mother, stepmother, or primary female caretaker and your father, stepfather, or primary male caretaker were relaxed and interacting with you from self-territory? For example, think of times when you spent quality time with a relative or special adult. What circumstances are present when one adult steps out of multitasking and relates in one interaction at a time?
- How could you tell when your grandparent(s) related with you from self-territory?
- How could you tell when your sibling(s) and/or peers related with you from self-territory?
- If none of these individuals could show self-territory to you, who from your childhood years was able to share aspects of self-presence with you?
- Who shares their self-territory with you currently? If you cannot think of anyone, what might get in the way of your being in the present moment with other people?
- **How do you share self-territory with your child? If this act seems like new territory to you, start today to relate one interaction at a time with one person in your life.** Make the space to focus your awareness solely on one conversation, one particular interaction, involving one person. When your mind wanders, bring back your attention for listening simply by taking a deep breath, which will cue your self-territory. Do not feel discouraged if this seems next to impossible. You have lived a lot of years in which you multitasked your way through one chore and then, a little breathless, moved right into the next tasks of the day. Be patient. Make a conscious effort to breathe more deeply and slowly. Stay curious about the process.
- As you experiment with one person today, make a plan to add a second person with whom to focus this space and attention on tomorrow. If you do not select a child initially, make a plan to include a child in one interaction at a time soon.

9

LEARN TO CONNECT THE DOTS IN SELF-TERRITORY

Each second we live is a new and unique moment of the universe . . . and what do we teach our children in school? We teach them that two and two make four . . . when will we also teach them what they are? We should say to each of them . . . you are a marvel. You are unique . . . in the millions of years that have passed, there has never been a child like you. . . . You may become a Shakespeare, a Michelangelo, a Beethoven. You have the capacity for anything . . . and when you grow up, can you then harm another who is, like you a marvel? You must cherish one another.

—Pablo Casals, Spanish cellist and composer,
Joys and Sorrows (written at age 93)

Like Rumpelstiltskin, writers weave words and wounds into gold. The last conversation between my husband and me might have included these very words:

"What's it all about, Alfie?"[1]

"I'm still figuring it out, but it has something to do with relationships."

"Did we give our children enough of what they really needed to learn in life?"

"We gave them what we knew at the time."

"If we could go back and do it over, could we be better parents?"

"Yes, if we knew then what we know now."

"We ended up learning more than they did!"

"Yes, they raised us as parents and taught us what's really important in life."

"What *is* really important in life?"

"Many things, but perhaps one of the most important things rests upon knowing how to raise your own self, with your own sense of well-being, in the midst of constant change."

While this dialogue with my husband never happened with these exact words, renditions of similar dialogues did occur between us on many occasions. The last words my husband did say to me were, "I'm going out to mow." Not five minutes later, he was "out," dead in our front lawn beside our red lawn mower. Fortunately, I salvaged a precious few final other words he said just prior to his heart attack: "When are you going to write your book?"

I demurred that afternoon when my husband asked me about writing. I said, "I don't know," which it turns out, was the most accurate response possible. However, in my mind's eye, I had cleared my work calendar and drawn a blueprint of writing productivity for one week, to set into motion the very next day. You see, my husband's unmet plan was to head out of town the next morning on a weeklong business trip. I anticipated joining him in Denver after that week for vacation, and I planned to roll out the fledgling first pages of my manuscript as we weaved our way through mountain passes in Colorado. My husband and I were seldom without plans. At the time, our son was a recent college graduate, and our daughter had left home just a few weeks earlier to begin her college career. All four of us were transitioning on an odyssey of uncharted developmental terrain—empty-nester parents, firstborn's first professional job, and second child's maiden voyage into collegiate territory. It was time for personal reflection for everyone. Then my husband died.

We cannot know what experiences the next five minutes or the next five years will bring to us and our children. Different stressors occur at different developmental stages for every family. However, each family has the same daily raising agenda; energy, discipline, creativity, belonging, and ability needs apply to everyone. *It Takes a Child to Raise a Parent* offers a guide to mapping our personality story-houses through our sometimes smooth, and sometimes treacherous, developmental transitions.

We are born. Our biological parents may or may not choose to be the caretakers who raise us. Whoever raises us may or may not do a very good job. Yet, as adults, we can come to understand and accept our personality story. As we gain insight into our personality roles, we can evolve our story and learn how to raise up the next generation with better decisions. Even without insight, we fantasize how *different* outcomes would occur in our lives if something else had happened at a particular developmental stage. Or we make up false endings to what happened to us when we tell another person our story, embellishing our tale to make ourselves look "good." While some personality story-house remodeling jobs are botched attempts, just like some of the remodeling we attempt on our homes, other remodeling totally transforms our living spaces. Likewise, our reinterpreted stories that we learn to tell ourselves can sustain change in behavior.[2]

FAMILY STORIES CONTAIN STRESS

Entire families experience much stress in the new millennium. With our basic physical security questioned in the shadow of wars, school shootings, hurricanes, tsunamis, and post-9/11 trauma, the uncertainty of our physical safety unnerves both parents and children. Additionally, a shifting world economy taxes the financial security of many families. Still, those fortunate parents with jobs race from home to work and from work to home. How did our parents and grandparents manage?

In every era, raising children and raising ourselves as adults entails stress for parents. No one can anticipate tomorrow's bumpy raising roads. Many children are raised by only one adult. Mothers, fathers, grandparents, and even great-grandparents raise children solo. Mothers often work outside the home; some choose this role, but many are single moms with few choices and too many hours pledged to bill paying. Time-strapped caretakers strain to meet a child's needs, often ignoring their own. Work-shift demands consume much time and thinking. The "second shift"[3] of child care and home care shrinks possibilities for parents to reflect that they will raise their children in the present, one interaction at a time. Tedium with baskets of laundry mixes with tedium for in/out baskets of office work. As the various chores of modern life increase, our children's needs pile up as one more load of laundry on some days. Who can take the time to sort out delicate-cycle problems from the regular-load needs of the day?

When *do* we finally grow *up*? (Hopefully, we keep growing up until the day we die.) When *do* we know which needs to meet first? **Each caretaker has to reconfigure their own recycling escalator of needs as they grow up daily. Caretakers model ways of meeting basic needs for children, and children often model ways for caretakers.** The map for the raising road of meeting everyone's basic needs is not without potholes. We sometimes feel like the twelve-year-old child who anguished over the terrorist attack on the United States on September 11, 2001: "It's too big. . . . I'm too young [in experience]. . . . I can't understand it. . . . I'm sure it's worse than I can imagine." Most family stories contain life and death issues, challenging parents with worse-than-they-ever-imagined details. All of us have to embrace problem solving in our lives whether we are ready or not.

When a close friend of mine nearly died before her heart surgery, she received a heart-shaped pillow with stitches down its creased center to take home with her. A small, hopeful label attached to the broken-heart pillow stated "Mended Heart." All of us can learn to mend our own emotions into meaningful stories and learn to grow up through our crisis periods. We have daily opportunities to connect the dots to mend hearts many, many times along the raising road for both ourselves and our children.

AND FAMILY STORIES CONTAIN GROWTH

This book tells stories for the growth of the whole family and the whole community. Our lives evolve one story at a time in our families, extended families, and adopted families of relatives and friends. Evolving stories gather children, parents, grandparents, friends, and teachers in real-life interactions, and those interactions challenge each person to keep growing up through the daily dilemmas of meeting basic needs. **Every person's story includes opposite personality roles and documents developmental shifts. Each family member sometimes heads backward and sometimes forward, but they usually change directions several times in the same day.**

One person in the family acts in a particular way to meet one basic need in energy, discipline, creativity, belonging, or ability. Then, like a speedy chameleon changing colors, the same individual darts off in a different direction to meet a different need. Another family member responds. Possibly a third and fourth family member join the interaction. Who knows which direction the family will head next? Both caretakers and children are like chameleons with dozens of colorful personality poses and roles. Immobile one moment, a person can bolt into overdrive as a response to the first family member's role. Family members move from personality role to personality role with speed. By now, a variety of family members' personality poses and roles are showing up to meet basic needs, but each person seems to have a different need in the present moment.

Where does the parent in training turn when everyone seems headed in a different direction to meet a different need? How can caretakers raise chameleon children? How can children *listen* to a chameleon caretaker? Both caretakers and children can learn to interact in their families and communities one interaction at a time. I start family therapy sessions by asking for the "pluses," or positive behaviors, that parents and children see in each other; then I ask for any changes that each family member wants to see in the others. Some people are baffled. They expected to start telling me "the problems" of someone in their family instead of telling about anything positive. Recalling alternative behaviors requires a different personality part from the part that is filled with complaints.

This beginning dialogue is fascinating. At times, a parent cannot put their desired changes into words. It is as if they believe that their child should know automatically what is expected—a version of the Nike ad, "Just do it." But what is *it* that a child must do? Other parents express concrete tasks, like, "Go to bed when I say *it* is bedtime." Still other parents offer abstract comments with lots of possibilities for miscommunication. This beginning dialogue for clarity in meeting basic needs in the family is diagnostic for me. The flexibility or rigidity of the family members' positions becomes readily apparent.

Psychotherapy does not "cure" the ills of a family. Rather, I have been privileged to travel along with some special people as they traversed developmental roads with their families. In the words of Swiss psychologist Carl Jung, "There is no once-and-for-all cure . . . that is unconditionally valid over a long period of time. Life has always to be tackled anew . . . because the constant flow of life again and again demands fresh adaptation."[4] All of us have to adapt to the hairpin twists and turns in traveling along unforeseeable roadways in life. This book offers a method for creating new maps along life's unpredictable journey.

ONE INTERACTION AT A TIME PLUS ONE INTERACTION AT A TIME PLUS . . .

Children and parents in training all struggle to meet the same daily basic needs for energy, discipline, creativity, belonging, and ability. When we see our children flit in some wayward direction, we initially may not recognize their intent. After all, we have needs of our own, and often the need of a particular caretaker does not travel well with the needs of a particular child. Take an extended family gathering as one example. Grandparents host a holiday gathering. A parent looks forward to seeing aunts, uncles, and cousins who rarely get together anymore. The parent's intentions of staying late, talking endlessly, reminiscing, and laughing relate to their belongingness needs.

However, a young child's energy needs demand a different route from their parent's needs. Sleep energy needs of a youngster often clash with the belonging needs of a parent. The child begins whimpering, and like a soft rain that disintegrates abruptly into a tornado, a tantrum launches itself in the middle of the relatives' family room. The social parent, bewildered at their child's rapid change from charmer to ballistic whirling dervish, turns first to their embarrassed role; then they turn to their angry role. **When the family story takes an unexpected U-turn, the parents in training temporarily lose their internal compass, their self-territory.**

Children who take us out of our comfort zone with their chameleon roles have something to teach us, and we seldom can guess what we might learn in the next family episode. Think about your own personality story-house; consider all the lessons you have learned throughout the years. We gather many of our most important lessons from the difficult developmental transition points in our lives and the personality story-house of memories that accompany them.

A RAISING ROAD TRAVELED TOGETHER

You are on a journey in your current life story-house. Your personality story-house comes from your genes, family values, memories, and the many personality poses and roles you have assembled to handle your basic needs. **Just as European Renaissance houses of worship are built on the sacred sites of earlier religions, your children are building their own story-houses on the footprint of *your* story-house foundation.**

Are there any renovations you wish to make in your story-house? What personality poses and roles are you handing down to the next generation? Have you found space for self-territory? All of us search for meaning and a core sense of well-being as our many life transitions jolt us. As we think of the different roles of our personality, we learn to separate them from self-territory, an inner compass in our mind. We learn to invest in present moments in one interaction at a time.

When parents in training and their children learn to connect with one another in one interaction at a time, they travel the raising road with a partner or team spirit. Every time a parent and child connect well in one interaction at a time, it leads them closer to the possibility of another good connection in the next transition point. These close connections help each person in the family share values dialogues of respect and fairness. Each affirms the strengths of the others. And each helps others learn to meet their basic needs.

Each child presents us with new opportunities to learn how to answer the question, "Who am I as a parent?" We learn much of our parenting skill from parenting a particular child, in particular transitions, throughout the child's lifetime. Each child juggles needs differently in various life transitions, so each child "raises" us as parents in certain aspects. As our child experiences growth pains in a particular developmental passage, we come face to face with our own growth pains. Yet each new phase of parenting can bring new learning; we are parents in training throughout most of our lives.

Everyone at one time or another fantasizes for wizardly solutions to problems, but they don't realize that wish fulfillment in life mostly consists of an "inside" job. When we come to accept the raising roads we have traveled so far, our remodeling efforts of our personality story-house can provide us with insight and wisdom. We can add on space in which resilience and a sense of overall well-being have "room" to flourish on a daily basis. We can "open up" our personalities for both self-acceptance and acceptance of others. Our self-knowledge is a life-affirming gift, a map to "making it" through difficult times.

Our job as caretakers of children requires that we raise our own self-awareness for all ways in which we interact with our children. As parents, we raise our potential for a satisfying life through making space for listening to our children one interaction at a time. Parents in training learn how to find self-territory, and then they model such self-awareness for their children.

DISCIPLINE REVISITED

Do you remember the "common" discipline story in chapter 4?

A mother drives her children and a friend's child to music lessons. A territorial scuffle slips out from the seat-belted encampments. An argument over which child touched the other one first burns parental ears: "Did not!" "Did too!" "Did not!" "Did too!" The frazzled mother raises her voice and presses down on the accelerator: "If I told you once, I told you a hundred times—there is no arguing in the car." The loud children raise their bantering flags higher . . .

Now envision the carpool discipline story with a different ending:

The mother remembers to take some deep breaths. She flashes on a scene from her own childhood. Her mother was yelling at her to change some childish behavior. Leaving her mother's shrill voice in the distance, she sighs. She has reminded herself over and over that she does not intend to be a carbon copy of "what never worked" in her family of origin. Calmly, the mother flicks her turn signal, slows her speed, and pulls off into the parking lane. She turns off the car. She looks into the eyes of the child in the copilot front seat for several seconds. Then she turns and looks equally long into the eyes of the backseat-driver child. Her silence and the car's silence penetrate the thick air.

Momentarily stunned, the children cease their verbal repartee. The mother considers several options in this silence, discarding the punitive option that ends with, "You both are grounded from watching TV for a week." Taking another deep breath, she considers the most important need in this interaction for all concerned. Energy, discipline, creativity, belonging and ability needs flash in front of her eyes. She takes another deep breath. She briefly engages her children in "we" language: "We cannot drive together safely when everybody's mad energy is bouncing off each other in every direction. What can we do next so that we can drive safely?" A bright-eyed child calls out from the backseat: "How about we sing 'Bingo' until we get there?" The music lesson starts early.

> . . . when it's over, I want to say: All my life
> I was a bride married to amazement.
> —Mary Oliver, *New and Selected Poems, Volume One*

SCANNER PROBLEM SOLVING (SPS) SHORTCUT

In just a few moments' time, this caring mother *solves* the headed-for-disaster car problem. She becomes a savvy traveler along the raising road. She takes a few deep breaths. Instead of thinking SOS, she remembers, **"SPS: *scan* this *problem* and *solve* it."** She scans her situation by asking a few key questions:

- What is my basic need right now?
- What is each child's basic need right now?
- What are my alternatives in the *present* moment?
- Which choice is best?

Later, when she successfully has dropped off the trio at their music lesson, she recalls her brief processing and decides which part of her personality navigated this choice. She smiles to herself when she considers that her personality role of "Socrates" thought of asking her children what *they* could do to help solve the dilemma. Self-awareness is critical for successful parenting. Parenting interventions that focus on learning a few techniques without helping parents engage their own personality issues are less effective.[5] There is no substitute for knowing your *own* basic needs, met and unmet, and how they affect others.

Another example comes to mind. A father takes his toddler and infant on a zoo outing. The toddler's basic need is ability. She loves this excursion and wants to keep saying the names of new animals. However, her baby brother is communicating his energy needs through crying. He is hungry (again), and he needs a diaper change. While the toddler tugs at her father's pant leg to keep moving, the patient Dad finds a bench, pulls off a soiled diaper, and breaks into song! His rendition of "Row, Row, Row Your Boat" models positive action for his active toddler. For the short time that it takes to attend to his infant's needs, this father wisely makes the choice to distract his daughter momentarily with a song she knows. The father's music-lover role handles his need for toddler discipline. An off-key duet creates smiles for everyone who walks by.

International travel journalist Judith Fein tells about her New Zealand camper-van adventure in which she traveled with a Maori chief and twenty-seven people in his extended family. The wise chief stopped travel immediately whenever family conflicts broke out. Fein recalls how everyone had to get out of their van, and on one occasion, the entire family stood in the middle of a freeway on the island. The first step in problem solving was the singing of Maori songs. After singing, the initial problem was solved quickly.[6] Singing comes from a different personality role than the role(s) involved in conflict start-ups. Perhaps we attach a second motto to our **SPS**, **or "*Scan* this *problem* and *solve* it"** motto, and also endorse "*Scan* this *problem* and *sing* it!"

CONNECTING THE DOTS BETWEEN CHILDHOOD AND ADULTHOOD

Some of us only dimly remember our previous developmental crises and the lessons we learned at earlier stages of life until we bump into a child going through some rocky transition. Suddenly, our memory cascades with stories from our own childhoods. In the words of psychiatrist Dan Siegel and parent educator Mary Hartzell, "Our children's attachment to us will be influenced by what happened to us when we were young if we do not come to process and understand those experiences. . . . Your children give you the opportunity to grow and challenge you to examine issues left over from your own childhood."[7] **A child "raises" our parenting potential through helping us to connect the dots between our own childhood and adulthood transitions along the way.**

As caretakers, we help children construct their personality storyhouses of life memories. We not only improve our parenting skills through relating to our children's actions one interaction at a time, but we also can improve our schools by helping them attune to developmental differences among children. We can look closely at our educational curricula to determine if we are making the best use of schoolchildren's time. As psychologist Robert Sternberg suggests, our schools have a preoccupation with teaching cognitive skills to children. They are making a mistake by not developing *wisdom* in learners. Wisdom includes a practical intelligence that addresses not only intrapersonal and interpersonal issues but also takes the larger community of humanity into daily discussion: "In wisdom, one certainly may seek good ends for oneself, but one also seeks common good outcomes for others."[8] This wisdom encompassing the Golden Rule requires teaching in both our homes and schools.

Our journey as caretakers takes us on roads we can never anticipate. While my daughter was studying in Northern Ireland, our family took a driving trip to the edges of Ireland. While touring the famous Ring of Kerry, we had four flat tires—two at a time, within two hours, with two different drivers. I wryly suggested we might enter *The Guinness Book of World Records*, but the seriousness of the situation was daunting. Trial number one was a tire-slashing event along a high curb when map reading was confusing and directions came too late ("Turn right, no turn left!"). Trial number two was a heart-pounding face-off with a white van headed straight at us on a curve; I chose the brambly, rock-studded embankment and blew out the two brand-new tires we replaced earlier. Officers of the Garda, Ireland's police force, nodded politely at our misery and then brought snacks, as it was Christmas Eve afternoon and towing was not readily available. What map skills did we lack? For extra-challenging roads, what preparation might have prevented our skirmishes?

Prevention of parental skirmishes along the raising road of learning how to meet basic needs never reaches 100 percent, just like driving narrow, curving roads in a different country never qualifies as 100 percent safe. However, living your family values; acknowledging your personality roles and poses; and meeting your basic needs of energy, discipline, creativity, belonging, and ability, along with making space for self territory, are road signs that can help you on your parenting journey. This book suggests a pattern of parent skill development for handling many common childhood issues and enhancing the potential of each family member. Through the various mapping exercises, caretakers can learn to steer their way along unfamiliar roads with more presence for one interaction at a time.

WHAT HAPPENS WHEN THE CHILDREN LEAVE HOME?

If you experienced one flat tire after another along the raising road of parenting, you have another chance to discover belongingness after your children leave home. **Hopefully, the transition of your children leaving home provides you with a wealth of information, both about your children as young adults and about yourself.**

Initially, though, a sense of shock unsettles many empty-nester parents. Meals require less food, laundry loads level off, curfew checking stops, and phones ring much less often. Every part of the house—and your life—seems quieter. You become interested in knowing what your children took away from their childhoods. You may again ask yourself the age-old question, "What's it all about?"

Now that you have moved off the raising road of meeting your child's basic needs seven days a week, you have more time to consider your own needs. You have time for self-reflection. You have more opportunities to embark on a journey to remodel your personality story-house of lifetime memories. You might begin to acknowledge more space in self-territory. You might review both your child's progress in meeting basic needs and your own progress so far. What needs have you ignored in your life? What are your choices for living well the rest of your life? All of us are in transition on one level or another all the time. We face new beginnings frequently.

As we put our childhood personality story-house into perspective, we gain wisdom about life that allows us to view self-definitions with acceptance. All of us have a rich story-house, or collection of our past memories, in our history. While we do not remember all of our past stories with either ease or appreciation, we learn to embrace our family, peer, and school stories. Comprehension of where we come from allows us to grasp meaning for parenting both the future generation and ourselves. We learn why we behave in the ways we behave today, understanding which values highlight our actions. Recognizing our values inheritance, or accumulated values from our families, allows us to choose which values we use to raise our children.

CONNECTING THE DOTS BEYOND ONE'S FAMILY

The Albert Einstein Planetarium of the National Air and Space Museum in Washington, D.C., had a wonderful sky show on the nature of infinity. As my adult son and I settled back in our chairs to catch the right angle for "sky" viewing, I secretly hoped this program was not another encounter with "black holes;" our last visit to a planetarium show struck me with both awe and fear. Happily, this sky show on outer space took us galaxy hopping: "There are billions of galaxies . . ." When I heard that, I began to feel curious about the actual size of that number, "billions," and I wondered if each galaxy is as unique as a snowflake. Then I realized that a galaxy and a snowflake are worlds apart! Or are they? Each one must be a special creation, yet they're somehow linked.

The planetarium show paraded pictures from the Hubble telescope of how galaxies "cluster," or band together, in space. Surprisingly, two galaxies can merge, forming one entity. I leaned over to my son and whispered that even galaxies have sex. What a marvel our universe is! And what a wonder it is that two people can merge to form a precious, new entity! That wonder, however, drops off quickly for too many parents. It is a monumental challenge to parent children when there seem to be no road maps for the difficult journey. Most of us would not think of getting into our car for a family vacation without studying a map first, or downloading directions on our computer, or using GPS in our car. What maps are available for parents along the developmental trip? Where can basic training for parenting exist in our culture?

The immensity of this dilemma poses one of our most important challenges in family development. **We need a better road map to the planet's future. Our hope lies with a new generation of parents in training.** Because ideal raising-road conditions are not always possible, this book is an effort to steer parents and potential parents in a direction that provides guideposts for effective childrearing.

The focus for enhanced parent development centers upon the present moment. Caretakers take a few deep breaths and experience the present moment in their day. In one interaction at a time, in one teachable moment, caretakers experience self-territory, along with the increased capacity to view self-territory in a child. Following these parenting-trip tips can help caretakers travel their raising road, filling up the parental gas tank with here-and-now awareness that will affect family functioning for generations. Ideal road conditions are not always possible, but parents in training can embark on an odyssey of discovering the everyday miracles in connections with their children. And that, dear reader, is what I hope *It Takes a Child to Raise a Parent* has taught you.

"What's it all about, Alfie?"

"I'm still figuring it out, but it has something to do with relationships, belonging to others, as well as belonging to one's *self-territory . . . one interaction at a time.*"

NOTES

INTRODUCTION: CHILDREN RAISE PARENTS, AND PARENTS RAISE CHILDREN

1. Anthony Storr, *The Integrity of the Personality* (New York: Ballantine, 1992), 6–7.

2. U.S. Census Bureau, Census 1990, 2000.

3. Mount Vernon tour.

4. Abraham H. Maslow, *Motivation and Personality*, 2nd ed. (New York: Harper and Row, 1970).

5. Richard C. Schwartz, *Internal Family Systems Therapy* (New York: Guilford, 1994).

1. LET'S UNDERSTAND THE FIVE BASIC NEEDS

1. Daniel C. Molden and Carol S. Dweck, "Finding 'Meaning' in Psychology: A Lay Theories Approach to Self-Regulation, Social Perception, and Social Development," *American Psychologist* 61 (2006): 192–203.

2. *The Random House Dictionary of the English Language*, unabridged ed., s.v. "raise."

3. Elizabeth Barrett Browning, *Aurora Leigh, Book I* (London: J. Miller, 1864), line 48.

4. William Glasser, *Reality Therapy: A New Approach to Psychiatry* (New York: Harper and Row, 1965), 9.

5. Daniel Miller, "How Infants Grow Mothers in North London," in *Consuming Motherhood*, ed. Janelle S. Taylor, Linda L. Layne, and Danielle. F. Wozniak (New Brunswick, NJ: Rutgers University Press, 2004), 32.

6. Glasser, *Reality Therapy*, 11.

7. *The World Book Encyclopedia*, vol. 6 (Chicago: World Book, 2004), 356.

8. *How It Works: Science and Technology*, 3rd ed. (Tarrytown, NY: Marshall Cavendish Corporation, 2003), 820–21.

9. *The Random House Dictionary*, s.v. "interaction."

10. Schwartz, *Internal Family Systems Therapy*, 37.

11. Frank Gonzalez-Crussi, *On Being Born and Other Difficulties* (Woodstock, NY: Overlook, 2004), 61.

12. Albert E. Schflen, *Body Language and the Social Order: Communication as Behavioral Control* (Englewood Cliffs, NJ: Prentice-Hall, 1972), 1.

13. *The Random House Dictionary*, s.v. "territory."

14. Julian P. Keenan, *The Face in the Mirror: The Search for the Origins of Consciousness* (New York: HarperCollins, 2003), 137.

15. William Morris and Mary Morris, *The Morris Dictionary of Word and Phrase* (New York: Harper Row, 1971), s.v. "story."

16. Michael White and David Epston, *Narrative Means to Therapeutic Ends* (New York: W. W. Norton, 1990), 79.

17. Sanjay Srivastava et al., "Development of Personality in Early and Middle Adulthood: Set Like Plaster or Persistent Change?" *Journal of Personality and Social Psychology* 84 (2003): 1041–53.

18. Srivastava et al., "Development of Personality," 1041.

19. Paul Wink and Ravenna Helson, "Personality Change in Women and Their Partners," *Journal of Personality and Social Psychology* 65 (1993): 597–606.

20. Daniel J. Siegel and Mary Hartzell, *Parenting from the Inside Out: How a Deeper Self-Understanding Can Help You Raise Children Who Thrive* (New York: Jeremy P. Tarcher/Putnam, 2003), 20.

21. Dan P. McAdams, *The Stories We Live By: Personal Myths and the Meaning of the Self* (New York: William Morrow, 1993), 27–28.

22. Monisha Pasupathi, "Social Construction of Memory and Self in Storytelling: Listener Effects" (paper presented at the annual meeting for American Psychological Association, Toronto, Canada, August 6, 2003).

23. Dan Kindlon and Michael Thompson, *Raising Cain: Protecting the Emotional Life of Boys* (New York: Ballantine, 2000), 151.

24. Arnold Gesell, Frances L. Ilg, and Louise Bates Ames, *The Child from Five to Ten*, revised ed. (New York: Harper and Row, 1977), 1.

25. Jonathon Lazear and Wendy Lazear, *Meditations for Parents Who Do Too Much* (New York: Simon and Schuster, 1993), 19.

26. JoAnn Deak, *Girls Will Be Girls: Raising Confident and Courageous Daughters*, with Teresa Barker (New York: Hyperion, 2002), 135.

27. Laurence Steinberg, *Crossing Paths: How Your Child's Adolescence Triggers Your Own Crisis* (New York: Simon and Schuster, 1974), 60.

28. Nick Lyons and Tony Lyons, eds., *The Quotable Dad* (Guilford, CT: Lyons, 2002), 198.

29. *The Random House Dictionary*, s.v. "dumb."

30. Candace B. Pert, *Molecules of Emotion: The Science Behind Mind-Body Medicine* (New York: Simon and Schuster, 1997), 137.

31. *The Random House Dictionary*, s.v. "pose."

32. Julius Fast, *Body Language: The Essential Secrets of Non-verbal Communication* (New York: M. Evans, 1970), 161.

33. Fast, *Body Language*, 13.

34. Sally Planalp, "Varieties of Emotional Cues in Everyday Life," in *The Nonverbal Communication Reader*, ed. Laura K. Guerrero, Joseph A. DeVito, and Michael L. Hecht, 2nd ed. (Prospect Heights, IL: Waveland, 1999), 272–73.

35. Albert Mehrabian, "Communication Without Words," *Psychology Today* 2 (1968): 53–55.

36. Susan Aposhyan, *Body-Mind Psychotherapy: Principles, Techniques, and Practical Applications* (New York: W. W. Norton, 2004), 12.

37. Babette Rothschild, *The Body Remembers: The Psychophysiology of Trauma and Trauma Treatment* (New York: W. W. Norton, 2000), xv.

38. Kristin D. Neff, Stephanie S. Rude, and Kristin L. Kirkpatrick, "An Examination of Self-Compassion in Relation to Positive Psychological Functioning and Personality Traits," *Journal of Research in Personality* 42 (2007): 908–16.

39. Geoffrey Canada, *Reaching Up for Manhood: Transforming the Lives of Boys in America* (Boston: Beacon, 1998), 31.

2. DISCOVER WHAT A PERSONALITY STORY-HOUSE SAYS ABOUT US

1. McAdams, *The Stories We Live By*, 13.

2. "This Is the House That Jack Built," Nursery Rhymes Lyrics and Origins, accessed January 6, 2010, www.rhymes.org.uk/this_is_the_house_that_jack_built.htm .

3. Steven Pinker, *The Blank Slate: The Modern Denial of Human Nature* (New York: Penguin, 2002), 225.

4. Alma Luz Villanueva, *Planet with Mother, May I?* (Tempe, AZ: Bilingual Press, 1993), 13–14.

5. Pinker, *The Blank Slate*, 253–54.

6. Helen Fisher, *Why We Love: The Nature and Chemistry of Romantic Love* (New York: Henry Holt, 2004), 47–48.

7. Fisher, *Love*, 75.

8. Fisher, *Love*, 78–79.

9. Fisher, *Love*, 96–98.

10. Michelle Bryner, "Some Pregnancies May Not Be So Accidental," *Psychology Today* 38 (2005): 32.

11. Sharon Thompson, *Going All the Way: Teenage Girls' Tales of Sex, Romance and Pregnancy* (New York: Farrar, Strauss and Giroux, 1995), 27.

12. Karen Gravelle, *What's Going On Down There? Answers to Questions Boys Find Hard to Ask* (New York: Walker, 1998), 62–63.

13. Debra Fulghum Bruce and Samuel Thatcher, *Making a Baby: Everything You Need to Know to Get Pregnant* (New York: Ballantine, 2000), 5; Rebecca A. Clay, "Battling the Self-Blame of Infertility," *American Psychological Association Monitor on Psychology* 37 (2006): 44–45; Bruce and Thatcher, *Baby*, 39, 70–89.

14. Lynne Cudmore, "Infertility and the Couple," in *Partners Becoming Parents*, ed. Christopher Clulow (Northvale, NJ: Jason Aronson, 1997), 60.

15. Cudmore, "Infertility," 62.

16. Elizabeth Harper Neeld, *Tough Transitions: Navigating Your Way Through Difficult Times* (New York: Warner, 2005), 145–46.

17. Marie Allen and Shelly Marks, *Miscarriage: Women Sharing from the Heart* (New York: John Wiley, 1993), 47.

18. Allen and Marks, *Miscarriage*, 53–54.

19. Martha S. Rinehart and Mark S. Kiselica, "Helping Men with the Trauma of Miscarriage, *Psychotherapy: Theory, Research, Practice, Training* 47 (2010): 288–95.

20. Allen and Marks, *Miscarriage*, 178.

21. Andrew Samuels, "The Good-Enough Father of Whatever Sex," in *Partners Becoming Parents*, ed. Christopher Clulow (Northvale, NJ: Jason Aronson, 1997), 104.

22. Ruta Nonacs, *A Deeper Shade of Blue: A Woman's Guide to Recognizing and Treating Depression in Her Childbearing Years* (New York: Simon and Schuster, 2006), 25.

23. Dan P. McAdams and Phillip J. Bowman, "Narrating Life's Turning Points: Redemption and Contamination," in *Turns in the Road: Narrative Studies of Lives in Transition*, ed. Dan P. McAdams, Ruthellen Josselson, and

Amia Lieblich (Washington, DC: American Psychological Association, 2001), 19.

24. Doula Network, accessed November 26, 2012, www.xmarks.com/site/www.Doulanetwork.com/ .

25. Canada, *Manhood*, 155.

26. Nonacs, *Deeper Shade*, 35.

27. Jane L. Rankin, *Parenting Experts: Their Advice, The Research, and Getting It Right* (Westport, CT: Praeger, 2005), 39–41.

28. Erik H. Erikson, *Childhood and Society*, 2nd ed. (New York: W. W. Norton, 1996), 273–74.

29. Nonacs, *Deeper Shade*, 238.

30. Brooke Shields, *Down Came the Rain: My Journey Through Postpartum Depression* (New York: Hyperion, 2005), 123–32.

31. Fiona Shaw, *Composing Myself: A Journey Through Postpartum Depression* (South Royalton, VT: Steerforth, 1998), 25.

32. Frederic M. Hudson, *The Adult Years: Mastering the Art of Self-Renewal* (San Francisco, CA: Jossey-Bass, 1991), 165–66.

33. Lee Salk, *My Father, My Son: Intimate Relationships* (New York: G. P. Putnam, 1982), 249.

34. Carl G. Jung, "Psychology and Religion" in *The Collected Works of C. G. Jung*, volume 11, *Psychology and Religion: West and East*, trans. R. F. C. Hull, Bollingen Series XX (New York: Pantheon, 1938), par. 133.

35. Schwartz, *Internal Family Systems Therapy*, 42.

36. Regina A. Goulding and Richard C. Schwartz, *The Mosaic Mind: Empowering the Tormented Selves of Child Abuse Survivors* (New York: W. W. Norton, 1995), 174–77.

37. Hal Stone and Sidra Stone, *Partnering: A New Kind of Relationship: How to Love Each Other Without Losing Yourselves* (Novato, CA: New World, 2000), 49.

38. Daniel N. Stern, *The Present Moment in Psychotherapy and Everyday Life* (New York: W. W. Norton, 2004), 55–56.

39. McAdams, *The Stories We Live By*, 35–36.

40. Dan P. McAdams and Jennifer L. Pals, "A New Big Five: Fundamental Principles for an Integrative Science of Personality," *American Psychologist* 61 (2006), 204–17.

41. Don Miguel Ruiz, *The Four Agreements: A Toltec Wisdom Book* (San Rafael, CA: Amber-Allen, 1997), 54–56.

42. Schwartz, *Internal Family Systems Therapy*, 27–28.

43. Schwartz, *Internal Family Systems Therapy*, 46–52.

44. Allan Combs and Mark Holland, *Synchronicity: Science, Myth, and the Trickster* (New York: Paragon House, 1990), 105.

45. Susan Mineka et al., "Observational Conditioning of Snake Fear in Rhesus Monkeys," *Journal of Abnormal Psychology* 93 (1984), 355–72.

46. Carla Hannaford, *Smart Moves: Why Learning Is Not All in Your Head*, 2nd ed. (Salt Lake City, UT: Great River, 2005), 64–65.

47. T. Berry Brazelton, *Families: Crisis and Caring* (Reading, MA: Addison-Wesley, 1989), 38.

48. Daniel N. Stern and Nadia Bruschweiler-Stern, *The Birth of a Mother: How the Motherhood Experience Changes You Forever* (New York: Basic, 1998), 12.

49. Lenore Terr, *Unchained Memories: True Stories of Traumatic Memories, Lost and Found* (New York: Basic, 1994), 12.

50. Keenan, *The Face in the Mirror*, 61; Keenan, *The Face in the Mirror*, 35.

51. Jerome Kagan, *Unstable Ideas: Temperament, Cognition, and Self* (Cambridge, MA: Harvard University Press, 1989), 233.

3. ENERGY NEEDS: ARE YOU AN ENGINEER, OR ARE YOU ENSLAVED TO ENNUI?

1. David H. Levy, *Eclipse: Voyage to Darkness and Light* (New York: Simon and Schuster, 2000), 29.

2. Shad Helmstetter, *Predictive Parenting: When You Talk to Your Kids* (New York: William Morrow, 1989), 28–30.

3. Helmstetter, *Predictive Parenting*, 16–17.

4. Kathleen Brehony, *Awakening at Midlife: A Guide to Reviving Your Spirit, Re-creating Your Life, and Returning to Your Truest Self* (New York: Riverhead, 1996), 253.

5. Diane Ehrensaft, *Spoiling Childhood: How Well-Meaning Parents Are Giving Children Too Much—but Not What They Need* (New York: Guilford, 1997), 237.

6. Daniel J. Siegel, "The Developing Mind and the Resolution of Trauma: Some Ideas About Information Processing and an Interpersonal Neurobiology of Psychotherapy," in *EMDR as an Integrative Psychotherapy Approach*, ed. Francine Shapiro (Washington, DC: American Psychological Association, 2002).

7. Judith Rich Harris, *The Nurture Assumption: Why Children Turn Out the Way They Do* (New York: Free Press, 1998), 23.

8. Matt Ridley, *Genome: The Autobiography of a Species in 23 Chapters* (New York: HarperCollins, 1999), 162.

9. Paul H. Mussen, John J. Conger, and Jerome Kagan, *Child Development and Personality*, 2nd ed. (New York: Harper and Row, 1963), 9.

10. Ridley, *Genome*, 165.

11. Lea Winerman, "The Mind's Mirror," *American Psychological Association Monitor on Psychology* 36 (2005), 48–50.

12. Siegel and Hartzell, *Parenting from the Inside Out*, 65–66.

13. Siegel and Hartzell, *Parenting from the Inside Out*, 34.

14. John Welwood, *Toward a Psychology of Awakening: Buddhism, Psychotherapy, and the Path of Personal and Spiritual Transformation* (Boston, MA: Shambhala, 2000), 22.

15. Mel Roman and Patricia E. Raley, *The Indelible Family: How the Hidden Forces in Your Family Determine Who You Are Today* (New York: Rawson, Wade, 1980), 34–36.

16. Jhumpa Lahiri, *The Namesake* (Boston, MA: Houghton Mifflin, 2003), 28.

17. Brehony, *Awakening at Midlife*, 275.

18. Elaine Hatfield, John Cacioppo, and Richard L. Rapson, *Emotional Contagion* (New York: Cambridge University Press, 1994).

19. Pert, *Molecules of Emotion*, 141.

20. Antonio Damasio, *Looking for Spinoza: Joy, Sorrows, and the Feeling Brain* (Orlando, FL: Harcourt, 2003), 30.

21. Damasio, *Looking for Spinoza*, 43–45.

22. Damasio, *Looking for Spinoza*, 63.

23. Damasio, *Looking for Spinoza*, 85.

24. Damasio, *Looking for Spinoza*, 161–62.

25. Sharon Lamb, *The Secret Lives of Girls: What Good Girls Really Do—Sex Play, Aggression, and Their Guilt* (New York: Free Press, 2001), 46.

26. Lazear and Lazear, *Meditations for Parents*, "September 12."

27. John Gottman, *The Heart of Parenting: Raising an Emotionally Intelligent Child* (New York: Simon and Schuster, 1997), 178.

28. Ashley Montagu, *Growing Young* (New York: McGraw-Hill, 1981), 131.

29. Tori DeAngelis, "What's to Blame for the Surge in Super-Size Americans?" *Monitor on Psychology* 35 (2004), 46–49.

30. Eric Schlosser, *Fast Food Nation: The Dark Side of the All-American Meal* (New York: HarperCollins, 2002), 3.

31. Michael Pollan, *The Omnivore's Dilemma: The Secrets Behind What You Eat* (New York: Dial, 2009), 103.

32. Pollan, *The Omnivore's Dilemma*, 102–4.

33. Schlosser, *Fast Food Nation*, 262.

34. Lawrence J. Cohen, *Playful Parenting* (New York: Ballantine, 2001), xi.

35. Armin A. Brott, *The Single Father: A Dad's Guide to Parenting Without a Partner* (New York: Abbeville, 1999), 112.

36. Mary Pipher, *Hunger Pains: The Modern Woman's Tragic Quest for Thinness* (New York: Ballantine, 1995), 5.

37. Boston Women's Health Book Collective, *Ourselves and Our Children: A Book by and for Parents* (New York: Random House, 1978), 97.

38. Linda Eyre and Richard Eyre, *How to Talk to Your Child About Sex: It's Best to Start Early, but It's Never Too Late—a Step-by-Step Guide for Every Age* (New York: St. Martin's, 1998), 4.

39. Mark Greer, "Strengthen Your Brain by Resting It," *American Psychological Association Monitor on Psychology* 35 (2004), 60–62.

40. Better Sleep Council, accessed November 26, 2012, www.bettersleep. org/better-sleep/the-science-of-sleep-statistics-research/survey-results .

41. Vivian Gussin Paley, *Bad Guys Don't Have Birthdays: Fantasy Play at Four* (Chicago: University of Chicago Press, 1988), ix.

42. Scott Sleek, "After the Storm, Children Play Out Fears," *American Psychological Association Monitor* 29 (1998), 12.

43. Jennifer J. Freyd, "Dynamic Mental Representations," *Psychological Review* 94 (1987), 427–38.

44. Paley, *Bad Guys*, 66.

45. Harris, *The Nurture Assumption*, 241.

46. Hannaford, *Smart Moves*, 107–17.

47. David Souden, *Stonehenge Revealed* (New York: Facts On File, 1997), 131–37.

4. DISCIPLINE NEEDS: ARE YOU A DISCIPLE, OR ARE YOU DISORGANIZED IN DISORDER?

1. Neeld, *Tough Transitions*, 43.

2. *The Random House Dictionary*, s.v.v. "disciple," discipline."

3. Sogyal Rinpoche, *The Tibetan Book of Living and Dying* (San Francisco, CA: Harper, 1993), 23.

4. Jacob Azerrad and Paul Chance, "Why Our Kids Are Out of Control," *Psychology Today* 34, no. 5 (2001), 43–46.

5. Gesell, Ilg, and Ames, *The Child from Five to Ten*, 159–60.

6. Mark Bryan, *Codes of Love: How to Rethink Your Family and Remake Your Life* (New York: Pocket Books, 1999), 160.

7. Susan Faludi, *Stiffed: The Betrayal of the American Man* (New York: William Morrow, 1999), 35.

8. Jennifer Keeley, *Case Study: Appleton Central Alternative Charter High School's Nutrition and Wellness Program* (East Troy, WI: Michael Fields Agricultural Institute, 2004), www.thewholeplate.yihs.net/wp-content/uploads/2010/02/Appleton-school-food-study.pdf .

9. Mary Pipher, *In the Shelter of Each Other: Rebuilding Our Families* (New York: Ballantine, 1996), 245–46.

10. Hara Estroff Marano, *A Nation of Wimps: The High Cost of Invasive Parenting* (New York: Broadway, 2008), 45.

11. Abraham H. Maslow, *Motivation and Personality*, 2nd ed. (New York: Harper and Row, 1970), 35–51.

12. Diana West, *The Death of the Grown-Up: How America's Arrested Development Is Bringing Down Western Civilization* (New York: St. Martin's, 2007), 25.

13. Lynda Madison, *Parenting with Purpose: Progressive Discipline from Birth to Four* (Kansas City, KS: Andrew McNeel, 1998), 90.

14. Wayne Dosick, *Golden Rules: The Ten Ethical Values Parents Need to Teach Their Children* (New York: HarperCollins, 1995).

15. Alan E. Kazdin, *The Kazdin Method for Parenting the Defiant Child with No Pills, No Therapy, No Contest of Wills* (New York: Houghton Mifflin, 2008), 105.

16. Eugene T. Gendlin, *Let Your Body Interpret Your Dreams* (Wilmette, IL: Chiron, 1986), 49.

17. Robert Coles, *The Moral Life of Children* (Boston: Houghton Mifflin, 1986), 16.

18. Coles, *The Moral Life*, 32.

19. Coles, *The Moral Life*, 44.

20. Sidney B. Simon, Leland W. Howe, and Howard Kirschenbaum, *Values Clarification* (New York: Hart, 1972), 15–19.

21. Simon, Howe, and Kirschenbaum, *Values Clarification*, 20.

22. Howard Kirschenbaum, "An Interview with Howard Kirschenbaum," *Newsletter for Educational Psychologists, American Psychological Association* 24 (2001), 5–8.

23. Louis Edward Raths, Merrill Harmin, and Sidney B. Simon, *Values and Teaching* (Columbus, OH: Charles E. Merrill, 1966).

24. Janis Clark Johnston and Patricia Fields, "School Consultation with the 'Classroom Family,'" in *Family Counseling: The School Counselor's Role* 29 (1981), 140–46.

25. Rima Shore, *What Kids Need: Today's Best Ideas for Nurturing, Teaching, and Protecting Young* (New York: Carnegie Foundation, 2002).

26. Irwin A. Hyman, "School Psychology and the Culture Wars: 40 Years of Advocacy, Research and Practice," *NASP Communique* 32 (2004), 18–21.

27. Gesell, Ilg, and Ames, *The Child from Five to Ten*, 56.

28. Hudson, *The Adult Years*, 158.

29. Betty Friedan, *The Fountain of Age* (New York: Simon and Schuster, 1993), 250.

30. Howard Gardner, *The Disciplined Mind: Beyond Facts and Standardized Tests, the K-12 Education That Every Child Deserves* (New York: Penguin, 2000), 33.

31. Gardner, *The Disciplined Mind*, 28.

32. Kindlon and Thompson, *Raising Cain*, 6.

33. Kindlon and Thompson, *Raising Cain*, 1.

34. William Damon, *The Moral Child: Nurturing Children's Natural Moral Growth* (New York: Free Press, 1988), 2.

35. Helmstetter, *Predictive Parenting*, 26.

36. Charlene C. Giannetti and Margaret Sagarese, *Parenting 911: How to Safeguard and Rescue Your 10- to 15-Year-Old from Substance Abuse, Depression, Sexual Encounters, Violence, Failure in School, Danger on the Internet, and Other Risky Situations* (New York: Broadway, 1999), 185.

37. Deak, *Girls Will Be Girls*, 135.

38. Lamb, *The Secret Lives*, 44.

39. Theodore Zeldin, *An Intimate History of Humanity* (New York: Harper-Collins, 1994), 33–34.

40. Glasser, *Reality Therapy*, 58.

41. Glenn and Nelson, *Raising Self-Reliant Children*, 169.

42. Kim Paleg, *Kids Today, Parents Tomorrow* (Oakland, CA: New Harbinger, 1999), 77.

43. Gesell, Ilg, and Ames, *The Child from Five to Ten*, 107.

44. Ruth Bell, "The Middle Years," in *Ourselves and Our Children: A Book by and for Parents:* Boston Women's Health Book Collective (New York: Random House, 1978), 69.

45. Myrna B. Shure, *Raising a Thinking Preteen: The "I Can Problem Solve" Program for 8- to 12-Year-Olds* (New York: Henry Holt, 2000), 214.

46. Riane Eisler, *The Power of Partnership: Seven Relationships That Will Change Your Life* (Novato, CA: New World Library, 2002), 33.

47. Hudson, *The Adult Years*, 145.

48. Ralph W. Hingson et al., "Magnitude of Alcohol-Related Mortality and Morbidity Among U.S. College Students Ages 18–24," *Journal of Studies on Alcohol* 63 (2002), 136–44.

49. Sadie F. Dingfelder, "A Two-Front War on Alcoholism," *Monitor on Psychology* 36 (2005), 38–39.

50. Don Elium and Jeanne Elium, *Raising a Son: Parents and the Making of a Healthy Man* (Hillsboro, OR: Beyond Words, 1992), 201.

51. Jean Lush, *Mothers and Sons: Raising Boy to Be Men*, with Pamela Vredevelt (Grand Rapids, MI: Baker, 1988), 63.

52. James Snyder et al., "The Contributions of Ineffective Discipline and Parental Hostile Attribution of Child Misbehavior to the Development of Conduct Problems at Home and School," *Developmental Psychology* 41 (2005), 30–41.

53. Ehrensaft, *Spoiling Childhood*, 233–34.

54. Eisler, *The Power of Partnership*, 5.

55. Kindlon and Thompson, *Raising Cain*, xiii.

5. CREATIVITY NEEDS: ARE YOU A COMPOSER, OR ARE YOU A CLONE TO CONFORMITY?

1. K. Eileen Allen and Lynn R. Marotz, *By the Ages: Behavior and Development of Children Pre-birth Through Eight* (Albany, NY: Delmar, 2000), 115.

2. Sam Keen, *To Love and Be Loved* (New York: Bantam, 1997), 191.

3. Mihaly Csikszentmihalyi, *The Evolving Self: A Psychology for the Third Millennium* (New York: HarperCollins, 1993), 116.

4. Allen and Marotz, *By the Ages*, 128.

5. Judith Viorst, *Imperfect Control: Our Lifelong Struggles with Power and Surrender* (New York: Fireside, 1999), 164.

6. Gesell, Ilg, and Ames, *The Child from Five to Ten*, 216–17.

7. Lazear and Lazear, *Meditations for Parents*, "April 3."

8. Mihaly Csikszentmihalyi, *Creativity Flow and the Psychology of Discovery and Invention* (New York: HarperCollins, 1996), 12.

9. Robert Kegan, *The Evolving Self: Problem and Process in Human Development* (Cambridge, MA: Harvard University Press, 1982), 11.

10. Roger Schank, *Coloring Outside the Lines: Raising a Smarter Kid by Breaking All the Rules* (New York: HarperCollins, 2000), 130.

11. Sam Goldstein and Robert Brooks, "Does It Matter How We Raise Our Children?" *National Association of School Psychologists Communique* 38 (2009), 19.

12. Deborah Herman, *The Complete Idiot's Guide to Motherhood* (New York: Macmillan, 1999), 161.

13. Edward De Bono, *Serious Creativity: Using the Power of Lateral Thinking to Create New Ideas* (New York: HarperBusiness, 1992), 42.

14. Michael Michalko, *Cracking Creativity: The Secrets of Creative Genius* (Berkeley, CA: Ten Speed Press, 2001), 4.

15. Myrna B. Shure, *I Can Problem Solve: An Interpersonal Cognitive Problem-Solving Program—Preschool* (Champaign, IL: Research Press, 1992); Shure, *I Can Problem Solve*, 9–32.

16. Myrna B. Shure, *Raising a Thinking Child Workbook: Teaching Young Children How to Resolve Everyday Conflicts and Get Along with Others*, with Theresa Foy DiGeronimo (Champaign, IL: Research Press, 2000), 11.

17. Shure, *Raising a Thinking Child*, 56–57.

18. Shure, *Raising a Thinking Preteen*, 29.

19. Shure, *Raising a Thinking Child*, 158.

20. Shure, *Raising a Thinking Preteen*, 132–33.

21. Janis Clark Johnston, Dennis Simon, and Alice Zemitzsch, "Balancing an Educational Mobile Through Problem-Solving Conference," in *Advances in Therapies for School Behavior Problems*, ed. Jeffrey J. Cohen and Marian C. Fish (San Francisco: Jossey-Bass, 1993).

22. Shure, *Raising a Thinking Preteen*.

23. Schwartz, *Internal Family Systems Therapy*.

24. Julia Cameron, *The Vein of Gold: A Journey to Your Creative Heart* (New York: Jeremy P. Tarcher/Putnam, 1996), 12.

25. Gesell, Ilg, and Ames, *The Child from Five to Ten*, 94.

26. Elium and Elium, *Raising a Son*, 27.

27. Samuel Osherson, *Wrestling with Love: How Men Struggle with Intimacy with Women, Children, Parents, and Each Other* (New York: Fawcett Columbine, 1992), 214.

28. Jane M. Healy, "How to Find Out Whether Your Child Is Creative," *The Brown University Child and Adolescent Behavior Letter: Parenting Solutions* (Providence, RI: Manisses, 1998), 2–12.

29. Nancy Carlsson-Paige and Diane E. Levin, *Who's Calling the Shots? How to Respond Effectively to Children's Fascination with War Play and War Toys* (Philadelphia, PA: New Society, 1990), 61.

30. Carlsson-Paige and Levin, *Who's Calling the Shots?*, 82–83.

31. Cohen, *Playful Parenting*, xii.

32. Gesell, Ilg, and Ames, *The Child from Five to Ten*, 218–19.

33. Gottman, *The Heart of Parenting*, 179.

34. Pipher, *The Shelter of Each Other*, 14.

35. Brian Wilcox et al., *APA Task Force on Advertizing and Children* (Washington, DC: American Psychological Association, 2004).

36. Neil Postman, *Technopoly: The Surrender of Culture to Technology* (New York: Knopf, 1992), 75.

37. Beth M. Miller et al., *I Wish the Kids Didn't Watch So Much TV: Out-of-School Time in Three Low Income Communities* (Wellesley, MA: Center for Research on Women, 1996), 6–7.

38. John Condry, "Thief of Time, Unfaithful Servant: Television and the American Child," *Daedalus* 122 (1993), 259–78.

39. Glenn and Nelson, *Raising Self-Reliant Children*, 42.

40. Brott, *The Single Father*, 113.

41. Dorothy G. Singer and Jerome Singer, *Partners in Play: A Step-by-Step Guide to Imaginative Play in Children* (New York: Harper and Row, 1977), 19.

42. Cohen, *Playful Parenting*, 4–6.

43. Kindlon and Thompson, *Raising Cain*, 104.

44. Judith Viorst, *Necessary Losses: The Loves, Illusions, Dependencies, and Impossible Expectations That All of Us Have to Give Up in Order to Grow* (New York: Fawcett Columbine, 1986), 16.

45. Viorst, *Necessary Losses*, 249.

46. Howard Gardner, *Leading Minds: An Anatomy of Leadership* (New York: Basic Books, 1995), 25–28.

47. Gardner, *Leading Minds*, 9–11.

48. Teresa A. Amabile, *Growing Up Creative: Nurturing a Lifetime of Creativity* (New York: Crown, 1989).

49. Julia Cameron, *The Artist's Way: A Spiritual Path to Higher Creativity* (New York: Jeremy P. Tarcher/Putnam, 1992), 9–10.

6. BELONGING NEEDS: ARE YOU A BUDDY OR ARE YOU BELITTLED BY "BELONGING BLUES"?

1. Jean Baker Miller, "The Development of Women's Sense of Self," in *Women's Growth in Connection: Writings from the Stone Center*, ed. Judith V. Jordan et al. (New York: Guilford, 1991), 12; Erikson, *Childhood and Society*, 247–68.

2. Peter Blos, "Modifications in the Traditional Psychoanalytic Theory of Female Adolescent Development," in *Adolescent Psychiatry VIII*, ed. Sherman Feinstein (Chicago: University of Chicago Press, 1980), 21.

3. Alexandra G. Kaplan, Rona Klein, and Nancy Gleason, "Women's Self Development in Late Adolescence," in *Women's Growth in Connection: Writings from the Stone Center*, ed. Judith V. Jordan et al. (New York: Guilford Press, 1991), 125.

4. Dana Crowley Jack, *Silencing the Self: Women and Depression* (New York: HarperCollins, 1991), 8.

5. Rachel Adelson, "Detecting Deception," *American Psychological Association Monitor on Psychology* 35 (2004): 70–73.

6. James F. Masterson, *The Search for the Real Self: Unmasking the Personality Disorders of Our Age* (New York: Free Press, 1988), 7.

7. Jean Baker Miller and Irene Pierce Stiver, *The Healing Connection: How Women Form Relationships in Therapy and in Life* (Boston: Beacon, 1997), 11.

8. Martin Buber, *I and Thou*, trans. Walter Kaufmann (New York: Scribner, 1970), 62.

9. Zeldin, *An Intimate History*, 32.

10. Maurice J. Elias, Steven E. Tobias, and Brian S. Friedlander, *Raising Emotionally Intelligent Teenagers: Parenting with Love, Laughter, and Limits* (New York: Harmony, 2000).

11. Miller and Stiver, *The Healing Connection*, 16–17.

12. Robert Spencer, "Symposium: Boys to Men—Masculinity and Boys' Socioemotional and Academic Development" (paper presented at the annual meeting for the American Psychological Association, Toronto, Canada, August 7–10, 2003).

13. Siegel and Hartzell, *Parenting from the Inside Out*, 64–65.

14. Siegel and Hartzell, *Parenting from the Inside Out*, 70.

15. Eisler, *The Power of Partnership*, 1.

16. Eisler, *The Power of Partnership*, xiv.

17. Edward M. Hallowell, *Worry: Controlling It and Using It Wisely* (New York: Pantheon, 1997), 296.

18. *The Random House Dictionary*, s.v. "religion."

19. Gary Kowalski, *Science and the Search for God* (New York: Lantern, 2003), 23.

20. Micki Pulleyking, "Children as Spiritual Creatures," *The Family Psychologist* 20 (2004), 17–19.

21. Tobin Hart, *The Secret Spiritual World of Children* (Novato, CA: New World Library, 2003), 156.

22. Stern, *The Present Moment*, 22.

23. Alan Loy McGinnis, *The Friendship Factor: How to Get Closer to the People You Care For* (Minneapolis, MN: Augsburg, 1979), 53.

24. Joseph Bruchac, *The Circle of Thanks: Native American Poems and Songs of Thanksgiving* (Mahwah, NJ: Bridge Water, 1996).

25. Rahima Baldwin Dancy, *You Are Your Child's First Teacher: What Parents Can Do with and for Their Children from Birth to Age Six* (Berkeley, CA: Celestial, 2000), 169.

26. Dan Kindlon, *Tough Times, Strong Children: Lessons from the Past for Your Children's Future* (New York: Hyperion, 2003), 38.

27. Gottman, *The Heart of Parenting*, 93.

28. Friedan, *The Fountain of Age*, 70.

29. Frans B. M. de Waal, *Chimpanzee Politics: Power and Sex Among Apes* (New York: Harper and Row, 1982), 40–41.

30. de Waal, *Chimpanzee Politics*, 47.

31. Eisler, *The Power of Partnership*, 75.

32. Bertrand Cramer, *The Scripts Parents Write and the Roles Babies Play: The Importance of Being Baby* (Northvale, NJ: Jason Aronson, 1997), 38.

33. John Bowlby, *Attachment and Loss*, vol. 1, *Attachment* (New York: Basic, 1969), 207.

34. Daniel N. Stern, The *Interpersonal World of the Infant: A View from Psychoanalysis and Developmental Psychology* (New York: Basic, 1985), 195–97.

35. Hudson, *The Adult Years*, 136.

36. Charlene C. Giannetti and Margaret Sagarese, *Cliques: 8 Steps to Help Your Child Survive the Social Jungle* (New York: Broadway, 2001), 11.

37. Kathryn R. Wentzel, Carolyn McNamara Barry, and Kathryn A. Caldwell, "Friendships in Middle School Influences on Motivation and School Adjustment," *Journal of Educational Psychology* 96 (2004): 195–203.

38. Stanley I. Greenspan, *Playground Politics: Understanding the Emotional Life of Your School-Age Child* (Reading, MA: Addison-Wesley, 1993), 81.

39. Boston Women's Health Book Collective, *Ourselves and Our Children*, 81.

40. Stern and Bruschweiler-Stern, *The Birth of a Mother*, 229.

41. Deak, *Girls Will Be Girls*, 106.

42. Brehony, *Awakening at Midlife*, 178.

43. Kindlon and Thompson, *Raising Cain*, 255.

44. Brehony, *Awakening at Midlife*, 168.

45. Jaana Juvonen, "Peer Harassment as a Personal Plight and as a Collective Problem: Implications for Intervention," *Psychological Science Agenda* 14 (2001), 7–8.

46. James Synder et al., "Observed Peer Victimization During Early Elementary School: Continuity, Growth, and Relation to Child Antisocial and Depressive Behavior," *Child Development* 74 (2003): 1–18.

47. Amie E. Grills and Thomas H. Ollendick, "Peer Victimization, Global Self-Worth, and Anxiety in Middle School Children," *Journal of Clinical Child and Adolescent Psychology* 31 (2002): 59–68.

48. Nan Stern, *Bullyproof: A Teacher's Guide on Teasing and Bullying for Use with Fourth and Fifth Grade Students* (Wellesley, MA: Wellesley College Center for Research on Women, 1996), 6.

49. Steven Landau et al., "You Really Don't Know How Much It Hurts: Children's and Preservice Teachers' Reactions to Childhood Teasing," *School Psychology Review* 30 (2001): 330.

50. Richard Sennett, *The Corrosion of Character: The Personal Consequences of Work in the New Capitalism* (New York: W. W. Norton, 1998), 145.

51. Edward M. Hallowell and John J. Ratey, *Answers to Distraction* (New York: Bantam, 1996), 65.

52. Christopher Peterson and Martin E. P. Seligman, *Character Strengths and Virtues: A Handbook and Classification* (Washington, DC: American Psychological Association; New York: Oxford University, 2004), 304.

53. Karen Kersting, "Accentuating the Positive," *Monitor on Psychology* 35 (2004): 64–65.

54. Giannetti and Sagarese, *Cliques*, 103.

55. Greenspan, *Playground Politics*, 113.

56. "Safe School Ambassadors Program (SSA)," Community Matters, accessed July 5, 2010, http://community-matters.org/programs-and-services/safe-school-ambassadors .

57. "Don't Laugh at Me," accessed November 26, 2012,www.steveseskin.com/music.

58. Operation Respect, *2010 Annual Report*, accessed November 26, 2012, www.operationrespect.org/Operation_Respect_Annual_Report.pdf.

59. Hey U.G.L.Y. website, accessed July 5, 2010, http://heyugly.org/about.php .

60. Landau et al., "You Really Don't Know," 339.

61. Marjorie Taylor, *Imaginary Companions and the Children Who Create Them* (New York: Oxford University Press, 1999), 4.

62. Taylor, *Imaginary Companions*, 116.

63. Todd E. Feinberg, *Altered Egos: How the Brain Creates the Self* (New York: Oxford University Press, 2001), 84.

64. Martha Beck, *Finding Your Own North Star: Claiming the Life You Were Meant to Live* (New York: Three Rivers, 2001), 2.

65. Zeldin, *An Intimate History*, 380.

66. Zeldin, *An Intimate History*, 60–61.

67. Zeldin, *An Intimate History*, 61–69.

68. John O'Donohue, *Anam Cara: A Book of Celtic Wisdom* (New York: HarperCollins, 1997), xix.

69. Marc McCutcheon, *Roget's Super Thesaurus*, 2nd ed. (Cincinnati, OH: Writer's Digest Books), 338.

7. ABILITY NEEDS: ARE YOU AN ARCHER, OR ARE YOU ALIENATED WITH APATHY?

1. Kindlon and Thompson, *Raising Cain*, 49.

2. Walter Isaacson, *Einstein: His Life and Universe* (New York: Simon and Schuster, 2007), 8–9.

3. Janis Clark Johnston, "Family Interaction Patterns and Career Orientation in Late Adolescent Females" (EdD dissertation, Boston University, 1973).

4. Robert Rosenthal and Lenore Jacobson, *Pygmalion in the Classroom: Teacher Expectation and Pupils' Intellectual Development* (New York: Rinehart and Winston, 1968).

5. Howard Gardner, *To Open Minds* (New York: Basic, 1989), 6.

6. Sternberg and Grigorenko, *Parenting 911*, 255–56.

7. Gardner, *To Open Minds*, 6.

8. Ellen J. Langer, *On Becoming an Artist: Reinventing Yourself Through Mindful Creativity* (New York: Ballantine, 2005), xv–5.

9. William Gibson, *The Miracle Worker: A Play for Television* (New York: Random House, 1957).

10. Kathy Hirsh-Pasek, Roberta Michnik Golinkoff, and Diane Eyer, *Einstein Never Used Flash Cards: How Our Children Really Learn—and Why They Need to Play More and Memorize Less* (New York: Rodale, 2003), 14–15.

11. Jane Nelsen, Cheryl Erwin, and Roslyn Ann Duffy, *Positive Discipline for Preschoolers: Raising Children Who Are Responsible, Respectful and Resourceful* (Rocklin, CA: Prima, 1998), 107.

12. Adele Faber and Elaine Mazlish, *Siblings Without Rivalry: How to Help Your Children Live Together So You Can Live Too* (New York: W. W. Norton, 1987), 99.

13. Hirsh-Pasek, Golinkoff, and Eyer, *Einstein Never Used*, 99.

14. Sylvia Rimm, *Dr. Sylvia Rimm's Smart Parenting: How to Raise a Happy, Achieving Child* (New York: Crown, 1996), 79.

15. Howard Gardner, *Multiple Intelligences: The Theory in Practice* (New York: Basic, 1993), 10–11.

16. Stanley I. Greenspan, *The Growth of the Mind and the Endangered Origins of Intelligence* (Reading, MA: Addison-Wesley, 1997), 7.

17. Schank, *Coloring Outside the Lines*, xxii.

18. Debra K. Meyer and Julianne C. Turner, "Discovering Emotion in Classroom Motivation Research," *Educational Psychology* 37 (2002), 107–14.

19. Pert, *Molecules of Emotion*, 144.

20. Marian Diamond and Janet Hopson, *Magic Trees of the Mind: How Nurture Your Children's Intelligence, Creativity, and Healthy Emotions from Birth Through Adolescence* (New York: Dutton, 1998), 12–13.

21. Rimm, *Smart Parenting*, 79.

22. American Association of University Women (AAUW) Educational Foundation, *How Schools Shortchange Girls: The AAUW Report* (New York: Marlowe, 1995), 4.

23. AAUW, *How Schools Shortchange Girls*, 19.

24. Peggy Orenstein, *School Girls: Young Women, Self-Esteem, and the Confidence Gap* (New York: Doubleday, 1994), 111–32.

25. Emily Hancock, *The Girl Within: Recapture the Childhood Self, the Key to Female Identity* (New York: E. P. Dutton, 1989), 142–43.

26. Elium and Elium, *Raising a Son*, 30.

27. Kindlon and Thompson, *Raising Cain*, 23.

28. AAUW, *How Schools Shortchange Girls*, 29–30.

29. Robert J. Sternberg and Elena Grigorenko, *Our Labeled Children: What Every Parent and Teacher Needs to Know About Learning Disabilities* (Reading, MA: Perseus, 1999), 63.

30. Dawn D. Matthews, ed. *Learning Disabilities Sourcebook*, 2nd ed. (Detroit, MI: Omnigraphics, 2003), 5.

31. Sternberg and Grigorenko, *Our Labeled Children*, 19–20.

32. Richard Lavoie, *It's So Much Work to Be Your Friend: Helping the Child with Learning Disabilities Find Social Success* (New York: Simon and Schuster, 2005), 253–63.

33. Faber and Mazlish, *Siblings Without Rivalry*, 122.

34. Eisler, *The Power of Partnership*, 33.

35. William S. Pollack, *Real Boys' Voices* (New York: Random House, 2000), 384.

36. Peter A. Levine and Maggie Kline, *Trauma Through a Child's Eyes: Awakening the Ordinary Miracle of Healing* (Berkeley, CA: North Atlantic, 2007), 17.

37. Greenspan, *The Growth of the Mind*, 71.

38. Martha Wakenshaw, *Caring for Your Grieving Child: Engaging Activities for Dealing with Loss and Transition* (Oakland, CA: New Harbinger, 2002), 57.

39. Ariadne V. Schemm, "Conjoint Behavioral Consultation: Meeting the Needs of Students at Risk of Dropping Out," *The School Psychologist* 58 (2004): 48–49.

40. Brown University, "Report Indicts Juvenile Justice System for a Lack of Treatment," *The Brown Child and Adolescent University Behavior Letter* 21 (2005): 6.

41. Robin Tepper Jacob, Susan Stone, and Melissa Roderick, *Ending Social Promotion in Chicago: Impacts on Instruction* (Chicago: Consortium on Chicago School Research, 2004).

42. Brenda Goodman, "When Pass Is a Four-Letter Word," *Psychology Today* 37 (2004): 24.

43. Gardner, *The Disciplined Mind*, 39.

44. Tamera B. Murdock, Lynley H. Anderman, and Sheryl A. Hodge, "Middle-Grade Predictors of Students' Motivation and Behavior in High School," *Journal of Adolescent Research* 15 (2000): 327–51.

45. Nathan Thornburgh, "Dropout Nation," *Time*, April 9, 2006, 30–40.

46. Deak, *Girls Will Be Girls*, 108.

47. Carol Orsborn, *Enough Is Enough: Exploding the Myth of Having It All* (New York: G. P. Putnam's Sons, 1986), 165.

48. Osherson, *Wrestling with Love*, 206.

49. Giannetti and Sagarese, *Parenting 911*, 39.

50. Jie-Qi Chen, Mara Krechevsky, and Julie Viens, *Building on Children's Strengths: The Experience of Project Spectrum* (New York: Teachers College, 1998), 23–24.

51. Gardner, *Multiple Intelligences*, 87.

52. Gardner, *The Disciplined Mind*, 72.

53. Chen, Krechevsky, and Viens, *Building on Children's Strengths*, 59.

54. Mihaly Csikszentimihalyi, Kevin Rathunde, and Samuel Whalen, *Talented Teenagers: The Roots of Success and Failure* (Cambridge, UK: Cambridge University, 1997), 249.

55. Deborah Stipek and Kathy Seal, *Motivated Minds: Raising Children to Love Learning* (New York: Henry Holt, 2001), 15.

56. Csikszentimihalyi, Rathunde, and Whalen, *Talented Teenagers*, 10–14.

57. Mihaly Csikszentimihalyi, *Flow: The Psychology of Optimal Experience* (New York: Harper and Row, 1990).

58. Csikszentimihalyi, Rathunde, and Whalen, *Talented Teenagers*, 14–16.

59. Csikszentimihalyi, Rathunde, and Whalen, *Talented Teenagers*, 31–32.

60. Linda Sapadin and Jack Maguire, *It's About Time! The Six Styles of Procrastination and How to Overcome Them* (New York: Penguin, 1997).

61. William Sears and Martha Sears, *The Successful Child: What Parents Can Do to Help Kids Turn Out Well* (Boston, MA: Little, Brown, 2002), 173–76.

62. Orsborn, *Enough Is Enough*, 72–73.

63. Rimm, *Smart Parenting*, 166–71.

64. The Brookings Institution, "A New Report Reveals That Homework in the United States Is an Easy Load," news release, October 1, 2003, www.brookings.edu/about/media-resources/news-releases/2003/20031001brown.

65. Bridget Murray, "Rewards Should Be Given When Defined Goals Are Met," *American Psychological Association Monitor* 52 (1997): 26.

66. Stipek and Seal, *Motivated Minds*, 3.

67. John D. Bransford, Ann L. Brown, and Rodney R. Cocking, eds. *How People Learn: Brain, Mind, Experience, and School* (Washington, DC: Commission on Behavioral and Social Sciences and Education, 2000), 104–8.

68. Jeffrey C. Valentine et al., "Out-of-School Activities and Academic Achievement: The Mediating Role of Self-Beliefs," *Educational Psychologist* 37 (2002): 245–56.

8. YOU CAN MAP YOUR PERSONALITY

1. Brehony, *Awakening at Midlife*, 18–19.

2. Ralph E. Ehrenberg, *Mapping the World: An Illustrated History of Cartography* (Washington, DC: National Geographic, 2006), 156.

3. Stern, *The Present Moment*, 14–24.

4. Stern, *The Present Moment*, 33–35.

5. Charles Hartshorne, *Whitehead's Philosophy: Selected Essays, 1935–1970* (Lincoln, NE: University of Nebraska, 1972), 119.

6. Stern, *The Present Moment*, 42–44.

7. Carl G. Jung, *Word and Image*, ed. Aniela Jaffe (Princeton, NJ: Princeton University Press, 1979), 228.

8. Anthony Storr, *The Integrity of Personality* (New York: Ballantine, 1992), 197.

9. Carl R. Rogers, *On Becoming a Person* (Boston: Houghton Mifflin, 1961), 75.

10. Schwartz, *Internal Family Systems Therapy*, 57–58.

11. Richard C. Schwartz, *Introduction to the Internal Family Systems Model* (Oak Park, IL: Trailheads, 2001), 48.

12. Eckhart Tolle, *The Power of Now: A Guide to Spiritual Enlightenment* (Novato, CA: New World, 1999), 52.

13. Joan Borysenko, *A Woman's Journey to God: Finding the Feminine Path* (New York: Riverhead, 1999), 84.

14. O'Donohue, *Anam Cara*, 58.

15. John O'Donohue, *Beauty: The Invisible Embrace: Rediscovering the True Sources of Compassion, Serenity, and Hope* (New York: HarperCollins, 2004), 16.

16. Csikszentmihalyi, *The Evolving Self*, 179–86.

17. Aristotle, "The Essential Whatness," in *Soul: An Archaelogy*, ed. Phil Cousineau (New York: HarperCollins, 1994), 11.

18. Keenan, *The Face in the Mirror*, 3–4.

19. Keenan, *The Face in the Mirror*, 251–52.

20. Keenan, *The Face in the Mirror*, 188–89.

21. Keenan, *The Face in the Mirror*, 94–95.

22. Gesell, Ilg, and Ames, *The Child from Five to Ten*, 175.

23. Masterson, *The Search for the Real Self*, 49.

24. Osherson, *Wrestling with Love*, 209.

25. Marvin Minsky, *The Society of Mind* (New York: Simon and Schuster, 1985), 39.

26. Sheldon Bach et al., "Definition of the Self," *Journal of Infant, Child, and Adolescent Psychotherapy* 1 (2000): 20–22.

27. Abraham H. Maslow, *Toward a Psychology of Being*, 2nd ed. (New York: Van Nostrand Reinhold, 1968), 26.

28. Maslow, *Motivation and Personality*, 35–51.

29. Maslow, *Motivation and Personality*, 128.

30. Maslow, *Motivation and Personality*, 207.

31. Maslow, *Motivation and Personality*, 214.

32. James Hollis, *Finding Meaning in the Second Half of Life: How to Finally, Really Grow Up* (New York: Gotham, 2005), 148.

33. Salvador Minuchin, *Families and Family Therapy* (Cambridge, MA: Harvard University Press, 1974).

34. Helen B. Landgarten, "Family Art Psychotherapy," in *Family Play Therapy*, ed. Charles E. Schaefer and Lois J. Carey (Northvale, NJ: Jason Aronson, 1994), 224.

35. Betty Edwards, *Drawing on the Right Side of the Brain* (New York: Jeremy P. Tarcher/Perigee, 1989), 3.

36. Otto Weininger, *Time-in Parenting: How to Teach Children Emotional Self-Control, Life Skills, and Problem Solving by Lending Yourself and Staying Connected* (Toronto, ON: Rinascente, 2002), 113.

37. Joseph Campbell and Bill Moyers, *The Power of Myth* (New York: Doubleday, 1988), 120.

9. LEARN TO CONNECT THE DOTS IN SELF-TERRITORY

1. "Burt Bacharach—Alfie lyrics," AllTheLyrics.com , accessed July 5, 2010, www.allthelyrics.com/lyrics/burt_bacharach/alfie-lyrics-591462.html .

2. Timothy D. Wilson, *Redirect: The Surprising New Science of Psychological Change* (Boston: Little, Brown, 2011).

3. Arlie Russell Hochschild, *The Second Shift: Working Parents and the Revolution at Home* (New York: Avon, 1989).

4. Joan Chodorow, ed., *Encountering Jung: Active Imagination* (Princeton, NJ: Princeton University Press, 1997).

5. Debbie W. Leung and Amy M. Smith Slep, "Predicting Inept Discipline: The Role of Parental Depressive Symptoms, Anger, and Attributions," *Journal of Consulting and Clinical Psychology* 74 (2006): 524–34.

6. Judith Fein, "The Richness of Relationships," *Hemispheres* magazine, July 2007, 128.

7. Siegel and Hartzell, *Parenting from the Inside Out*, 4–8.

8. Robert J. Sternberg, "Why Schools Should Teach for Wisdom: The Balance Theory of Wisdom in Educational Settings," *Educational Psychologist* 34 (2001): 227–45.

REFERENCES

Adelson, Rachel. "Detecting Deception." *American Psychological Association Monitor on Psychology* 35 (2004): 70–73.

Allen, Marie, and Shelly Marks. *Miscarriage: Women Sharing from the Heart*. New York: John Wiley, 1993.

Allen, K. Eileen., and Lynn R. Marotz. *By the Ages: Behavior and Development of Children Pre-birth Through Eight*. Albany, NY: Delmar, 2000.

Amabile, Teresa A. *Growing Up Creative: Nurturing a Lifetime of Creativity*. New York: Crown, 1989.

American Association of University Women (AAUW) Educational Foundation. *How Schools Shortchange Girls: The AAUW Report*. New York: Marlowe, 1995.

Aposhyan, Susan. *Body-Mind Psychotherapy: Principles, Techniques, and Practical Applications*. New York: W. W. Norton, 2004.

Aristotle. "The Essential Whatness." In *Soul: An Archaeology*, edited by Phil Cousineau. New York: HarperCollins, 1994.

Azerrad, Jacob, and Paul Chance. "Why Our Kids Are Out of Control." *Psychology Today* 34, no. 5 (2001): 43–46.

Bach, Sheldon, Linda Mayes, Anne Alvarez, and Peter Fonagy. "Definition of the Self." *Journal of Infant, Child, and Adolescent Psychotherapy* 1 (2000): 20–22.

Beck, Martha. *Finding Your Own North Star: Claiming the Life You Were Meant to Live*. New York: Three Rivers, 2001.

Bell, Ruth. "The Middle Years." In *Ourselves and Our Children: A Book by and for Parents*, Boston Women's Health Book Collective. New York: Random House, 1978.

Blos, Peter. "Modifications in the Traditional Psychoanalytic Theory of Female Adolescent Development." In *Adolescent Psychiatry VIII*, edited by Sherman Feinstein. Chicago: University of Chicago Press, 1980.

Borysenko, Joan. *A Woman's Journey to God: Finding the Feminine Path*. New York: Riverhead, 1999.

Boston Women's Health Book Collective. *Ourselves and Our Children: A Book by and for Parents*. New York: Random House, 1998.

Bowlby, John. *Attachment and Loss*. Vol. 1, *Attachment*. New York: Basic, 1969.

Bransford, John D., Ann L. Brown, and Rodney R. Cocking, eds. *How People Learn: Brain, Mind, Experience, and School*. Washington, DC: Commission on Behavioral and Social Sciences and Education, 2000.

Brazelton, T. Berry. *Families: Crisis and Caring*. Reading, MA: Addison-Wesley, 1989.

Brazelton, T. Berry, and Joshua D. Sparrow. *Discipline the Brazelton Way*. Cambridge, MA: Perseus, 2003.

Brehony, Kathleen. *Awakening at Midlife: A Guide to Reviving Your Spirit, Re-creating Your Life, and Returning to Your Truest Self*. New York: Riverhead, 1996.

Brookings Institution, "A New Report Reveals That Homework in the United States Is an Easy Load," news release, October 1, 2003, www.brookings.edu/about/media-resources/news-releases/2003/20031001brown .

Brott, Armin A. *The New Father, the Single Father: A Dad's Guide to Parenting Without a Partner*. New York: Abbeville, 1999.

Brown University. "Report Indicts Juvenile Justice System for a Lack of Treatment." *The Brown Child and Adolescent University Behavior Letter* 21 (2005): 6.

Browning, Elizabeth Barrett. *Aurora Leigh, Book I*. London: J. Miller, 1864.

Bruce, Debra Fulghum, and Samuel Thatcher. *Making a Baby: Everything You Need to Know to Get Pregnant*. New York: Ballantine, 2000.

Bruchac, Joseph. *The Circle of Thanks: Native American Poems and Songs of Thanksgiving*. Mahwah, NJ: Bridge Water, 1996.

Bryan, Mark. *Codes of Love: How to Rethink Your Family and Remake Your Life*. New York: Pocket, 1999.

Bryner, Michelle. "Some Pregnancies May Not Be So Accidental." *Psychology Today* 38 (2005): 32.

Buber, Martin. *I and Thou*. Translated by Walter Kaufmann. New York: Scribner, 1970.

Campbell, Joseph, and Bill Moyers. *The Power of Myth*. New York: Doubleday, 1988.

Clay, Rebecca A. "Battling the Self-Blame of Infertility." *American Psychological Association Monitor on Psychology* 37 (2006): 44–45.

Cameron, Julia. *The Artist's Way: A Spiritual Path to Higher Creativity*. New York: Jeremy P. Tarcher/Putnam, 1992.

Cameron, Julia. *The Vein of Gold: A Journey to Your Creative Heart*. New York: Jeremy P. Tarcher/Putnam, 1996.

Canada, Geoffrey. *Reaching Up for Manhood: Transforming the Lives of Boys in America*. Boston: Beacon, 1998.

Carlsson-Paige, Nancy, and Diane E. Levin. *Who's Calling the Shots? How to Respond Effectively to Children's Fascination with War Play and War Toys*. Philadelphia, PA: New Society, 1990.

Chen, Jie-Qi, Mara Krechevsky, and Julie Viens. *Building on Children's Strengths: The Experience of Project Spectrum*. New York: Teachers College, 1998.

Chodorow, Joan, ed. *Encountering Jung: Active Imagination*. Princeton, NJ: Princeton University Press, 1997.

Coles, Robert. *The Moral Life of Children*. Boston: Houghton Mifflin, 1986.

Cohen, Lawrence J. *Playful Parenting*. New York: Ballantine, 2001.

Combs, Allen, and Mark Holland. *Synchronicity: Science, Myth, and the Trickster*. New York: Paragon House, 1990.

Condry, John. "Thief of Time, Unfaithful Servant: Television and the American Child," *Daedalus* 122 (1993): 259–78.

Cramer, Bertrand. *The Scripts Parents Write and the Roles Babies Play: The Importance of Being Baby*. Northvale, NJ: Jason Aronson, 1997.

Csikszentmihalyi, Mihalyi. *Creativity Flow and the Psychology of Discovery and Invention*. New York: HarperCollins, 1996.

Csikszentimihalyi, Mihalyi. *Flow: The Psychology of Optimal Experience*. New York: Harper and Row, 1990.

Csikszentimihalyi, Mihalyi. *The Evolving Self: A Psychology for the Third Millennium*. New York: HarperCollins, 1993.

Csikszentimihalyi, Mihalyi, Kevin Rathunde, and Samuel Whalen. *Talented Teenagers: The Roots of Success and Failure*. Cambridge, UK: Cambridge University, 1997.

Cudmore, Lynne. "Infertility and the Couple." In *Partners Becoming Parents*. Edited by Christopher Clulow. Northvale, NJ: Jason Aronson, 1997.

Damasio, Antonio. *Looking for Spinoza: Joy, Sorrows, and the Feeling Brain*. Orlando, FL: Harcourt, 2003.

Damon, William. *The Moral Child: Nurturing Children's Natural Moral Growth.* New York: Free Press, 1988.

Dancy, Rahima Baldwin. *You Are Your Child's First Teacher: What Parents Can Do with and for Their Children from Birth to Age Six.* Berkeley, CA: Celestial, 2000.

Deak, JoAnn. *Girls Will Be Girls: Raising Confident and Courageous Daughters.* New York: Hyperion, 2002.

DeAngelis, Tori. "What's to Blame for the Surge in Super-size Americans?" *Monitor on Psychology* 35 (2004): 46–49.

DeBono, Edward. *Serious Creativity: Using the Power of Lateral Thinking to Create New Ideas.* New York: HarperBusiness, 1992.

de Waal, Franz B. M. *Chimpanzee Politics: Power and Sex Among Apes.* New York: Harper and Row, 1982.

Diamond, Marian, and Janet Hopson. *Magic Trees of the Mind: How Nurture Your Children's Intelligence, Creativity, and Healthy Emotions from Birth Through Adolescence.* New York: Dutton, 1998.

Dingfelder, Sadie F. "A Two-Front War on Alcoholism." *Monitor on Psychology* 36 (2005): 38–39.

Dosick, Wayne. *Golden Rules: The Ten Ethical Values Parents Need to Teach Their Children.* New York: HarperCollins, 1995.

Edwards, Betty. *Drawing on the Right Side of the Brain.* New York: Jeremy P. Tarcher/Perigee, 1989.

Ehrenberg, Ralph E. *Mapping the World: An Illustrated History of Cartography.* Washington, DC: National Geographic, 2006.

Eisler, Riane. *The Power of Partnership: Seven Relationships That Will Change Your Life.* Novato, CA: New World Library, 2002.

Ehrensaft, Diane. *Spoiling Childhood: How Well-Meaning Parents Are Giving Children Too Much—but Not What They Need.* New York: Guilford, 1997.

Elias, Maurice J., Steven E. Tobias, and Brian S. Friedlander. *Raising Emotionally Intelligent Teenagers: Parenting with Love Laughter, and Limits.* New York: Harmony, 2000.

Elium, Don, and Jeanne Elium. *Raising a Son: Parents and the Making of a Healthy Man.* Hillsboro, OR: Beyond Words, 1992.

Erikson, Erik H. *Childhood and Society.* 2nd ed. New York: W. W. Norton, 1996.

Eyre, Linda, and Richard Eyre. *How to Talk to Your Child About Sex: It's Best to Start Early, But It's Never Too Late—A Step-by-Step Guide for Every Age.* New York: St. Martin's, 1998.

Faber, Adele, and Elaine Mazlish. *Siblings Without Rivalry: How to Help Your Children Live Together So You Can Live Too.* New York: W. W. Norton, 1987.

Faludi, Susan. *Stiffed: The Betrayal of the American Man.* New York: William Morrow, 1999.

Fast, Julius. *Body Language: The Essential Secrets of Non-verbal Communication.* New York: M. Evans, 1970.

Feinberg, Todd E. *Altered Egos: How the Brain Creates the Self.* New York: Oxford University Press, 2001.

Fisher, Helen. *Why We Love: The Nature and Chemistry of Romantic Love.* New York: Henry Holt, 2004.

Fraiberg, Selma H. *The Magic Years: Understanding and Handling the Problems of Early Childhood.* New York: Scribner, 1959.

Freyd, Jennifer J. "Dynamic Mental Representations." *Psychological Review* 94 (1987): 427–38.

Friedan, Betty. *The Fountain of Age.* New York: Simon and Schuster, 1993.

Gardner, Howard. *The Disciplined Mind: Beyond Facts and Standardized Tests, the K–12 Education That Every Child Deserves.* New York: Penguin, 2000.

Gardner, Howard. *Leading Minds: An Anatomy of Leadership.* New York: Basic, 1995.

Gardner, Howard. *Multiple Intelligences: The Theory in Practice.* New York: Basic, 1993.

Gardner, Howard. *To Open Minds.* New York: Basic, 1989.

Gendlin, Eugene T. *Let Your Body Interpret Your Dreams.* Wilmette, IL: Chiron, 1986.

Gesell, Arnold, Frances L. Ilg, and Louise Bates Ames. *The Child from Five to Ten*. Revised ed. New York: Harper and Row, 1974.

Giannetti, Charlene C., and Margaret Sagarese. *Cliques: 8 Steps to Help Your Child Survive the Social Jungle*. New York: Broadway, 2001.

Giannetti, Charlene C., and Margaret Sagarese. *Parenting 911: How to Safeguard and Rescue Your 10- to 15-Year-Old from Substance Abuse, Depression, Sexual Encounters, Violence, Failure in School, Danger on the Internet, and Other Risky Situations*. New York: Broadway, 1999.

Gibson, William. *The Miracle Worker: A Play for Television*. New York: Random House, 1957.

Glasser, William. *Reality Therapy: A New Approach to Psychiatry*. New York: Harper and Row, 1965.

Glenn, H. Steven, and Jane Nelson. *Raising Self-Reliant Children in a Self-Indulgent World*. Rocklin, CA: Prima, 1988.

Goldstein, Sam, and Robert Brooks. "Does It Matter How We Raise Our Children?" *National Association of School Psychologists Communique* 38 (2009): 19.

Gonzalez-Crussi, Frank. *On Being Born and Other Difficulties*. Woodstock, NY: Overlook, 2004.

Goodman, Brenda. "When Pass Is a Four-letter Word," *Psychology Today* 37 (2004): 24.

Gottman, John. *The Heart of Parenting: Raising an Emotionally Intelligent Child*. New York: Simon and Schuster, 1997.

Goulding, Regina A., and Richard C. Schwartz. *The Mosaic Mind: Empowering the Tormented Selves of Child Abuse Survivors*. New York: W. W. Norton, 1995.

Gravelle, Karen. *What's Going On Down There? Answers to Questions Boys Find Hard to Ask*. New York: Walker, 1998.

Greenspan, Stanley I. *Playground Politics: Understanding the Emotional Life of Your School-Age Child*. Reading, MA: Addison-Wesley, 1993.

Greenspan, Stanley I. *The Growth of the Mind and the Endangered Origins of Intelligence*. Reading, MA: Addison-Wesley, 1997.

Greer, Mark. "Strengthen Your Brain by Resting It." *American Psychological Association Monitor on Psychology* 35 (2004): 60–62.

Grills, Amie E., and Thomas H. Ollendick. "Peer Victimization, Global Self-Worth, and Anxiety in Middle School Children." *Journal of Clinical Child and Adolescent Psychology* 31 (2002): 59–68.

Hallowell, Edward M. *Worry: Controlling It and Using It Wisely*. New York: Pantheon, 1997.

Hallowell, Edward M., and John J. Ratey. *Answers to Distraction*. New York: Bantam, 1996.

Hancock, Emily. *The Girl Within: Recapture the Childhood Self, the Key to Female Identity*. New York: E. P. Dutton, 1989.

Hannaford, Carla. *Smart Moves: Why Learning Is Not All in Your Head*. 2nd ed. Salt Lake City, UT: Great River Books, 2005.

Harris, Judith Rich. *The Nurture Assumption: Why Children Turn Out the Way They Do*. New York: Free Press, 1998.

Hart, Tobin. *The Secret Spiritual World of Children*. Novato, CA: New World Library, 2003.

Hartshorne, Charles. *Whitehead's Philosophy: Selected Essays, 1935–1970*. Lincoln, NE: University of Nebraska, 1972.

Hatfield, Elaine, John Cacioppo, and Richard L. Rapson. *Emotional Contagion*. New York: Cambridge University Press, 1994.

Healy, Jane M. "How to Find Out Whether Your Child Is Creative," *The Brown University Child and Adolescent Behavior Letter: Parenting Solutions*, 2–12. Providence, RI: Manisses, 1998.

Helmstetter, Shad. *Predictive Parenting: When You Talk to Your Kids*. New York: William Morrow, 1989.

Herman, Deborah Levine. *The Complete Idiot's Guide to Motherhood*. New York: Macmillan, 1999.

Hingson, Ralph W., Timothy Heeren, Rhonda C. Zakocs, and Andrea Kopstein, and Henry Wechsler. "Magnitude of Alcohol-Related Mortality and Morbidity Among U.S. College Students Ages 18–24," *Journal of Studies on Alcohol* 63 (2002): 136–44.

Hirsh-Pasek, Kathy, Roberta Michnik Golinkoff, and Diane Eyer. *Einstein Never Used Flash Cards: How Our Children Really Learn—and Why They Need to Play More and Memorize Less.* New York: Rodale, 2003.

Hochschild, Arlie Russell. *The Second Shift: Working Parents and the Revolution at Home.* New York: Avon, 1989.

Hollis, James. *Finding Meaning in the Second Half of Life: How to Finally, Really Grow Up.* New York: Gotham, 2005.

How It Works: Science and Technology. 3rd ed. Tarrytown, NY: Marshall Cavendish Corporation, 2003.

Hudson, Frederic M. *The Adult Years: Mastering the Art of Self-Renewal.* San Francisco, CA: Jossey-Bass, 1991.

Hyman, Irwin A. "School Psychology and the Culture Wars: 40 Years of Advocacy, Research and Practice," *NASP Communique* 32 (2004): 18–21.

Isaacson, Walter. *Einstein: His Life and Universe.* New York: Simon and Schuster, 2007.

Jack, Dana Crowley. *Silencing the Self: Women and Depression.* New York: HarperCollins, 1991.

Jacob, Robin Tepper, Susan Stone, and Melissa Roderick. *Ending Social Promotion in Chicago: Impacts on Instruction.* Chicago: Consortium on Chicago School Research, 2004.

Johnston, Janis Clark. "Family Interaction Patterns and Career Orientation in Late Adolescent Females," EdD dissertation, Boston University, 1973.

Johnston, Janis Clark, and Patricia Fields. "School Consultation with the 'Classroom Family.'" *Family Counseling: The School Counselor's Role* 29 (1981): 140–46.

Johnston, Janis Clark, Dennis Simon, and Alice Zemitzsch. "Balancing an Educational Mobile Through Problem-Solving Conference." In *Advances in Therapies for School Behavior Problems.* Edited by Jeffrey J. Cohen and Marian C. Fish. San Francisco: Jossey-Bass, 1993.

Jung, Carl G. "Psychology and Religion (the Terry Lectures)." In *The Collected Works of C. G. Jung.* Vol. 11, *Psychology and Religion: West and East.* Translated by R. F. C. Hull (Bollingen Series XX). New York: Pantheon, 1938.

Jung, Carl G. *Word and Image.* Edited by Aniela Jaffe. Princeton, NJ: Princeton University Press, 1979.

Juvonen, Jaana. "Peer Harassment as a Personal Plight and as a Collective Problem: Implications for Intervention." *Psychological Science Agenda* 14 (2001): 7–8.

Kagan, Jerome. *Unstable Ideas: Temperament, Cognition, and Self.* Cambridge, MA: Harvard University Press, 1989.

Kaplan, Alexandra G., Rona Klein, and Nancy Gleason. "Women's Self Development in Late Adolescence." In *Women's Growth in Connection: Writings from the Stone Center.* Edited by Judith V. Jordan, Alexandra G. Kaplan, Jean Baker Miller, Irene P. Stiver, and Janet L. Surrey. New York: Guilford Press, 1991.

Kazdin, Alan E. *The Kazdin Method for Parenting the Defiant Child with No Pills, No Therapy, No Contest of Wills.* New York: Houghton Mifflin, 2008.

Kegan, Robert. *The Evolving Self: Problem and Process in Human Development.* Cambridge, MA: Harvard University Press, 1982.

Keen, Sam. *To Love and Be Loved.* New York: Bantam, 1997.

Keenan, Julian P. *The Face in the Mirror: The Search for the Origins of Consciousness.* New York: HarperCollins, 2003.

Kersting, Karen. "Accentuating the Positive." *Monitor on Psychology* 35 (2004): 64–65.

Kindlon, Dan. *Tough Times, Strong Children: Lessons from the Past for Your Children's Future.* New York: Hyperion, 2003.

Kindlon, Dan, and Michael Thompson. *Raising Cain: Protecting the Emotional Life of Boys.* New York: Ballantine, 2000.

Kirschenbaum, Howard. "An Interview with Howard Kirschenbaum." *Newsletter for Educational Psychologists, American Psychological Association* 24 (2001): 5–8.

Kitzinger, Sheila. *Ourselves as Mother: The Universal Experience of Motherhood*. Reading, MA: Addison-Wesley, 1992.

Kowalski, Gary. *Science and the Search for God*. New York: Lantern, 2003.

Lamb, Sharon. *The Secret Lives of Girls: What Good Girls Really Do—Sex Play, Aggression, and Their Guilt*. New York: Free Press, 2001.

Landau, Steven, Richard Milich, Monica J. Harris, and Sarah E. Larson. "You Really Don't Know How Much It Hurts: Children's and Preservice Teachers' Reactions to Childhood Teasing," *School Psychology Review* 30 (2001): 330.

Landgarten, Helen B. "Family Art Psychotherapy." In *Family Play Therapy*. Edited by Charles E. Schaefer and Lois J. Carey. Northvale, NJ: Jason Aronson, 1994.

Lahiri, Jhumpa. *The Namesake*. Boston: Houghton Mifflin, 2003.

Langer, Ellen J. *On Becoming an Artist: Reinventing Yourself Through Mindful Creativity*. New York: Ballantine, 2005.

Lavoie, Richard. *It's So Much Work to Be Your Friend: Helping the Child with Learning Disabilities Find Social Success*. New York: Simon and Schuster, 2005.

Lazear, Jonathon, and Wendy Lazear. *Meditations for Parents Who Do Too Much*. New York: Simon and Schuster, 1993.

Leung, Debbie W., and Amy M. Smith Slep. "Predicting Inept Discipline: The Role of Parental Depressive Symptoms, Anger, and Attributions," *Journal of Consulting and Clinical Psychology* 74 (2006): 524–34.

Levine, Peter A., and Maggie Kline. *Trauma Through a Child's Eyes: Awakening the Ordinary Miracle of Healing*. Berkeley, CA: North Atlantic, 2007.

Levy, David H. *Eclipse: Voyage to Darkness and Light*. New York: Simon and Schuster, 2000.

Lush, Jean. *Mothers and Sons: Raising Boy to Be Men*. Grand Rapids, MI: Baker, 1988.

Lyons, Nick, and Tony Lyons, eds. *The Quotable Dad*. Guilford, CT: Lyons, 2002.

Madison, Lynda. *Parenting with Purpose: Progressive Discipline from Birth to Four*. Kansas City, KS: Andrew McNeel, 1998.

Marano, Hara Estroff. *A Nation of Wimps: The High Cost of Invasive Parenting*. New York: Broadway, 2008.

Maslow, Abraham H. *Motivation and Personality*. 2nd ed. New York: Harper and Row, 1970.

Maslow, Abraham H. *Toward a Psychology of Being*. 2nd ed. New York: Van Nostrand Reinhold, 1968.

Masterson, James F. *The Search for the Real Self: Unmasking the Personality Disorders of Our Age*. New York: Free Press, 1988.

Matthews, Dawn D., ed. *Learning Disabilities Sourcebook*. 2nd ed. Detroit, MI: Omnigraphics, 2003.

McAdams, Dan P. *The Stories We Live By: Personal Myths and the Meaning of the Self*. New York: William Morrow, 1993.

McAdams, Dan P., and Jennifer L. Pals. "A New Big Five: Fundamental Principles for an Integrative Science of Personality," *American Psychologist* 61 (2006), 204–17.

McAdams, Dan P., and Phillip J. Bowman. "Narrating Life's Turning Points: Redemption and Contamination." In *Turns in the Road: Narrative Studies of Lives in Transition*. Edited by Dan P. McAdams, Ruthellen Josselson, and Amia Lieblich. Washington, DC: American Psychological Association, 2001.

McGinnis, Alan Loy. *The Friendship Factor: How to Get Closer to the People You Care For*. Minneapolis, MN: Augsburg, 1979.

Mehrabian, Albert. "Communication Without Words." *Psychology Today* 2 (1968): 53–55.

Meyer, Debra K., and Julianne C. Turner. "Discovering Emotion in Classroom Motivation Research." *Educational Psychology* 37 (2002): 107–114.

Michalko, Michael. *Cracking Creativity: The Secrets of Creative Genius*. Berkeley, CA: Ten Speed, 2001.

Miller, Beth M., Susan O'Connor, Sylvia W. Sirignano, and Pamela Joshi. *I Wish the Kids Didn't Watch So Much TV: Out-of-School Time in Three Low Income Communities*. Wellesley, MA: Center for Research on Women, 1996.

Miller, Daniel. "How Infants Grow Mothers in North London." In *Consuming Motherhood.* Edited by Janelle. S. Taylor, Linda L. Layne, and Danielle. F. Wozniak, 31–51. New Brunswick, NJ: Rutgers University Press, 2004.

Miller, Jean Baker. "The Development of Women's Sense of Self." In *Women's Growth in Connection: Writings from the Stone Center.* Edited by Judith V. Jordan, Alexandra G. Kaplan, Jean Baker Miller, Irene P. Stiver, and Janet L. Surrey. New York: Guilford Press, 1991.

Mineka, Susan, Mark Davidson, Michael Cook, and Richard Keir. "Observational Conditioning of Snake Fear in Rhesus Monkeys." *Journal of Abnormal Psychology* 93 (1984): 355–72.

Minsky, Marvin. *The Society of Mind.* New York: Simon and Schuster, 1985.

Minuchin, Salvador. *Families and Family Therapy.* Cambridge, MA: Harvard University Press, 1974.

Molden, Daniel C., and Dweck, Carol S. "Finding 'Meaning' in Psychology: A Lay Theories Approach to Self-Regulation, Social Perception, and Social Development." *American Psychologist* 61 (2006): 192–203.

Montagu, Ashley. *Growing Young.* New York: McGraw-Hill, 1981.

Morris, William, and Morris, Mary. *The Morris Dictionary of Word and Phrase.* New York: Harper Row, 1971.

Murdock, Tamera B., Lynley H. Anderman, and Sheryl A. Hodge. "Middle-Grade Predictors of Students' Motivation and Behavior in High School." *Journal of Adolescent Research* 15 (2000): 327–51.

Murray, Bridget. "Rewards Should Be Given When Defined Goals Are Met." *American Psychological Association Monitor* 52 (1997): 26.

Mussen, Paul H., John J. Conger, and Jerome Kagan. *Child Development and Personality.* 2nd ed. New York: Harper and Row, 1963.

Neeld, Elizabeth Harper. *Tough Transitions: Navigating Your Way Through Difficult Times.* New York: Warner, 2005.

Neff, Kristin D., Stephanie S. Rude, and Kristin L. Kirkpatrick. "An Examination of Self-Compassion in Relation to Positive Psychological Functioning and Personality Traits." *Journal of Research in Personality* 42 (2007): 908–16.

Nelsen, Jane, Cheryl Erwin, and Roslyn Ann Duffy. *Positive Discipline for Preschoolers: Raising Children Who Are Responsible, Respectful and Resourceful.* Rocklin, CA: Prima, 1998.

Nonacs, Ruta. *A Deeper Shade of Blue: A Woman's Guide to Recognizing and Treating Depression in Her Childbearing Years.* New York: Simon and Schuster, 2006.

O'Donohue, John. *Anam Cara: A Book of Celtic Wisdom.* New York: HarperCollins, 1997.

O'Donohue, John. *Beauty, The Invisible Embrace: Rediscovering the True Sources of Compassion, Serenity, and Hope.* New York: HarperCollins, 2004.

Orenstein, Peggy. *SchoolGirls: Young Women, Self-Esteem, and the Confidence Gap.* New York: Doubleday, 1994.

Orsborn, Carol. *Enough Is Enough: Exploding the Myth of Having It All.* New York: G. P. Putnam's Sons, 1986.

Osherson, Samuel. *Wrestling with Love: How Men Struggle with Intimacy with Women, Children, Parents, and Each Other.* New York: Fawcett Columbine, 1992.

Paleg, Kim. *Kids Today, Parents Tomorrow.* Oakland, CA: New Harbinger, 1999.

Paley, Vivian Gussin. *Bad Guys Don't Have Birthdays: Fantasy Play at Four.* Chicago: University of Chicago Press, 1988.

Pasupathi, Monisha. "Social Construction of Memory and Self in Storytelling: Listener Effects." Paper presented at the annual meeting for the American Psychological Association, Toronto, Canada, August 6, 2003.

Pert, Candice B. *Molecules of Emotion: The Science Behind Mind-Body Medicine.* New York: Simon and Schuster, 1997.

Peterson, Christopher, and Martin E. P. Seligman. *Character Strengths and Virtues: A Handbook and Classification.* Washington, DC: American Psychological Association; New York: Oxford University, 2004.

Planalp, Sally. "Varieties of Emotional Cues in Everyday Life." In *The Nonverbal Communication Reader*. Edited by Laura K. Guerrero, Joseph A. DeVito, and Michael L. Hecht. 2nd ed. Prospect Heights, IL: Waveland, 1999.

Pinker, Steven. *The Blank Slate: The Modern Denial of Human Nature*. New York: Penguin, 2002.

Pipher, Mary. *Hunger Pains: The Modern Woman's Tragic Quest for Thinness*. New York: Ballantine, 1995.

Pipher, Mary. *In the Shelter of Each Other: Rebuilding Our Families*. New York, Ballantine, 1996.

Pollack, William S. *Real Boys' Voices*. New York: Random House, 2000.

Pollan, Michael. *The Omnivore's Dilemma: The Secrets Behind What You Eat*. New York: Dial, 2009.

Postman, Neil. *Technopoly: The Surrender of Culture to Technology*. New York: Knopf, 1992.

Pulleyking, Micki. "Children as Spiritual Creatures." *The Family Psychologist* 20 (2004), 17–19.

The Random House Dictionary of the English Language. Unabridged ed. New York: Random House, 1967.

Rankin, Jane L. *Parenting Experts: Their Advice, the Research, and Getting It Right*. Westport, CT: Praeger, 2005.

Raths, Louis Edward, Merrill Harmin, and Sidney B. Simon. *Values and Teaching*. Columbus, OH: Charles E. Merrill, 1966.

Ridley, Matt. *Genome: The Autobiography of a Species in 23 Chapters*. New York: HarperCollins, 1999.

Rimm, Sylvia. *Dr. Sylvia Rimm's Smart Parenting: How to Raise a Happy, Achieving Child*. New York: Crown, 1996.

Rinehart, Martha S., and Mark S. Kiselica. "Helping Men with the Trauma of Miscarriage." *Psychotherapy: Theory, Research, Practice, Training* 47 (2010): 288–95.

Rinpoche, Sogyal. *The Tibetan Book of Living and Dying*. San Francisco, CA: Harper, 1993.

Rogers, Carl R. *On Becoming a Person*. Boston: Houghton Mifflin, 1961.

Roman, Mel, and Patricia E. Raley. *The Indelible Family: How the Hidden Forces in Your Family Determine Who You Are Today*. New York: Rawson, Wade, 1980.

Rosenthal, Robert, and Lenore Jacobson. *Pygmalion in the Classroom: Teacher Expectation and Pupils' Intellectual Development*. New York: Rinehart and Winston, 1968.

Rothschild, Babette. *The Body Remembers: The Psychophysiology of Trauma and Trauma Treatment*. New York: W. W. Norton, 2000.

Ruiz, Don Miguel. *The Four Agreements: A Toltec Wisdom Book*. San Rafael, CA: Amber-Allen, 1997.

Salk, Lee. *My Father, My Son: Intimate Relationships*. New York: G. P. Putnam, 1982.

Samuels, Andrew. "The Good-Enough Father of Whatever Sex." in *Partners Becoming Parents*. Edited by Christopher Clulow. Northvale, NJ: Jason Aronson, 1997.

Sapadin, Linda, and Jack Maguire. *It's About Time! The Six Styles of Procrastination and How to Overcome Them*. New York: Penguin, 1997.

Schemm, Ariadne, V. "Conjoint Behavioral Consultation: Meeting the Needs of Students at Risk of Dropping Out." *The School Psychologist* 58 (2004): 48–49.

Schflen, Albert E. *Body Language and Social Order: Communication as Behavioral Control*. Englewood Cliffs, NJ: Prentice-Hall, 1972.

Schlosser, Eric. *Fast Food Nation: The Dark Side of the All-American Meal*. New York: HarperCollins, 2002.

Schwartz, Richard C. *Internal Family Systems Therapy*. New York: Guilford Press, 1994.

Schwartz, Richard C. *Introduction to the Internal Family Systems Model*. Oak Park, IL: Trailheads, 2001.

Schank, Roger. *Coloring Outside the Lines: Raising a Smarter Kid by Breaking All the Rules*. New York: HarperCollins, 2000.

Sears, William, and Martha Sears. *The Successful Child: What Parents Can Do to Help Kids Turn Out Well*. Boston: Little, Brown, 2002.

Sennett, Richard. *The Corrosion of Character: The Personal Consequences of Work in the New Capitalism*. New York: W. W. Norton, 1998.

Shaw, Fiona. *Composing Myself: A Journey Through Postpartum Depression*. South Royalton, VT: Steerforth, 1998.

Shields, Brooke. *Down Came the Rain: My Journey Through Postpartum Depression*. New York: Hyperion, 2005.

Shore, Rima. *What Kids Need: Today's Best Ideas for Nurturing, Teaching, and Protecting Young*. New York: Carnegie Foundation, 2002.

Shure, Myrna B. *I Can Problem Solve: An Interpersonal Cognitive Problem-Solving Program—Preschool*. Champaign, IL: Research Press, 1992.

Shure, Myrna B. *Raising a Thinking Child Workbook: Teaching Young Children How to Resolve Everyday Conflicts and Get Along with Others*. Champaign, IL: Research Press, 2000.

Shure, Myrna B. *Raising a Thinking Preteen: The 'I Can Problem Solve' Program for 8- to 12-Year-Olds*. New York: Henry Holt, 2000.

Siegel, Daniel J. "The Developing Mind and the Resolution of Trauma: Some Ideas About Information Processing and an Interpersonal Neurobiology of Psychotherapy." In *EMDR as an Integrative Psychotherapy Approach*. Edited by Francine Shapiro. Washington, DC: American Psychological Association, 2002.

Siegel, Daniel J., and Mary Hartzell. *Parenting from the Inside Out: How a Deeper Self-Understanding Can Help You Raise Children Who Thrive*. New York: Jeremy P. Tarcher/Putnam, 2003.

Simon, Sidney, Leland W. Howe, and Howard Kirschenbaum. *Values Clarification*. New York: Hart, 1972.

Singer, Dorothy G., and Jerome Singer. *Partners in Play: A Step-by-Step Guide to Imaginative Play in Children*. New York: Harper and Row, 1977.

Sleek, Scott. "After the Storm, Children Play Out Fears." *American Psychological Association Monitor* 29 (1998): 12.

Snyder, James, Monica Brooker, M. Renee Patrick, Abigail Snyder, Lynn Schrepferman, and Mike Stoolmiller. "Observed Peer Victimization During Early Elementary School: Continuity, Growth, and Relation to Child Antisocial and Depressive Behavior." *Child Development* 74 (2003): 1–18.

Snyder, James, Ann Cramer, Jan Afrank, and Gerald R. Patterson. "The Contributions of Ineffective Discipline and Parental Hostile Attribution of Child Misbehavior to the Development of Conduct Problems at Home and School." *Developmental Psychology* 41 (2005): 30–41.

Souden, David. *Stonehenge Revealed*. New York: Facts On File, 1997.

Spencer, Robert. "Symposium: Boys to Men—Masculinity and Boys' Socioemotional and Academic Development." Paper presented at the annual meeting for the American Psychological Association, Toronto, Canada, August 7–10, 2003.

Srivastava, Sanjay, Oliver D. John, Samuel D. Gosling, and Jeff Potter. "Development of Personality in Early and Middle Adulthood: Set Like Plaster or Persistent Change?" *Journal of Personality and Social Psychology* 84, no. 5 (2003): 1041–53.

Steinberg, Laurence. *Crossing Paths: How Your Child's Adolescence Triggers Your Own Crisis*. New York: Simon and Schuster, 1974.

Stern, Daniel N. *The Present Moment in Psychotherapy and Everyday Life*. New York: W. W. Norton, 2004.

Stern, Daniel N., and Nadia Bruschweiler-Stern. *The Birth of a Mother: How the Motherhood Experience Changes You Forever*. New York: Basic, 1998.

Stern, Nan. *Bullyproof: A Teacher's Guide on Teasing and Bullying for Use with Fourth and Fifth Grade Students*. Wellesley, MA: Wellesley College Center for Research on Women, 1996.

Sternberg, Robert J. "Why Schools Should Teach for Wisdom: The Balance Theory of Wisdom in Educational Settings." *Educational Psychologist* 34(2001): 227–45.

Sternberg, Robert J., and Elena Grigorenko. *Our Labeled Children: What Every Parent and Teacher Needs to Know About Learning Disabilities*. Reading, MA: Perseus, 1999.

Stipek, Deborah, and Kathy Seal. *Motivated Minds: Raising Children to Love Learning*. New York: Henry Holt, 2001.

Stone, Hal, and Sidra Stone. *Partnering, A New Kind of Relationship: How to Love Each Other Without Losing Yourselves*. Novato, CA: New World Library, 2000.

Storr, Anthony. *The Integrity of the Personality*. New York: Ballantine, 1992.

Tauber, Robert T. "Good or Bad, What Teachers Expect from Students They Generally Get! *ERIC Digest*. Washington, DC: ERIC Clearinghouse on Teaching and Teacher Education, 1998: ED426985.

Taylor, Marjorie. *Imaginary Companions and the Children Who Create Them*. New York: Oxford University Press, 1999.

Terr, Lenore. *Unchained Memories: True Stories of Traumatic Memories, Lost and Found*. New York: Basic, 1994.

Thompson, Sharon. *Going All the Way: Teenage Girls' Tales of Sex, Romance and Pregnancy*. New York: Farrar, Strauss and Giroux, 1995.

Thornburgh, Nathan. "Dropout Nation." *Time*, 30–40. April 9, 2006.

Tolle, Eckhart. *The Power of Now: A Guide to Spiritual Enlightenment*. Novato, CA: New World, 1999.

U.S. Census Bureau, Census 1990, 2000.

Valentine, Jeffrey C., Harris Cooper, B. Ann Bettencourt, and David L. DuBois. "Out-of-School Activities and Academic Achievement: The Mediating Role of Self-Beliefs." *Educational Psychologist* 37 (2002): 245–56.

Villanueva, Alma Luz. *Planet with Mother, May I?"* Tempe, AZ: Bilingual Press, 1993.

Viorst, Judith. *Imperfect Control: Our Lifelong Struggles with Power and Surrender*. New York: Fireside, 1999.

Viorst, Judith. *Necessary Losses: The Loves, Illusions, Dependencies, and Impossible Expectations That All of Us Have to Give Up in Order to Grow*. New York: Fawcett Columbine, 1986.

Wakenshaw, Martha. *Caring for Your Grieving Child: Engaging Activities for Dealing with Loss and Transition*. Oakland, CA: New Harbinger, 2002.

Weininger, Otto. *Time-in Parenting: How to Teach Children Emotional Self-Control, Life Skills, and Problem Solving by Lending Yourself and Staying Connected*. Toronto, ON: Rinascente, 2002.

Welwood, John. *Toward a Psychology of Awakening*. Boston: Shambhala, 2000.

Wentzel, Kathryn R., Carolyn McNamara Barry, and Kathryn A. Caldwell. "Friendships in Middle School Influences on Motivation and School Adjustment." *Journal of Educational Psychology* 96 (2004): 195–203.

West, Diana. *The Death of the Grown-Up: How America's Arrested Development Is Bringing Down Western Civilization*. New York: St. Martin's, 2007.

White, Michael, and David Epston. *Narrative Means to Therapeutic Ends*. New York: W. W. Norton, 1990.

Wilcox, Brian, Joanne Cantor, Peter Dowrick, Dale Kunkel, Susan Linn, and Edward Palmer. *APA Task Force on Advertizing and Children*. Washington, DC: American Psychological Association, 2004.

Wilson, Timothy D. *Redirect: The Surprising New Science of Psychological Change*. Boston: Little, Brown, 2011.

Wink, Paul, and Ravenna Helson. "Personality Change in Women and Their Partners." *Journal of Personality and Social Psychology* 65 (1993): 597–606.

Winerman, Lea. "The Mind's Mirror." *American Psychological Association Monitor on Psychology* 36 (2005): 48–50.

World Book Encyclopedia. Vol. 6. Chicago: World Book, 2004.

Zeldin, Theodore. *An Intimate History of Humanity*. New York: HarperCollins, 1994.

INDEX

ABOUT THE AUTHOR

Janis Clark Johnston, EdD, has worked as a school psychologist in public schools, a supervising psychologist at a mental health center, an employee assistance therapist, and a private practice family psychologist. She received the 2011 Founder's Award in appreciation for her dedication to the mission of Parenthesis Family Center, Oak Park, IL. Sarah's Inn, a domestic violence shelter and education center in Oak Park, IL, honored Johnston in 2002 with a Community Spirit Award for her support of teen dating violence prevention/intervention programming for local high school students. Johnston has published journal articles in a variety of journals and coauthored two book chapters. Currently, Johnston is a family psychologist and consultant in Oak Park, Illinois.

Photo by Monte Gerlach